IRAN AND THE RISE OF ITS
NEOCONSERVATIVES

IRAN AND THE RISE OF ITS NEOCONSERVATIVES

The Politics of Tehran's Silent Revolution

Anoushiravan Ehteshami and Mahjoob Zweiri

I.B. TAURIS

LONDON · NEW YORK

Published in 2007 by I.B.Tauris & Co Ltd
6 Salem Road, London W2 4BU
175 Fifth Avenue, New York NY 10010
www.ibtauris.com

In the United States of America and Canada
distributed by Palgrave Macmillan, a division of St. Martin's Press
175 Fifth Avenue, New York NY 10010

ISBN: 978 1 84511 388 9

A full CIP record for this book is available from the British Library
A full CIP record is available from the Library of Congress

Library of Congress Catalog Card Number: available

Typeset in Adobe Caslon Pro by Sara Millington, Editorial and
Design Services
Printed and bound in Great Britain by T.J. International Ltd,
Padstow, Cornwall

CONTENTS

PREFACE

As it happens, we began preparing this book a year before Ahmadinejad's rise to power. In 2004 we were keenly following the progress of the neoconservatives in the Majlis elections, and even then saw their success there as a prelude for a bid for the presidency. On various occasions we spoke publicly of the growth and the potential importance of the emergence of a New Right faction in Iran, both for the country itself and for the international community as a whole. This was still when President Khatami was in power, and most commentators were assuming that his successor would be a like-minded person who would successfully assume his mantle and also pursue ably policies consistent with Khatami's priorities and wishes.

While we were speaking of the broader dangers to the reformists and their agenda represented by the rise of the New Right, others were saying that the neoconservatives' success in the Majlis elections was little more than a bleep in the historical process of reform. Unlike so many other commentators, we refused to view the reform movement as part of a linear flow of history whose destiny had somehow been preordained. This was not an ahistorical and mechanical process – as Iran's own history had already shown. To assume that the reforms had a historical destiny also overlooked the fact that power, real power in terms of action and decisions, circulated in a complex way in the Islamic Republic. We were keenly aware of the dynamics of the Iranian political system and the importance of the place and the role of the Right in the system. However, we were also mindful of the structural weaknesses of the reform movement itself; it had been clear to us since the municipal elections of 2003 that the reform camp was running into the ground under its own weight, and also because of its inability to constructively respond to the challenges being posed by the Right. Their boycott of the elections seemed to us to be a woefully inadequate response to the political manipulation of the conservative forces. It seemed that the reformists had everything to lose – even without the Right trying to win it from them.

We were, therefore, anticipating a major conservative backlash to the Khatami years. What none of us could have predicted however was the neoconservatives' ability to emerge, in the course of the 2005 presidential elections, with their own independent voice. For reasons to be explained later in this book, this voice came to prominence in the form of Dr Ahmadinejad, despite the presence of more eminent conservative candidates, such as Bagher Qalibaf for example. How Ahmadinejad emerged to champion the Right faction and what his electoral success has meant for the conservatives and the traditionalists, and the reformists alike, forms the core of this study.

In completing this book we have been fortunate to have interacted with a large community of commentators, experts, policymakers and students of modern Iran. We have interacted with this large and well-informed community both under the auspices of the Centre for Iranian Studies here in Durham and also on our various travels to conduct our research and to exchange views about developments in Iran. We would very much like to acknowledge our debt of gratitude to our colleagues and friends who have helped us over the last two years to sharpen our ideas and to follow up leads that have enriched our own thinking about the exercise of power in the Iranian political establishment. We are particularly grateful to the secretariat and the wider membership of the Centre for Iranian Studies for helping us along the way with interesting suggestions, the provision of references that had not been made available to the public before, and the gathering of information about key events in Iran over the second term of President Khatami. However, any shortcomings in the book are entirely the authors' responsibility and we do hope that all of our interlocutors will be satisfied with the outcome of our efforts. Ultimately though, it is you, the reader, who will have the final say – so now that you have this text in your possession we take comfort from the thought that you too can share in the pleasure that we had in writing it.

Anoushiravan Ehteshami and Mahjoob Zweiri
Durham

INTRODUCTION

'Iran is unpredictable.' Such a brief statement can truly encapsulate the nature of Iranian politics over the last three decades. This is not just our view but also that of many Iran-watchers, and even certain Iranian officials themselves with whom we have had the pleasure of discussing our book. As a case in point, it was in the course of unpredictable events (and quite contrary to the reports of the Central Intelligence Agency (CIA) stationed in Tehran in 1978) that the imperial regime lost power within just ten months of largely unarmed street protests in the country. The fall of the Shah occurred within months of President Jimmy Carter daringly referring to Iran as an 'island of stability' in a volatile region. Within a short period of time the new fountainhead of the volatility that President Carter had referred to was to be his depicted 'island of stability' itself. In the end, the Pahlavi monarchy was not strong enough to survive the challenge of the conservative clergy who had thus far been portrayed by analysts as being weak, ineffective and disorganized. The unpredictable happened.

Just as unpredictable was the arrival of the 'reform revolution' in Iran in May 1997, which rose to pre-eminence under the authority of the mild-mannered cleric Hojjatoleslam Muhammad Khatami.

He pushed the boundaries of debate in the Islamic Republic to a level not seen in the Muslim Middle East, and was indeed credited for trying to overcome the gloom of a 'clash of civilizations' by encouraging an inclusive discourse, which was later to be dubbed the 'dialogue of civilizations' by the United Nations (UN). In his own country Khatami championed the rights of civil society.

Thus barely a decade after the revolution, and despite the consequences of the long and exhausting Iran–Iraq war in the 1980s and the commonly held belief that the war would weaken the Islamic Republic, the state had become, if anything, socially stronger and more united. The war itself of course had helped the religious leadership to consolidate their grip on power by purging a number of opposition political factions. These forces had been involved in the anti-monarchy revolution from the beginning but also had been against Ayatollah Khomeini's *Valiy-e Faqih* system, and for this they had to be dealt with. Such secular entities as the communist Tudeh party, the Islamist-leaning Mujahideen Khalaq and even the Nehzat-e Azadi (Freedom Movement) were marginalized or institutionally destroyed by the end of the war period, paving the way for further centralization of authority in the hands of Ayatollah Khomeini's chief allies.

Interestingly, despite the pressures of war, Iran had had at least half a dozen significant elections throughout the 1980s, which also helped to consolidate the Islamic elite's power base (in as much as helping them to legitimize their political control of the country through the medium of the ballot box). The same process also enabled the new revolutionary elite to introduce Islamic law into many realms of public and private life in Iran and to further weaken the presence of secular-leaning forces in the country. As with all revolutionary regimes, propaganda about the 'imposed war' and the 'enemy from outside' were used as justifications for the introduction of a whole host of new laws and regulations. That early revolutionary spirit has always been around and, in more recent times, has again been resurrected to chart a new path for the Republic.

By the end of the war, therefore, Iranian politics had become much better structured and had found for itself a strong institutional base, despite the economic challenges that had been created as a consequence of the revolution itself and the costs of war. Having said this, as the war ended the Islamic Republic of Iran appeared to have no clear direction in developmental and public policy terms; constitutionally it needed reform and its whole war-driven economic strategy was in urgent need of revision and overhaul. The main concern, of course, was the reconstruction of the shattered economy and a recovery plan for the years of inefficient central planning and of the restrictive 'war economy'. Interestingly, it was in 1365 (1986)[1] that Iran for the first time started to debate the issues of privatization, borrowing money from international financial institutions and liberalization of economic activity, but these debates did not make much legislative progress at that time. Alongside the debates about the state of the economy, however, concerned voices were beginning to be raised also about the cultural and political challenges facing the country. It was around this time that issues such as the needs, problems and aspirations of the youth – the Islamic Republic's first generation – were being aired publicly.

However, the war and the presence of Ayatollah Khomeini himself prevented these debates from germinating into action plans. That had to wait until the end of the war and the rise of the Rafsanjani administration in 1989. The reconstruction period (1989–97) had proved that Iran was suffering not only from a collapsed economy but also from profound international isolation. The eight years of war and the image of Iran as a country trying to export its ideology and exerting its influence in Middle Eastern politics had created a real challenge for policymaking at home and for foreign relations. But to succeed in reconstructing the Iranian economy, Iran was badly in need of assistance from the international community.

Perhaps one of the most important steps in this regard was taken at the sixth Organization of Islamic Conference (OIC) summit in Senegal in 1991. Rafsanjani (the recently elected Iranian president and former speaker of the Iranian parliament) attended this conference and his meetings with Islamic leaders were so effective that more than ten Islamic countries decided to renew their diplomatic relations with Iran, which in turn proved vital for convincing the rest of the international community that Iran was open for business. Equally important for the post-Khamenei president was, of course, to try and change the image of Iran in the West. However, the movement towards the West was slow and dominated by suspicion and fear, keeping relations at a fairly low level for much of the reconstruction period. The West itself also continued to have worries about Iran. Another impediment perhaps to warmer relations was Iran's rush to strengthen its relations with the Non-Aligned and Warsaw Pact countries, most notably the Soviet Union and China.

Until 1997, the contours of the state in Iran had been deeply shaped by Islamic ideology, revolutionary aspirations and singular political thought controlled by religious leaders. Such discourse changed dramatically after 1997, with the election of Muhammad Khatami with a new social, political and economic agenda and a movement demonstrating considerable prowess. The 78 per cent of votes he won in that year's presidential race was a surprising outcome, given the fact that the conservative leadership had given their full backing to their own clerical candidate, the Speaker of Majlis, Hojjatoleslam Nateq-Nouri.

This was the first time in post-revolution Iranian politics that Iranian voters were voting for political diversity, freedom of speech, freedom of knowledge, civil society, liberalization of the economy, political reform and the rule of law. The process that brought Muhammad Khatami to be the fourth president of the Islamic Republic should be understood as a new beginning for discourse in Iranian politics and the arrival of Iranian intellectuals to the centre stage.

Khatami was keen to change the nature of the state from authoritarian and intrusive to representative and accountable. These ideas were unexpected from a man who had spent his political life as a cleric in an Islamist-dominated revolutionary environment and close to the highest levels of revolutionary leadership. Khatami strived to establish a national spirit in the country, based on compromise and cooperation instead of mistrust and mutual confrontation. It was therefore not surprising to see a positive response from the Iranian people to Khatami's calls for a new political environment and infrastructure. However, it was more surprising to see those who had so wholly bought into Khatami's reforms so downhearted and disappointed by the end of his first term in office. Though they voted him in again, they nonetheless started blaming him more openly for not achieving his stated objectives, which he had repeatedly promised he would do.

Khatami's era has been attacked by conservatives and neoconservatives alike for not giving sufficient attention to the solving of Iran's economic problems and not addressing the people's daily economic concerns. For these critics, Khatami's main sin had been his neglect of the role of the state in the political economy of the country. For them, the promotion of political reforms was a misadventure and promise of a false dawn; the priority, they believed, was the improvement of the living standards of the Iranian people. Such concerns dominated the new march of the conservative forces back towards power. The new approach of the neoconservatives, who began to articulate a public platform only after their first victory in the municipal elections in 2003, brought the issue of the economy and economic reforms to the heart of the national agenda. Soon after, a new economic discourse began to appear about the direction of reforms in general in Iran and the place of economic reforms therein. The neoconservatives had found a new rallying cry: economic justice – one that resonated favourably with the masses. The conservatives also began to speak well of the so-called 'Chinese economic model', which dominated their economic discourse. The sum of this, it transpired, was to be economic liberalization under strong state patronage.

The election campaign of the neoconservatives in the Seventh Majlis elections in 2004 and also in the ninth presidential elections in 2005 further underlined their economy-based strategy. These two elections in Iran changed the country's political atmosphere, bringing with them a whole host of new faces to the seat of power. Looking at the make-up of political forces in Iran it can be argued that, since the revolution, three main forces within the establishment can be discerned: the traditional conservatives, the liberal reformists and the neoconservatives.

In this book we shall put much of our effort into examining the rise to power of the third political force, and into explaining how it emerged from within the state system in Iran to come to dominate it. However, we will not be ignoring the other two forces and are keen to explore the interplay between all three in order to provide a clearer understanding of the nature and basis of post-Khatami factional politics in the country.

This book is divided into five main chapters. Chapter I deals with reform in Iran and tries to understand the nature of the reform movement since 1997. It also tries to explain the divisions within the reformist camp itself and also the damaging consequences for them of the absence of clear definitions of the reform agenda at both the policy and theoretical levels. In addition, it also highlights the growing role of the military establishment in Iranian politics during the reform era, and traces the nature of the relationship between the Revolutionary Guards (the Sepah) and Khatami's government. The Sepah leadership and their traditional conservative allies understood the agenda of the reform movement as being a campaign for power in order to change the nature of the Khomeini-founded state. This critical perception generated a myriad of obstacles for the reform camp and challenged it at every step of the way. The tensions between the two camps of reformists and conservatives caused a serious imbalance in both the power and institutional relationships at the heart of the ruling establishment, inviting political engagement by the security forces of the state.

The chapter also explores the legacy and the achievements of the reform movement as a whole, despite the many serious obstacles that the movement faced. At the abstract level, the reform movement made possible open discussions of the questions of legitimacy of leadership, civil society, human rights, Islamic democracy and transparency in politics. It also, at the practical level, helped to encourage more debate about the nature of the Iranian state as a religious state in the twenty-first century, and the rule of law in Iranian politics within the parameters of a self-declared Islamic Republic. The chapter concludes by arguing that the reform movement has stopped at the state level, although some aspects of the movement and its discourse have become so central and embedded that even the neo-conservatives have had to adopt it in order to successfully chart their ascent to power.

Chapter II discusses in detail the neoconservatives' ability to change their strategy to gain power by distancing themselves from traditional conservatives and at the same time adhering to some aspects of reformist discourse. Their three election victories – at council, parliamentary and presidential level – have demonstrated the neoconservatives' ability to rise to a position of dominance in a very short period in the three bases of power in Iranian politics. Institutional and electoral politics, which took hold in the 1980s, provided the basis for the rotation of power in Iran, and the nature of power distribution made the smooth rise of the neoconservatives possible.

This chapter explores the issue of confrontation between the reformists and the traditional conservatives in the winning of the majority of seats in the councils elections, the seventh parliamentary elections and the ninth presidential elections. It also emphasizes the importance of the strategy followed by the traditional conservative forces, through such bodies as the powerful Guardian Council and the removal of the reformist camp from the electoral scene via the blatant disqualification of their candidates from standing for office. Direct intervention in the electoral process not only threatened to delegitimize the authority of the ruling system, but also directly affected the political environment of the elections and encouraged voter apathy.

Chapter III focuses on the meteoric rise of Iran's first neoconservative president. The 'Ahmadinejad phenomena' is explained through a close look at his family background, social roots, early political career and the factors and causes that have propelled him to office. It also discusses the impact of his background and the environment in which he lived on his presidential performance. It goes on to examine the intellectual roots of his policy statements and his relationship with the Sepah in particular and the traditional conservatives in general.

Chapter IV discusses the domestic political challenges of the presidency of Ahmadinejad. It focuses on the struggle for power between the traditional conservatives and neoconservatives on one side and the reformists on the other. It also draws attention to the much neglected divisions within the neoconservative front itself. This chapter is about the changing of the guard and the rise of the middle political generation in modern Iranian politics, and the relationship between this generation and the military. In addition, it will discuss the challenges that Ahmadinejad needs to tackle in managing the economic, political, social and cultural issues facing him and the country.

Chapter V focuses on Iran's regional role under the neoconservatives and it examines the new orientation of Iran's foreign policy. It tries to show the impact of this new political generation on the image of Iran abroad, and the challenges that they have created for the foreign policy of the country. This chapter argues that the new direction of foreign policy and the performance of the president himself have caused additional challenges for the country's foreign relations and role in the world. It also brings to the fore the clash of the neoconservatives within Iran with the United States of America (USA) on Iraq. It explores the regional and international concerns of Iranian influence in Iraqi politics post-Saddam, paying particular attention to the implications for the region of the growing concerns that are coming from many Arab capitals about Iran's growing influence in Arab affairs. This chapter also highlights the dangers of a confrontation between Sunni and Shia sects in the region as a result of the regime change in Iraq in 2003. In addition, the chapter deals with the Iranian nuclear issue and the concerns that have been raised by the international community and regional governments over this programme. It concludes by discussing the role of the USA in 'managing' the 'Iran crisis' and the range of policy options available to the international community for dealing with Iran's nuclear programme.

The conclusion of this book discusses the many facets of Ahmadinejad's time in office. It highlights the implications for Iran of the rise of the neoconservatives to power and the challenges that they face. Both domestically and externally, the new administration has had to deal with forces beyond its control, but nevertheless it has itself also been a catalyst for further change. The neoconservatives' rise, personnel, behaviour and also policies, we believe, have all further added to Iran's complexity, and also to the unpredictability of its politics.

I

REFORM IN IRAN – WHAT WENT WRONG?

One of the problems of reform was that there was no precise definition of reform and every individual and group involved thought they were reformists.

Hojjatoleslam Muhammad Khatami, 10 June 2006

INTRODUCTION

Without giving in to a deterministic view of modern Iranian political history, against which Gheissari and Nasr also strongly argue, it is still possible to discern a certain pattern in the reform process in Iran.[1] Indeed, five patterns of political discourse can be said to have dominated politics in twentieth-century Iran: 'the traditional patrimonialism of the Qajar era, democratic parliamentarianism of the constitutional era, modernizing autocracy of the Pahlavi era, revolutionary ideology of the Islamic Republic, and the end of the democratic pluralism of the reform movement'.[2] The latter ended officially with the election of President Mahmoud Ahmadinejad as the sixth Iranian president. This chapter will analyse how the reform movement played a significant role in helping the rise of Iran's neoconservative forces, who are ideologically Islamist, revolutionary in character, and populist in application and policy terms, to the heart of Iran's political institutions. This forms the basis of our definition of neoconservatism in Iran, which is a largely non-clerical force and is dominated by the security actors.[3]

Unpredictable change is how some commentators summarized developments in Iran after 1997. As mentioned previously, what has become known today as the Islamic Republic's reformist movement acquired international prominence in the wake of Hojjatoleslam Muhammad Khatami's overwhelming victory in the May 1997 presidential poll. Against all odds and expectations, this mild-mannered cleric's election victory promised to usher in a new era in post-revolutionary Iran. It is apparent from his first term in office that Khatami, former cabinet minister and close confidant of Ayatollah Khamenei, had very real electoral commitments to reforming the system and opening it up to public scrutiny and accountability. As evidence of this, we can point to the fact that by the end of his first term Khatami had not only managed to change and reshape the country's political agenda and introduce new and controversial dimensions to the national debate, but actually shifted the geography of the debate to the public arena, allowing the population to evaluate and make informed judgements about the very nature of the country's Islamic system of governance. While perhaps his administration proved less successful in actually implementing the wide range of social and political reforms promised, his reformist agenda nonetheless set the benchmark by which the Islamic Republic was to be judged by Iranians themselves as well as by an ever attentive international community.

President Khatami unashamedly championed reform of the governing system in Iran, proposed comprehensive changes to the country's civil-state relations, and sought to make the Islamic system more in tune with the aspirations of the people. Observers of modern Iran cannot help but be struck by the historical parallels between Khatami's 'revolutionary' agenda for reform and the two earlier occasions in which the desire for political change had become the country's defining force. The first of these was the 1905–6 Constitutional Revolution, which gave Iran its first taste of 'modernity' and, in the process, brought the Qajar Dynasty to an unceremonious end. The second was Iran's 1979 revolution against the Pahlavi regime and its westernized system of governance.

Looking at the two revolutions, the Constitutional Revolution, despite its early successes, did not manage to institutionalize the aspirations of Iran's modernizers and early democrats. On the other hand, the 1979 Islamic Revolution, having given birth to an altogether new and unique political order, was said to be the embodiment of the Iranian people's historic and spiritual aspirations. Yet, barely 20 years after the Islamic Revolution, we find Iran yet again in the grips of another period of rapid change and deep-seated transformation, facing the same fundamental questions as in 1905. In this context it is pertinent to raise the question, how much socio-political progress did Iran really make through the course of the late twentieth century? To answer this question adequately, one needs to trace the origins and nature of the reform process today and to consider some of its consequences.

The evolution of Iran's political system in the 1990s, characterized by some key constitutional reforms in 1989 following the end of the Iran–Iraq war and the death of the founder of the new Republic, Ayatollah Khomeini, can be divided into two distinct periods: the pragmatist-reconstructionist Rafsanjani presidency (1989–1997); and, the pragmatist-pluralist Khatami presidency (1997–2005). President Rafsanjani, a seasoned politician, close ally of Ayatollah Khomeini and a central figure in the Islamic revolutionary elite since the revolution itself, became Iran's first executive president in 1989, winning 13.5 million out of the 14.2 million votes cast in that year's presidential poll. Despite the customary level of horse-trading in appointments to senior posts, the make-up of Rafsanjani's cabinet largely reflected his administration's core objectives: reconstruction of the shattered country and reform of the economy and the bureaucracy. To this end, he assembled a team of largely Western-educated technocrats and social reformers. He set up what he himself dubbed 'the cabinet for reconstruction', with Khatami as one of its key social reformers.

By any measure his agenda was a reformist one, albeit largely limited to the reform of the economy and creation of the right conditions for growth. His proposed reforms, which won praise from the conservative forces who later came to oppose President Khatami's political and social reforms, hinged on the introduction

3

of sweeping market reforms, privatization and structural adjustment. So comprehensive was his brief that his economic reform strategy won the approval of the International Monetary Fund (IMF) for its thoroughness and depth.

Rafsanjani gained the support of the *Faqih* (Ayatollah Khomeini), as well as the backing of the Majlis. The Majlis was gradually won over as Rafsanjani slowly dropped his social reform agenda (including Khatami himself from his cabinet) in favour of practical measures that would move the economy towards the free-market system. Support from the Majlis, however, had to be 'engineered', and a pro-economic reform majority from the ranks of the conservative and right-wing forces had to be found. Thus, in the course of the early 1990s, Rafsanjani led a successful campaign against the so-called étatist and Islamic leftist and populist forces, which led to their wholesale exclusion from the Fourth Majlis (which begun work in 1992) at a particularly critical time in the reform process. Once in place the conservatives supported most of the Rafsanjani administration's economic programme, but there was continued opposition to the liberalization of foreign trade and unhindered foreign investment (and support for the maintenance of subsidies on certain foodstuffs and primary inputs), despite the removal of the architect of the economic reforms, Mohsen Nourbakhsh, from the cabinet. In this fashion, the conservative forces gained control of the Majlis, and were to keep it until the Sixth Majlis elections in February 2000.

The price for the Rafsanjani–conservative partnership was the wholesale removal of political and social reforms from Rafsanjani's reform agenda. To put this in the context of the shift in Rafsanjani's agenda, suffice to note that Rafsanjani himself entered the Majlis race with the conservative camp and against the Khatami reformers in the Sixth Majlis elections. This is testimony to the relationship he had struck with the conservative forces in the early and mid-1990s and the gap that had appeared between him and his reform agenda and that of Khatami. Even more telling was the very low support that he and his family received from the electorate: his daughter, who has been a close ally of the reformers, was not elected, his brother was not elected and he himself abandoned the chase after it was made clear that his presence in the Majlis would not be welcomed. This is perhaps the sorry end of the first phase of reform in Iran since the late 1980s.

KHATAMI'S RISE TO POWER

The second reform period began rather unexpectedly and was marked by the stunning election victory of Hojjatoleslam Khatami in the presidential poll of May 1997, the seventh such elections held in Iran since 1979. His victory shocked conservative forces and pundits alike. Despite a great media campaign and senior clerical support from the *Faqih* (Supreme Leader) downwards for the conservative candidate, speaker of the Majlis since May 1992 and former cabinet minister Hojjatoleslam Nateq-Nouri, Iran's youthful electorate, female voters and the majority of town dwellers turned their back on the conservatives and their champion. The profound rejection of the conservatives is reflected in the election result itself: with some 20 million votes, Khatami secured 69 per cent of the almost 30 million votes cast in the election, compared with Nateq-Nouri's figure of just 26 per cent. There were very few strongholds to be identified for the conservatives. The message from the Iranian people was loud and clear: 'We want change!' – as many cried during the election campaign.

Khatami and his allies have become known as the '2nd Khordad movement' (the date of the election in the Persian calendar) and are characterized by their advocation of pluralism and growth, and development of Iran's civil society. More specifically, he and some prominent members of his 'rainbow coalition' – which included the old Islamic leftist-populist forces edged out of the public arena by Rafsanjani in the early and mid-1990s, modernists, technocrats and Islamic liberals – have spoken of the need to introduce large-scale political and economic reforms and the empowerment of the citizen. Detailed policy initiatives included the call for more personal freedoms, social justice, privacy, tolerance, public participation in the affairs of the state, consolidation of the rule of law, an open and free

5

press, establishment of political parties, transparency in government, accountability and an end to corruption. A breath-taking agenda for any government, it has to be said – not least for one still gripped by ideology and dogma.

Ironically, in many ways the 2nd Khordad movement marked the final unravelling of ideology from the Islamic Republic's policies and underlined the policymaking processes that President Rafsanjani had championed for much of his term in office. However, as subsequent developments testify, Khatami's key success from the outset was his ability to move the reform agenda forward and to associate himself with the deeply felt wishes and desires of the Iranian people. It is this latter issue that is most interesting, for it is not so much that Khatami was ever ahead of the people but rather, in a manner of speaking, alongside them. All the evidence suggests that it has been the majority of Iranian people who have been pushing open the doors of debate and reform in the country, egging the reformers on, and, by virtue of asking for a better future, demanding change at all levels of society, culture and government. In many ways, it is they and their actions that had given substance and a sense of purpose to the reform agenda of the Khatami administration.

DEVELOPMENT OF THE 2ND KHORDAD MOVEMENT

The 2nd Khordad movement's aims are clear: to overhaul the Islamic Republic; modernize its structures; rationalize its bureaucracy; and put in place a more accountable and responsive system of government. In short, the movement seemed to be looking to 'normalize' the state (in terms of brining it more into line with other modern states and systems of government) and for it to be a force for positive change in the international system. While different groups of the 2nd Khordad coalition pursued slightly different priorities, on the whole they were committed to the process of change championed by Khatami.

In a striking fashion, the team assembled by the president reinforced the reformist nature of his government. Of the 22 cabinet members he presented to the Majlis for ratification in 1997, no less than seven had PhDs, eight were engineers (*mohandes*) and all three clerics had advanced theological degrees. Moreover, one of the three clerical members of his 1997 cabinet, Hojjatoleslam Nouri, was one of the most outspoken members of the new team on social reform.

The 2nd Khordad movement consolidated its May 1997 gains with victories in the February 1999 municipal elections and the February 2000 elections for the Sixth Majlis. In the municipal elections, they secured control of virtually every major city and a majority of towns as well. These elections marked the first time that the Iranian people had directly elected their mayors and other local representatives. As such, the municipal elections were the reformists' first stab at the decentralization of power in a highly centralized state. Through this election victory they took control of the country's key constituencies.

Meanwhile in the Majlis elections, the pro-Khatami list won over 60 per cent of the seats. The 2nd Khordad coalition candidates, representing some 20 parties, organizations and groups, took almost all of Tehran's 30 seats – arguably the most important constituency in the country – and the majority of seats in a host of other towns and cities. As this was arguably the Islamic Republic's most openly contested parliamentary election, it is reasonable to draw some lessons from it. First, despite the coalition nature of the reform movement, its candidates were disciplined and all followed the same agenda in their campaigns. Second, the reformist candidates scored highly across the country, sometimes replacing popular candidates who had allied themselves too closely with the centrist list (which also supported the former president, Rafsanjani). The problem for the technocratic centrist camp was the close association of one of their leaders, Rafsanjani, with the conservatives. The electorate punished the centrist front for this association, despite the fact that many of its members had very close and long-standing links with the leaders of the 2nd Khordad movement. The elections for the Sixth Majlis thus provide anecdotal support for the contention that, for the first time in its history, the Iranian electorate discovered the true meaning of tactical voting and took great care to ensure that its true spokespersons entered the new Majlis.

One final observation is linked to the fact that a remarkably small number of clerics actually entered the Sixth Majlis. After a long period of monopoly control of the parliament, over time their numbers have shrunk – from over 150 in the First and Second Majlises in the early and mid-1980s to fewer than half a dozen in the early twenty-first century. Whether this trend indicates an extrication of religion from the key elected offices of the Islamic Republic, or the regime's total, and therefore passive, control of the political system remains to be seen. But the clerics' growing absence from such important bodies as the legislature must be indicative of a still changing and evolving political topology in an avowedly Islamic state.

The 2nd Khordad movement's other major achievement was its ability to modernize and liberalize the media. With over 40 newspapers, weeklies and other papers in circulation (until the conservative backlash of the late 1990s), newspaper kiosks across the country were a hub of activity and debate after the May 1997 elections. The reformist newspapers shouted the loudest, raised the most important issues in a challenging manner, engaged in debate and dared to criticize authority. Through their sheer audacity, they managed to break many of the taboos in this largely patriarchal Muslim society. Many of Iran's recent cultural openings owe much to the efforts of these newspapers. Despite recent setbacks of the reformist press we can conclude that the print media has managed to establish its place as perhaps the most important source of ideas and as an unrestricted forum for wide-ranging and free debate in the country.

THE REFORMIST ELITE AND ITS CHALLENGES

After eight years, the question remains as to whether it was Khatami or Iranian society that got reform wrong. In other words, were the Iranian people content with what President Khatami had achieved or not? To make this clear, we need to go back and take a look at the circumstances under which reform started in Iran, along with the people who were behind it and their background.

The shaping of reform that the world witnessed between 1997 and 2005 went back to the April 1992 Majlis elections and the time the Guardian Council prevented the so-called Islamic left candidates (for example, Behzad Nabavi[4] and Ali Akbar Mohtashmi[5]) from running in the elections. This event established two new divisions within the revolutionary forces. Since then, a new political class has formed from amongst the politicians and former senior officials who served the regime after the revolution. This led to the argument that reform in Iran was not far away from the political elite who were behind establishing the Islamic Republic of Iran, and therefore any change will be affected (positively or negatively) by the nature of the regime.

The reform process under President Khatami depended on three main forces. The first factor was key personnel, such as Said Hajarian. Hajarian was a member of the reformist elite and paid a heavy price for his leadership support role in the reform movement; he was disabled after he was attacked by Said Askar, a member of the hardline vigilante group Guruh-e Feshar. Hajarian joined the Ministry of Intelligence and National Security (MINS) in 1984, and in 1989 he left MINS and started working at the Centre for Strategic Studies, which was linked with the Ministry of Foreign Affairs and a sub-committee of the Supreme National Security Council. Serving in such a place helped Hajarian to attract some former officials of the security–intelligence apparatus to join the reform process. Together they would push the reform movement ahead. As a consequence, such individuals as Akbar Ganji,[6] Mohsen Armin,[7] Abbas Abdi,[8] Hamid-Reza Jalaipor,[9] Muhammad Moussavi-Khoeiniha,[10] Ebrahim Asghar-Zadeh[11] and Mohsen Sazegaran became core allies of Khatami.[12]

Second, the reform process depended on institutional support. One can note the role of four important institutions in this regard: Saseman Mojahedine Enghelabe Eslami (Organization of the Mojahedin of the Islamic Revolution – OMIR), the Majma'a

Rohaneeyoon Mobarez (Forum of Militant Clergy – FMC), the Daftare Tahkeem Vahdat (Office for Fostering Unity – OFU)[13] and the Nehzat-e Azadi-e Iran (Freedom Movement of Iran – FMI).

The third element of the reform movement was the print media. Such publications as *Iran-e Farda* and *Kian* magazines reflected the opinions of the Islamic left and became powerful mouthpieces of the movement. *Iran-e Farda* was also reflecting the viewpoints of the FMI. *Kian*, which was lead by Mashallah Shamolvaezin,[14] became an intellectual fountainhead for former senior officials and senior ex-Islamic Revolutionary Guards Corps (IRGC)[15] personnel.

These three forces were, by calling for change within the political system, working together indirectly and were at the same time creating the reform conditions that would feed into the daily life of ordinary citizens. The 2nd Khordad movement would not have developed without the partnership between Khatami and this powerful reformist elite. This partnership allowed each side to do its job and simultaneously support the other.

In 1999, after students from Tehran University were attacked by hard-line vigilante group Guruh-e Feshar and three were killed, President Khatami delivered a speech, albeit three months after the event, on the occasion of the Student Day, where he defended his reform programme and reiterated the founding principles of his government. This important speech focused on the need to reform the Islamic Republic of Iran system from within, arguing for the preservation of its 'Islamic' and its 'Republican' characters. He spoke of his strategy of 'tolerance' and 'dialogue', which was exemplified in his proud declaration, 'I did not sue anyone' and the claim that the reform movement has made real and important achievements; namely in creating a 'criticizable' and 'responsible' government and in reforming the intelligence system into one 'that works for the safety of the citizens rather than against them'.[16] President Khatami used this platform and this important occasion in the calendar of the country's student movement to respond to the criticisms tabled against him by the Right as well as those coming from the Left who were dissatisfied with the pace of change.[17] He directly accused what he called 'the radical groups' of creating more problems and obstacles for his reform plan.[18] Halfway through his term, we note, Khatami was openly acknowledging that the movement was facing many unforeseen challenges that in turn were slowing the rate of reform.

The challenges that he was referring to were rooted in the Right's efforts to stop the reform process, or at least to limit its scope and impact. The Right's first target was the press. By the end of 2002, nearly 100 newspapers were closed down by the judicial authorities and their editors jailed, including such prominent papers as *Jameeh* (Society), *Tous*, *Salaam*, *Neshat*, *Asr-e Azadegan* (Era of the Free), *Sobh-e Emrooz* and *Iran-e Farda*.

Again, Khatami's response to this challenge was muted and his message of toleration was not well received by his supporters.[19] His enemies and allies alike saw this as a weakness in the face of the Supreme Leader's expression of discontent with the reformist newspapers and his green light for the closures. While Khatami was urging the press to moderate their line, many of the pro-reform journalists were finding themselves in jail on charges of spreading propaganda against the Islamic Republic, publishing falsehoods, offending public decency and insulting Islam.[20] This confrontation also illustrated the deep roots of the power of the Right and their ability to use Iran's judiciary as effective weapons against Khatami's reform campaign. In retrospect, this latest confrontation had marked the beginning of the decline of support enjoyed by the reformist government and was to manifest itself in a notable decline in public support for Khatami's second presidency in 2001.

Evidence suggests that between 1997 and 2001 a fierce battle was raging in Iran between the administration and the hard-liner conservative forces based in many of the non-elected bodies of the regime. These forces had enough support from the judicial authorities to use their interpretations of *shariah* law to great effect against the reformists. At the same time, Khatami's administration was facing new challenges from the Ministry of Intelligence, whose personnel were eventually implicated in the murder of five Iranian intellectuals. This so-called 'war with hidden guns' proved to be another test of

11

the resilience of the movement and of President Khatami's ability to advance his popular cause. In the course of these confrontations, the Right also began targeting Khatami's allies within his movement.

Abdullah Nouri, Khatami's Minster of Interior, ran afoul of the conservative faction in the Majlis and in 1999 was sent to prison for five years after the Clerical Court convicted him on 15 charges. Said Hajarian, Khatami's closest adviser, was attacked by one of the Basij (state militia) and suffered long-term injuries. Hajarian and Akbar Ganji attempted to use the 1998 case of the killing of the five intellectuals to highlight the contradictions within the regime and also to draw attention to the role of groups who were supported by the conservatives. Their strategy was based on the need to show that the killings of the five intellectuals must have been carried out with a *fatwa* (religious decree) to justify them on religious grounds. The individuals concerned paid a heavy price for their role in the reform movement.[21] They were not the only ones to have paid a heavy price, and, as we will see later, as more individuals fell prey to the Right's campaign so the reformists raised the ante and started questioning the authority and role of the *Faqih* himself in the system, along with his role in the counter-reform campaigns of the conservatives.

The second level of pressure on the reformists was the increasing level of censorship by proscription of the Internet and satellite television. The strategy of the Right was a simple one: make communication as difficult as possible. The Iranian conservatives had campaigned against the Internet for the previous eight years, arguing that it had been used as a key publicity medium by the reformists to publicize their policies (and also to publicize to the world the conditions that they were facing in Iran). In 1996, there were only 2,000 Internet users in the country. However, this number steadily rose to 5,000 in 1997, the year in which Khatami was elected president. In 1998 the figure increased to 22,000, a 440 per cent increase. This jumped again to 130,000 users in 2000 and by 2002 the number of Internet users was a massive 1.3 million.[22]

The 'war' on the Internet was key for a number of reasons. First, there were concerns that the Internet was being used to contact the so-called 'enemies of the regime'; second, there were concerns that Islamic values were being undermined through exposure to it. Thus, by the summer of 2003, 10,000 foreign porn sites and a further 200 Iranian sites were being blocked.[23] The desire of the Iranian youth to be able to use the Internet and to maintain the service put pressure on the regime. The regime had difficulties containing the impact of the Internet in any case, but it was also acutely aware of the employment opportunities that the related Internet technologies were creating. Indeed, 'Experts had predicted that if the number of Internet users grows at the existing rate, 150,000 jobs will be created each year in Internet-related fields, which means that at least 700,000 jobs have been created in the last five years.'[24] It is worth noting that the third five-year economic plan (2000–5) had predicted that some 800,000 new jobs would have to be created to keep pace with population growth. The same war was being waged on satellite television and it was being said that the 'enemies of the regime' were trying to penetrate the society through satellite broadcasting and encouraging Iranians to resist the regime's policies. For the conservatives, these were the new battle lines in the realm of ideas. For them, the reform movement represented the internal face of those who wanted to obliterate the Islamic Revolution and they tended to justify their actions on the basis of being the defenders of the revolution's values and legacy.

We can further demonstrate the intensity of the campaign against the reform camp with a review of the workings of the Sixth Majlis in 2000. The reformists came to dominate the Majlis and, with a majority of nearly 200 MPs, gave President Khatami a solid base on which to build his strategy. The reformist coalition (the 2nd Khordad Front and Islamic Iran Participation Front 'Moshareket') dominated the Sixth Majlis and had given hope that the movement would be successful in defeating the Right through the operation of competitive politics. As already noted above, before 2000 there was little confidence that President Khatami could work alone and without the support of the Majlis. Until 2000 the Right, who had held the majority of seats in the Fifth Majlis, had effectively blocked the legislative

13

drive of the administration. So now new hope was being given to the movement and the Sixth Majlis was the reformists' second chance to advance their national liberalization agenda. It was expected that the huge majority in the Sixth Majlis would easily institutionalize the reform process, and enact laws and rules that would effectively transfer more power to civil society.

By 2003 President Khatami was sufficiently confident to take the next bold step, by advocating the institutionalization of the rule of law and the definition of powers of representatives of the regime. Thus, he submitted two key bills to the Majlis, said to be aimed at 'limiting the powers of the Right wing by stripping the Guardian Council of its right to vet candidates for public office and enable the president to challenge the judiciary', and also 'to assess the position of the president as the number-two figure in the state after the Supreme Leader'.[25] Khatami's proposed legislation faced tough opposition from the beginning from the Right, who considered this an attempt to weaken their power base and the first step towards revising the constitution again in order to limit the powers of the Leader. There were also parallels being drawn with the 1905–6 Constitutional Revolution, for then despite the clerics' critical role within the movement they were ultimately marginalized by secular forces, who came to dominate Iranian politics until 1979.

Despite his majority support in the Sixth Majlis and much public support for the proposed legislation to redefine the powers of various unelected institutions in the country, in the end the president was forced to withdraw the bills. This was because of both massive pressure from the Right and his own real concerns that the bills could provide the opportunity for his opponents to also challenge the authority of the presidency itself.[26]

If the failure to institute legislative change was not enough, Khatami was also having to fight on another front with the conservatives, namely over the economic agenda. In his second year in office, in 1998, he was already calling for the implementation of the so-called Economic Rehabilitation Plan (ERP). This plan listed the *dagdageha* (concerns) of the government: high unemployment and the urgent need to create jobs; a shortage of investment funds and the need to secure financing to underwrite productive projects; bringing the country's economic monopolies under government control; and the need to repeal statutes inimical to investment and growth. Other concerns raised in the plan related to the budget's heavy reliance on oil export revenues, the need to improve the treasury's fiscal structure, control high inflation in order to protect the people's purchasing power and guarantee their minimum living standard, and finally to reduce the imbalances in the country's external payments and improve Iran's position with its major trading partners.[27]

Khatami's administration, therefore, undertook a review of the legislation regarding foreign investment, proposing to encourage investment in all sectors including the oil industry. Looking at some of his administration's economic initiatives, it is clear that his economic strategy was based on absorbing foreign and domestic capital as part of the privatization strategy of the government. The Privatization Organization was established in 2001 as a new initiative of the administration. The government also provided incentives for Iranians to buy shares and invest in these companies. The plan was to accelerate the sale to the public by offering some $1.5 billion worth of public securities. The target for fulfilling this plan was March 2003, which in the end was not achieved due to political wrangling.[28] The government also established the oil reserve fund in the Central Bank of Iran. High oil prices encouraged the government to create this fund, and by the time of its introduction in the early 2000s, oil exports were generating over $23 billion a year in revenue for the government.[29]

Finally, it is worth noting that these new initiatives did succeed in creating an average of 255,000 jobs a year in 1997-2000 period,[30] short of the third five-year economic plan (2000-5) target of 800,000 jobs, but still fairly impressive given the economic climate. Iran also succeeded in convincing the World Bank to approve loans totalling $432 million to the country, following the World Bank's decision to resume lending to Iran in May 2000.[31]

MILITARIZATION OF POLITICS IN IRAN SINCE THE IRAN–IRAQ WAR

The armed forces and the Sepah are accountable to the Supreme Leader Ayatollah Ali Khamenei as their commander-in-chief, but during Rafsanjani's first administration (1989–93) the Artesh's (Army's) position was re-established as the defender of the country's territorial integrity, and the Sepah was encouraged to embrace a single administrative structure with the Artesh as its backbone. Management lines were reformed and simplified and the newly established National Security Council was given the all-important task of threat assessment and evaluation.

Towards the end of his first term and throughout his second, however, Rafsanjani was hampered by the activities of a resurgent (New) Right, which had capitalized on the demise of the left–centrist forces at his hands in order to build a powerful institutional base across the governing framework; they found a strong foothold in the Leader's office, the Majlis, the judiciary, the Intelligence Ministry and the Sepah. The neoconservative New Right was so firmly in place by the mid-1990s that its leadership seemed poised to take over the presidency as well, which was becoming vacant in 1997. Several Sepah and Basij leaders openly nailed their colours to the Right's mast at that time and supported the candidacy of Hojjatoleslam Nateq-Nouri, who until then had been the Speaker of Parliament. However, largely thanks to their greed and monopolistic tendencies, the neoconservatives in the end had not only precipitated the rise of their own anti-thesis – the mass-based 2nd Khordad reform front – but actually had encouraged, through their socially conservative policies, the social backlash against their own camp.

It should be recalled that the conservative wing rose rapidly because by 1990, barely two years after the end of the ideologically driven war, the issue of moral corruption had become a major social concern. The neoconservatives, championed by the Leader and managed by such figures as Nateq-Nouri, were anxious to use this problem both as a ladder to climb the power pyramid and as a

16

means of undermining the public policies of the Rafsanjani administration. With around 63 per cent of the population under the age
of 25, the clerical elite were increasingly concerned that the majority
of Iranians were now net consumers of not only goods and services
but also of ideas and habits. The latter were increasingly being acquired from the West. The Leader had mused openly on several
occasions about the youth's addiction to Western culture, and had
expressed the fear that the children of the revolution could develop
a dependence on it – a dependence which, if not broken, would
eventually consume the Islamic state in its entirety. The regime, it
was suggested, should try hard to identify and eradicate the causes
of moral corruption.

By the mid-1990s the moral crusade was in full swing, but its
operation had been compounded by a nervous executive branch that
had the unenviable task of reconciling the problem of providing for
the material well-being of such a young society with a mounting
national debt of over $25.0 billion and stagnant income from the
production of hydrocarbons. The Islamic regime also faced a further
problem: despite years of Islamization, the Iranian youth proved
much harder to 'control' than originally anticipated. Khatami was a
pioneer amongst Iranian leaders, readily admitting that the nature
of the world in which we live is such that today's youth, irrespective
of background and upbringing, is not only highly cosmopolitan and
culturally diverse, but is also open to new ideas and receptive of 'alien'
habits. He further recognized that the country's limited outlets for
social activity and entertainment were driving the youth away from
the regime and into the arms of what the Islamists called 'satanic
cultures'. Worse still, the youth seemed to accept readily and identify with the 'MTV culture' (received illegally by satellite by most of
Iran's average-income urban dwellers), and also to develop a degree
of fondness for the pre-revolution past (the latter trend being fed by
the older generation who reminisced nostalgically about the 'good
life' before the revolution). These trends in turn tended to reinforce
the country's secularizing tendency, which had been developing apace
throughout the 1990s.[32]

17

The combination of political impasse and the economic failures that had gripped the country before the election of President Khatami in May 1997 provides an explanation for the vehemence with which the traditionalist and rightist factions (particularly the New Right) in the elite sought to impose a stricter Islamic code of behaviour on society. They tried to do this through such Islamic-populist parastatal bodies as the Basij. Cynics would say that cultural identity is in a sense all that the Iranian Islamist leaders have to show for the Islamic Revolution, and therefore they will do their utmost to protect their achievements in this regard. To the traditionalist and rightist forces, moreover, the cultural realm is the only, all-important, dimension that distinguishes Iran from other developing (even Muslim) countries. In economic policy terms, it can be argued, most of the ideologues of these groups are free marketers with deep roots in Iran's commercial centres of power; even in foreign policy terms they seem reconciled to the reformers' line. All that remains distinct and unique to them is the fundamental values of the Islamic state, its religious–cultural underpinnings. In short, Iran's neoconservatives see the cultural fundamentals of the Islamic Republic as all that remains distinct from a fading Islamic Revolution, and is therefore worth protecting.

It is within this social context that the regime encouraged groups such as Ansar-e Hezbollah and the Basij to enter the fray. The Basijis themselves, many of whom are youthful and ambitious individuals, began training for the attack on 'cultural impurities' that they perceived were continuing to infect the Islamic Republic. In this sense, the concern of the New Right had been more to try and contain the growing extension of American culture, which ironically has elsewhere accompanied the expansion of capitalism and free enterprise, rather than the economics of 'Americanization'. Iran's New Right fully understood the language of market capitalism; what it objected to was its American garb under the conditions of globalization.

Domestically political tensions, continued in-fighting and the prolonged economic crisis tended to increase the Rafsanjani administration's reliance on its coercive machinery. Of course, national political

18

tensions during the Rafsanjani period had much to do with Iran's economic fortunes as well.[33] Actual gross national product (GNP) per capita in Iran in the 1990s, for example, did not get much above the $1,500 mark and remained well below the needs of an average family (of 5.5 children). Another measure of the economic situation can be taken from increases in food prices in recent years, with increases of over 350 per cent by the late 1990s, which of course has had a devastating impact on the fixed-wage sectors of society (that is, the majority of the country's workforce) and a not inconsiderable impact on the core of the regime's urban poor power base as well.

In other areas too the 1990s brought many uncertainties for Iranians. Changes in the social and economic positions of different strata followed the introduction of privatization, which hit some of the elite's vested interests while enriching others. And multiple exchange rates, which were abolished in Khatami's second term, adversely affected the bazaar and money-changing communities. In a nutshell, Rafsanjani's economic initiatives destabilized the social pyramid sufficiently for serious tensions to begin to appear in the edifice of the Republic, particularly in relations between state and civil society. These tensions began manifesting themselves in different ways – riots, strikes and sit-ins, political protests. They had at their core, however, problems associated with major changes in the Islamic state's responsibilities towards the 'deprived', its policies with regard to distribution of wealth and income, and the concentration of economic power in the hands of the regime's associates and inner core. Such tensions in turn slowly raised questions about the place of the military as a socio-political force in the new social environment.

Another interesting development impinging on civil–military relations was, and remains, that of factionalism. This has caused Iran's top leaders to recruit their own armed guards, ironically more so amongst the clerics. Such armed guards have in the past been deployed against rivals. The most public instances of such deployments were those between Ayatollahs Khomeini and Shariatmadari in the early 1980s, and between the Khamenei and Ayatollah Montazeri in the late 1980s, but they resurfaced in the Khatami era as violent attacks on the reformers intensified. After 1997, moreover, when factionalist politics escalated to the point of violence, not only did it embroil elements from the Pasdaran (IRGC) but it also posed serious challenges for the national security forces, whose primary function it was to keep order. The question was thus raised, do they try and keep order or do they step out of the way of legitimate demonstrations for reform? In the Khatami period they tended to do both, which of course complicated even further the command structures and the relations between the military and the civilian leadership. If armed gangs were to be deployed by various power centres, for example, the Artesh would have found it almost impossible to escape involvement, particularly if the (largely externally based) opposition groups were to capitalize on the regime's infighting to wage a protracted campaign of terror against its leading elements.

If on the other hand the Sepah was to feel that the regime in its entirety was under threat, it could legitimately deploy its forces 'in defence of the revolution', which under Article 150 it has the constitutional responsibility to do. While during the Rafsanjani period the clarity of the missions of the various military commands were not tested, during Khatami's presidency this problem emerged as one of the single most important issues affecting civil–military relations – the tone for which was already being set by the open support that General Mohsen Rezaie, Commander of the Sepah for 16 years, was providing for the conservative candidate in the presidential race of May 1997. General Rezaie also placed the explanation for the actions of the Sepah leadership during the election campaign in a much broader context. As he stated soon after the election of the new president in 1997:

> It is very difficult for the IRGC men who obey the instructions of the Vali [Leader] to see that there are persons amongst the associates of the president-elect who question the concept of absolute guardianship of the *Valiy-e Faqih* and even dare to consider the vote of the people above that of the Leader. In the meantime, Iran is the land of the 'Imam of the Time' and speaking about national sovereignty and man-made laws vis-à-vis the Divine laws, had made the dear Islamic Guards seriously concerned.[34]

MILITARIZATION OF POLITICS UNDER KHATAMI

Khatami's first term was dominated by civic activities and broad public participation in politics. The masses were truly energized by his stunning election victory and the message he had broadcast.[35] It was soon to manifest that Khatami's ability to win a massive popular mandate, also repeated in the February 2001 presidential race, would open new cleavages between the conservative segments of the elite, who were already well-lodged in the key institutions of state. The duality of leadership between the president and his realm and that of the Leader and the New Right factions would inevitably lead to the crystallization of the duality of power. Institutional-based social forces, such as the Basij and the Sepah, would eventually be forced to take sides.

This had two major consequences for civil-military relations. First, the posture that the security forces as a whole and the military in particular had adopted in the new order would inevitably leave a mark on the traditional balance of power within the elite. Second, it was an open question as to the extent to which revolutionary organizations would manage to keep within the rule of law and outside of politics (Khatami's primary concerns), despite their fears that reform would threaten both their considerable interests in the status quo and the very foundations of the Islamic Republic that they were required to protect. These were indeed uncertain times for all the actors and the first taste of how things might develop came in 1998, when in April the Sepah Commander, General Rahim Safavi, stated to a gathering of Sepah commanders that some of the reformers were 'hypocrites', going on to suggest that all those who threatened the Islamic Republic should be beheaded. He declared openly that pens will be broken and throats cut.[36]

In a meeting with Basiji students in the June of that year he again repeated these comments, adding that his earlier speech had been a provocation designed to expose what he classed as counter-revolutionaries in their midst:

We threw a stone in the nest of the poisonous snakes and we permitted all of them to come out of their nests … This was one of our tactics to identify them better. On June 8 there is the trial of one of those individuals.[37]

The trial of one such 'poisonous snake' that Safavi so candidly referred to was that of none other than the popular, pro-Rafsanjani reformist Mayor of Tehran, Gholam-Hussein Karbaschi. The Sepah leadership had defiantly nailed its colours to the mast of the anti-reformist camp, even going against their former spiritual comrade, Rafsanjani. So, in a public and threatening manner, Safavi had lined up the Sepah against the Khatami camp:

[W]e do not interfere in politics but if we see that the foundations of our system of government and our revolution is threatened … we get involved. When I see that a [political] current has hatched a cultural plot, I consider it my right to defend the revolution against this current. My commander is the exalted leader and he has not banned me [from doing this].[38]

A number of political developments seem to have had the effect of drawing out the military and bringing the Sepah leadership face-to-face with the executive. Looking back, the chain murders in 1998, the assassination attempts on political figures in the same year, the July 1999 student riots, the ultimatums made by the Sepah to the president over this tense period, the friction between power centres, the wider questions about the boundaries of power (including attempted prosecution in various courts of a big group of reformist MPs in the Sixth Majlis) and the student unrest in Khorramabad in 2000 all resulted in greater politicization of parts of the military – notably the Sepah and the Basij – and their direct action at key junctures. The immediate history of the democratic upheaval in Iran in the Khatami period can be written from the perspective of these things, with some critical periods highlighting the turning points in that struggle. With the benefit of hindsight we can say that after the initial excitement of Khatami's victory had subsided, within 12 months of his victory the domestic political fabric had begun to exhibit serious signs of stress.

Although some of the differences feeding into the inter-factional tensions were addressed at the political level, the fact remains that several extra-legal agencies have continued to operate.[39] Alongside such overtly anti-reform bodies as the Special Court for the Clergy and the Supreme Cultural Revolution Council were more shadowy organizations with links to the Sepah and the Intelligence Ministry. Of these, the creation of Sepah's own national intelligence agency (which is able to arrest suspects, question and even imprison them in secret locations) is of particular interest.[40] Prison No. 59 acts as one of the Sepah's main base camps, for instance, and is known as being a facility not open to any scrutiny.[41]

In the context of its intelligence- and security-related activities, and its encounters with the executive branch, it is clear that the Sepah has functioned very much as a political entity – at least this can be said to have been the case since the mid-1990s. With respect to civil–military relations, however, the turning point must be the student riots of July 1999 and the ease with which the demonstrators managed to burst onto the political dance floor and disrupt the careful choreography of the reformers and the neoconservatives. Not only had the scale of the violence unleashed been unprecedented since the heady days of 1979, but the demonstrations, and the security forces' response, created a very real crisis for the stability of the government machinery. First, there was the question of restoring order through the security forces without undermining the position of the students. While this was not an easy task, within weeks of the riots Khatami did manage to appease the students and at the same time collect some scalps from the security forces for the bloodshed and their mishandling of the crisis.

Second, the executive had to respond to the Sepah-orchestrated military challenge it was facing. Back in May 1998, General Safavi of the Sepah had charted for a sympathetic audience in Qom the general orientation of the Sepah in relation to political developments at home and its platform in the context of the reform process. He had stated, in contradistinction to the line espoused by President Khatami, that the Sepah, far from being apolitical, did indeed have a 'political line'. This political line was that of the hard-line 'Imam's line', which respected Iran's national authorities. However, he said, the Sepah respected one authority above all, and that was the guidance of the Leader, the *Faqih*. The president's allies were swift in their response:

> [Mr Safavi's] statements reveal a basic contempt for the popularly elected government that has a mandate to strengthen the rule of law and the roots of civil society. He seems also to have forgotten that the country has a constitution which clearly stipulates that the armed forces are forbidden interference in political affairs. The social reforms being undertaken and the ideas being floated are a natural progression that will only go forward. This is the will of the nation. Threats of violence by the head of our paramount military force will not stem this tide but obviously serve as a source of tension in the society and a potential flashpoint for worse.[42]

Despite the clear tensions between the executive and the Sepah, for a year or so after Hojjatoleslam Khatami's inauguration the two had managed to cohabit. In 1999, however, Safavi was openly lining up against the president. It is in fact a historic irony now that no more than a year after his famous speech in 1998, in which Safavi had outlined the boundaries of the permissible, the Sepah should be severely tested by no other force than a determined but unarmed student body. For it had been a local Basij leader who had declared in November 1998 that, 'our role is a cultural one, attracting students to Islam and fighting against the ideas and cultures imported to Iran from the West. The university is the cultural battleground.'[43] In the summer of 1999 'the University' became the actual battleground of ideas. The Sepah's direct political response to the student protests was the strongly-worded ultimatum letter to President Khatami in which 24 senior commanders of the force (excluding Safavi) issued an unveiled threat to the president and his allies.[44] In it the signatories expressed their frustration with government inaction over threats and challenges to the 'values of the system'. They retorted, 'how long should we have revolutionary patience while the system is being destroyed?' The signatories stated that the Sepah reserved for itself the right to intervene as its 'patience has ran out' and 'it cannot tolerate the continuation of this situation any longer'.

As Safavi had already suggested, the Sepah was more than capable of acting politically. This letter was a clear challenge to the popularly elected head of the executive. Its message clearer still: mend your ways and those of those around you, or face the wrath of the security forces. We now know that the day on which President Khatami received this letter his own defence minister had also been acting out of concert and had been putting further pressure on the beleaguered president. Shamkhani had stated on state television on 13 July 1999 that 'forces loyal to the values of the revolution ... will restore full security ... at any cost'.[45] Clearly, this provocative statement was consistent with the message that the Sepah had sent to the reformist camp and was designed to echo the same from the highest military level. If handled badly, the crisis could potentially have pitched the people (over 20 million of whom had already declared their support for Khatami and his reforms) against the guardians of the revolution and its ideals, and the Khomeini-founded *Faqih*-based Islamic system they purportedly defended.[46]

President Khatami's carefully crafted response to this challenge came in two forms. First, his convening of the National Security Council took the sting out of the tail of inter-agency rivalries and brought the issue of collective responsibility into play. His strategy was to attack in retreat; to take control without conceding political ground. As a result of President Khatami's deliberate 'institutionalization' of the regime's response to the crisis, the Artesh adopted the view that the defence establishment should not, as a rule, form a position on political matters. The president's allies capitalized on the position of the Artesh and built on the public mood against the signatories of the Sepah's ultimatum to argue strongly that the military should not be allowed to issue threats against the country's political leaders or be able to determine the fate of the country.[47] The military, pro-Khatami personalities publicly stated, should know its place and not be allowed to meddle in politics.

Second, the president chose to make his own response to the Sepah's challenge openly and publicly. Some three weeks after the student crisis, in a speech he delivered in the city of Hamedan, he suggested that the military should refrain from interference in government affairs, and that those who attacked the student dormitories during the demonstrations should be brought in front of the courts and be punished for their misdeeds. However as a sweetener to the Right camp, he also maintained that all (referring to the press and the government in particular) should recognize the important role that the Sepah and the Entazami forces were playing in establishing peace and security in the country. They were there, he implied, so people could engage in politics peacefully and without intimidation, and also in order to provide security for millions of citizens who were going about their daily lives.[48]

President Khatami's calculated response was seen as too little by both sides, however. His student supporters were disappointed by his apparent unwillingness to come to their aid and by his public endorsement of the very establishment against which they were rebelling. At the same time, his opponents remained unconvinced that he and his allies did not harbour a wish for wholesale reform of the given system of governance, bent on undoing the 'revolution'. In the last analysis, in a few short years after the devastating war with Iraq, during which the military had left the political space, civil–military relations had emerged in an unprecedented way as a core national issue for the country – beckoning profound changes in state–society relations for the best part of a century.

The impasse encouraged some of the reformist elite to raise the ante and directly and openly challenge the authority of to the Supreme Leader himself, who was the fountainhead of the armed forces and the legitimizing agency for the Sepah.

THE OUTCOME

The constitution of Iran provides a special place for the religious elite of the country. Based on an interpretation of the Shia school, it has enshrined the key concept of the *Velayat-e Faqih* to dominate the political system of Iran. In addition, the *Fuqaha* (community of religious scholars) have the right to interpret Quranic verses and other texts to suit the conditions of the day.[49] Despite forming a committee to review some of the articles of the constitution in 1989, which led to the easing of the requirements for the qualifications for the *Faqih*, the *Valiy-e Faqih* (Supreme Leader) has kept many of his office's constitutional powers – and indeed has acquired more, enabling him to dominate many aspects of the political, social and economic aspects of life in Iran.[50]

It was through the lens of the constitutional authority of the Leader that the right wing or conservative forces justified their criticism of the reformers and saw their initiatives as a direct challenge to the constitution and the place of the Leader therein. It should be underlined that one of the significant developments that came as a consequence of the reform movement was the wave of opinion being expressed about the religious state in Iran, the role of the *Faqih*, his source of legitimacy and authority, and the relationship between democracy and *Velayat-e Faqih*.

Soon after the victory of the revolution, with war raging and the factional battles in full swing, few people showed the inclination to follow the intricate internal debates about the theories of the Islamic state in Iran. Interested parties knew the history of the *Velayat-e Faqih* in Shia thought, but they were much less clear about where it fit in Shia genealogy. According to the Islamic Republic's constitution, the leader must be '*marji' al-taqlid*', a *Faqih*. Article 5 states that

> During the Occultation of the Wali al-Asr, the wilayah and leadership of the Ummah devolve upon the just ('*adil*) and pious (*muttaqi faqih*), who is fully aware of the circumstances of his age; courageous, resourceful, and possessed of administrative ability, will assume the responsibilities of this office in accordance with Article 107.[51]

Being a *Faqih*, just and wise, and possessing piety are therefore the essential qualifications for the Leader.[52]

The role of the *Valiy-e Faqih* fell under the spotlight in the reform era. Reformers began to question openly the wide-ranging authorities of the *Valiy-e Faqih*, whose office they saw as the main obstacle in the path of reform.

Thus in November 1997, just four months after President Khatami came to office, Ayatollah Hassan Ali Montazeri (Khomeini's successor designate until 1988), issued a strong statement criticizing what he saw as the excesses of the theocratic system in Iran. Based on his 600-page memoir, which was released through a website, he emphasizes that the authority of the Supreme Leader should be limited and open to discussion.[53] Montazeri was a critical figure in these debates, who believed in a somewhat modified 'interpretation of the theory of the Mandate of the Jurist that made the Supreme Jurist into [an] indirectly elected office'.[54] With the dawn of the reform era he was now aiming to put an end to the contradictions within the Iranian constitution, believing that the constitution should clarify whether the authority of the Supreme Leader should come from the nation or from God. He further asserted that it should be clarified whether *Valiy-e Faqih* should supervise (*nizart-e Faqih*) the workings of the state, or be involved fully in its day-to-day affairs for which he would need wide authority.[55] The Right saw his intervention as a direct attack on the legitimacy of the *Faqih* in Iran.

However, his intervention also opened the door to more criticisms of the constitution and the authority of the *Faqih*. Soroush, Kadiver and then Agajari became the lead figures in the questioning the *Faqih*'s legitimacy and authority, arguing that the authorities of this office should be defined and also limited. Bringing the issues of Shia political theories, the role of the clerics and the so-called 'official reading of religion'[56] into the political debate in Iran was significant. Abdolkarim Soroush had of course first raised these issues as far back as 1994, in discussion of the official reading of religion. He expressed his view via articles in *Kian* magazine and in such publications as *Mudara va Mudernity* [*Religious Democratic Government*], *Our Expectations of Religion, Maximalist Religion, Minimalist Religion, Ideologized Religion, Religious Ideology*, and *Religious Pluralism*.[57]

Later, Mohsen Kadiver raised the much bigger issue of political theory in Shia thought. In his book *Nazarrieh hayee Doulat dar Fiqh'h Shi'eh* [*The Theologies of State in Shiite Jurisprudence*], he spoke about nine theories of the state in Shia thought. His main message was that there is still a great deal of debate to be had about the nature of the Islamic state, and also that of 'the nation'. To what extent should they be linked?[58] The debate over the role of nation, and whether it should be the source of legitimacy, opened the door to a new discourse of asking for a review of the whole constitution and clarification of who is ruling Iran and who has this authority. Further questions followed: is this rule based on the constitution or does the *Faqih* rule in the name of God and the hidden Imam? This kind of debate was taboo in a country ruled by religious leaders; so it is understandable to see increasing pressure on reformists from religious and conservative groups in Iranian society.

CONCLUSION

The conservatives' defeat in the 1997 presidential race, the local elections of 1999, the Sixth Majlis elections of 2000 and the presidential poll in 2001 were soon overshadowed by their virtual routing in the municipal elections (Iran's first openly contested elections in its long history), where they failed to secure the control of any significant urban centre in the country. By then, the Sixth Majlis was already firmly in the hands of the reformers.

It is not surprising then, that as President Khatami's team became entrenched so the conservatives were galvanized into action. They forced the departure of several leading reformers and of President Khatami's advisers from the political scene (including Nouri and Mohajerani), the imprisonment of a number of the key figures in his camp and the suspension of over a dozen pro-Khatami newspapers. While a conservative backlash was regarded as more or less inevitable by observers, the extent of their fight back, and their methods, continued to cause concern. As Iran's political system is based on the smooth working of a number of competing institutions – the Majlis, the presidency, the ministries, the judiciary, the Expediency Council, the Guardian Council and finally the *Faqih*'s office – it was feared that the continued in-fighting would result in a general breakdown, destabilizing the entire government machinery and creating fertile conditions for the direct involvement in the political process of the anti-reform factions and of the military. There was also some concern that the struggle for power would weaken the reformist camp, increase the prospects for more violent encounters between the various factions, particularly between pro-Khatami students and the security forces, and end in the collapse of the reformist front. There was also concern about the role of vigilante groups who had understood political reform as a step to change the nature of state.

There is little doubt that the reform movement as a whole depended on one man, Khatami, who presented himself as an intellectual first and then a politician. There was no party-political machinery to support him, as most of the political parties had been banned. The political elite and intellectuals, who joined him, were pushing for wholesale reform without considering the nature of the regime or the consequences of their policy recommendations for the country's deeply entrenched socially and politically conservative forces. As Khatami himself put it some time later, the reform movement had in fact become a victim of those who had high and unrealistic expectations of the process.[59]

As we have tried to show, the reformists crossed virtually every 'Red Line' that had been established in Iranian politics, but their biggest sin appears to have been their questioning of the role of leadership, in particular that of the *Velayat-e Faqih*. In the end, the actions of the reformists brought a badly needed sense of cohesion to the Right and galvanized them into action. Using the apparent attacks on the *Faqih*, they rallied their forces and by 2004 they had returned as a viable and powerful political force. This new force however was significantly different from that of the 1990s. The new neoconservative hybrid had matured in the shadow of Khatami's reformers and as its elite looked back to the defeat of their faction in election after election, and in public debate after public debate, they committed themselves to winning both office and the argument as they prepared to fight the reformers on their own turf.

II

THE NEOCONSERVATIVES' MARCH TO POWER

Participation in the elections is not merely a right but a religious duty, and if the enemy fails in its efforts to encourage the [Iranian] nation to boycott the elections, as happened in the elections to the Seventh Majlis, it will accuse us [the Iranian regime] of various types of violations, whether in how the elections were conducted, or in [the nature of] our regime... The enemy opposes widespread, enthusiastic voting by the masses at the polling booths, but the [Iranian] nation is capable of holding authentic elections and of electing the best.

Ayatollah Ali Khamenei, June 2005

INTRODUCTION

The four harsh defeats that the right wing suffered in less than a decade, in the seventh presidential elections, eighth presidential elections, the 1999 local elections and elections for the Sixth Majlis, seemed to have permanently changed the political landscape of the country. Together, they marked the growing imbalance of power between the traditional conservatives, the neoconservatives and the reformists. The dynamism generated by the reform movement reflected the desire within Iranian society for change. Although President Khatami in his eight years in office may have failed to achieve in policy terms the desires and aspirations of his electorate, nonetheless, it is interesting that the groundswell of support for his reforms were such that between 1997 and 2004 he and his allies dominated the national scene. However, despite the rise and overwhelming presence of the reformists in many institutions of the Islamic Republic, the traditional conservative forces kept control of several of key instruments of power, namely the armed forces, the media, the judiciary and the major economic organizations such as the *Bonyads* (foundations).

At the same time, the timeline shows that alongside the electoral successes of the reform front, a more profoundly neoconservative force was also emerging, fearful of change and of the long-term consequences of the reform movement for the survival of the Republic in its existing form. This group included those individuals who remained loyal to the ideals of the revolution and the sacrifices made in the long and bloody war with Iraq in the 1980s.

Thus, there was real conflict on the ground between reformists and neoconservatives; a conflict in which all tools of power were ultimately deployed. To shed further light on the political situation post-1997, we will review the conservatives' strategy towards the reform camp at the height of the latter's political successes. Through this investigation we attempt to analyse how the so-called neoconservative forces emerged, what strategies they finally adopted to win back the support of the masses for their cause and who finally led them back to power. These questions will be answered through a detailed analysis of the first and second municipal elections in 1999 and 2003, the Seventh Majlis elections in 2004, and finally the ninth presidential elections of 2005.

Councils (Municipal) Elections

On 26 February 1999, the Iranian people voted to elect councils for the first time after the revolution. Around 300,000 candidates had registered to participate in this election.[1] The local councils and their role are defined in Chapter 7 of the Iranian constitution. This chapter includes seven articles describing the reasons behind the formation of these councils. It also identifies their tasks, their responsibilities and the eligibility of voters and candidates.[2] Both major camps have traditionally seen the local councils as fulfilling an important national function: 'Islamists who claimed the councils have roots in

Islam's "high priority to consultation" and the Left which saw them as instruments of workers control'.[3]

Local councils act as a strong mobilizing force in societies such as Iran and can generate grassroots support for the ideals of reform or those of the revolution in equal measure. While it is not fully clear why the government decided to implement the law in 1999, nonetheless, the elections in Iran were used as a tool to mobilize the people in support of the government. On the other side, the emerging neoconservative camp was optimistic that these elections presented the first opportunity for them to link with their traditional power base in the provinces and thus secure a massive victory as the first stage of their electoral fightback against the reformers. These elections, therefore, 'were greeted with enthusiasm'[4] by the neoconservatives, just as they had been by the reformists. The local elections were also to test the rural–urban divide that many conservatives believed existed in the support base of the reformers. More broadly, these elections were to feature 'two types of contests, each with its own unique characteristic, the highly politicized capital, Tehran, and to a lesser extent the urban hotspot of Isfahan', which 'mirrored Iran's national struggle between the forces of republicanism and those of traditional clerical power. This issue centered on broad questions of freedom, faith and democracy.'[5]

The outcome of the local councils elections showed that the neoconservatives did not, at that time, enjoy the support of those people who lived outside the major urban centres or even of those in rural areas. Indeed, the results showed that the reformist camp had captured more than 80 per cent of the votes cast. What was even more impressive was the reality that more than 26 million people had participated in this election, making it one of the largest of its kind in the entire Middle East. Perhaps not surprisingly, the reformist candidates won the majority of the seats, in particular in the council of Tehran, the capital. Hojjatoleslam Abdullah Nouri, a former interior minister who was leading the reformists' list in Tehran, 'won 589,000 votes out of 1.4 million ballots cast'.[6] While the reform camp celebrated, the lesson learnt by conservatives was that their political discourse looked old-fashioned and out of date. These elections, it should be remembered, were the first chance that the conservatives had had to test their agenda since their routing in the seventh presidential elections in 1997.

Four years later, on 28 February 2003, Iranians went to the polls again, in the second local elections. The outcome of the election in 2003 proved to be extraordinarily different from 1999. This time, the neoconservatives were to win the majority of seats nationally. The question is, how did this happen? This time, around 200,000 candidates contested local council seats nationally, including 5,000 women candidates. The number of the candidates had decreased from the 330,000 recorded in 1999.[7] This time round the candidates were competing for 180,000 seats nationally (905 city councils and 34,205 village councils).[8]

The turnout, according to Said Hajarian, was just 12–15 per cent of eligible voters in key cities like Tehran, Isfahan, and Mashhad, which was 'not the thing to be proud of'.[9] In Tehran, in which the neoconservatives won 14 out of 15 seats, just 12 per cent of eligible voters had participated.[10] The low turnout in urban areas provided the first tangible sign of the national disappointment in the implementation of the many reform initiatives being pursued by the Khatami administration – even though the fact that many of their candidates had been disqualified by the conservative-controlled committees that were vetting the suitability of candidates will have had something to do with their poor performance![11]

The turnout of the second councils elections (see Tables 1 and 2 in Appendix) was described as a national disaster. The former president, Hashemi Rafsanjani, in admitting that the number of voters at the polls had decreased after the eighth presidential elections in 2001, asked the experts to study 'the matter and clarify the cause'.[12] The 'sharper decline in people's turnout at the polls in different elections' was blamed on the political factionalism dominating the country.[13] Rafsanjani blamed both neoconservatives and reformists for the low turnout in the second councils elections:

In recent elections [councils elections 2003], even more so than some previous ones, there are claims that the Guardian Council's filter has resulted in such a low turnout but this was ruled out as representatives of all factions, from the religious–patriotic candidates and the Liberation Movement figures to the extremists and even those who introduce themselves as the opposition forces of the system were all present amongst the candidates[...] One of the newest hypotheses of the constantly declining number of voters in different elections is that the black picture presented by each of the two main ruling political factions of the other one, has led to the loss of the prestige of both, and this has [damaged] the whole system, leading to lowering the level of public participation.[14]

SEVENTH MAJLIS (PARLIAMENTARY) ELECTIONS

Thus the political atmosphere in Iran was already tense when the conservative Guardian Council announced that it had barred the registration of more than 2,500 hopeful candidates for the Seventh Majlis elections, including the president's own brother, a number of clerics and another several dozen of the incumbent MPs. The majority of the barred hopefuls belonged to the reformist camp, of course, which caused much consternation.

Understandably, the domestic and international reactions to the Guardian Council's decision, which was taken behind closed doors and without consultation with the national political elite, was one of shock and disbelief. The announcement of the decision was followed by loud protests from the reformist camp, a sit-in in the Majlis itself by a large group of MPs, public condemnation by President Muhammad Khatami and the Majlis Speaker (Hojjatoleslam Karroubi) and a request by the Leader (Ayatollah Khamenei) that the Guardian Council consider reviewing its decisions on all the barred candidates. They stood firm, allowing only for the registration of a few hundred of those on the barred list. The trauma of this daring move paralysed civil society and its many organs, thus depriving the reformist camp of a vital support base outside of the political arena itself at a crucial moment in its history. Externally, too, the Council's position was criticized. It was openly accused of trying to engineer the election of a pro-conservative and pro-Leader Majlis.

The candidate list of the neoconservative camp who called themselves the Islamic Iran Developers Coalition (Etelaf-e Abadgaran-e Iran-e Islami), was almost completely approved by the Guardian Council. This list had focused on the main cities, like Tehran; however they also had candidates in almost all other cities. Their main aim, their propaganda stated, was 'serving the Iranian people'. The fortuitous barring of dozens of reform candidates provided momentum for their electoral campaign and eased the way for their success in both the second councils elections and the Seventh Majlis elections of 2004. It was clear to all those who wished to look that the Guardian Council's decision to disqualify the reformist candidates had widened the gap between the traditional conservatives and the reformists. The conservatives openly used their institutional power to facilitate the neoconservatives' victory.

As already noted, their manipulation of the electoral system also brought strong criticism from the international community. The USA and European Union (EU) countries let their objections be made in public, and in strong terms. Many observers could not help but note that the neoconservatives had chosen a bad time, internationally at least, for 'rigging' the electoral system in their own favour but, in the last analysis, crisis did favour these forces.

The domestic and international outcry may have added to national tensions, but it did not change the new dynamics being injected into the system by the Right. The protests, objections and criticisms did not significantly change the political map that the Guardian Council had already drawn. The election week itself was marked by an odd mixture of complacency and apathy on the part of many voters, indecision on the part of others, immobility on the part of many pro-reform groups (the bulk of whom had chosen to 'withdraw' from the elections, a euphemism for a boycott) and a massive media drive (invoking both revolutionary and nationalist images) to encourage the electorate to turn out in force on 20 February 2004.

The media tide kept hitting the apparently solid wall of apathy – until, that is, the election day itself. Pundits inside and outside of the country were confidently predicting a voter turnout of 10 per cent or, at best, 30 per cent. On the other hand the participating reformists, now led by Majlis Speaker Karroubi, who had cobbled together a list of some 120 candidates, was confidently predicting a presence of some 100 seats in the Seventh Majlis. In the event, both proved to be spectacularly wrong: the turnout was healthy and the reformists gained far fewer than the expected 100 seats.

The reason for the unpredictability of the election result can be sought in the complexities of the Iranian political system itself. Voters were naturally deeply unhappy about the Guardian Council's behaviour, but faced a complex dilemma: by not voting they would leave the field free for conservative domination, yet by voting they would legitimize the undemocratic behaviour of the Guardian Council. Moreover, they were already so disappointed in the conduct of the Sixth Majlis and the paltry gains of the reformist MPs in terms of progressive legislation that they were not too sorry to see the reformers punished for their neglect of the popular agendas.[15]

In the event the neoconservatives secured over 150 of 290 seats in the Majlis, and the reform bloc secured some 60 seats. Turnout was around 50 per cent, much higher than was predicted but low enough to steal some of the conservative camp's thunder. The EU and its key three powers (France, Germany and the UK) saw the process and its outcome as a 'setback to democracy', and the USA condemned the outcome as a sham. Yet some observers put a very positive spin on the outcome. They claimed that the pro-reform forces were too naive in designing their strategies and setting their agendas. Furthermore it is argued that, for all their pluralist talk, actually they acted in a sectarian fashion. A period of 'exile', it was concluded, will force them to review their past behaviour and learn from their past mistakes.

While a neoconservative Seventh Majlis was not inclined to pursue the same socio-political reform agenda of the reformist-dominated Sixth Majlis, it nonetheless had to legislate for the reform of the economy, which inevitably forced an opening of society to the rest of the world. However the real arena to watch, some observers suggested, was the field of foreign affairs. It was suggested that the Seventh Majlis would be keen to do business with the West and was more likely to pursue both effective dialogue with the USA and peace and stability in the region – and deliver on both. In this regard, it was suggested to the authors that the neoconservatives mirrored their Likud counterparts in Israel: only they could break taboos and get away with it. The victory of the neoconservative forces in the Seventh Majlis elections was considered as their second step towards obtaining executive power in the country, and was viewed as a process that should be welcomed by the West!

This victory, important though it was, came as a result of three main reasons. First, the strategy that has been followed by the con-servative-dominated institution of the Guardian Council had a direct impact on the election process, public opinion and the outcome.[16] Disqualifying a large number of the reformists restricted their base and limited their opportunity to make real progress in the imple-mentation of their agenda.

Second, the political failure of the reform movement after eight years in power created real divisions amongst the camp in assessing the outcome of the movement. The main figure of reform, President Muhammad Khatami, believed that it was a long-term process and that it needed concerted effort and a clear vision, as well as power, to implement it in full. A real gap had opened up between the president and many of his allies and supporters over the pace of reform and its direction. He, of course, was dedicated to reform of the existing system while some of his allies had begun thinking about making radical changes to what had been created by Ayatollah Khomeini and sustained by his lieutenants. The differences between them had, in the end, cost them at the ballot box.

Third, the new image of conservatism in Iran had begun to change so radically by the mid-2000s that these forces were now able to project themselves as a viable and sound alternative to the failing 2nd Khordadis. Indeed, their success in the Seventh Majlis elections was such that it heralded the appearance of the neoconservatives as a new political force in Iranian politics. In addition, to distinguish themselves from the traditional conservatives, they used effectively the political agenda of the reform camp by admitting that political reform was a necessity. However, they cleverly put the reform of the economy at the top of their agenda for change, which was well received by the voters who were by now wholly disillusioned by the 2nd Khordad movement, as well as with the traditional Right who did not apparently any longer believe in social justice as a national value. The neoconservatives' prioritization of socio-economic change attracted many voters.

Comparing the results of Majlis elections, the participation rate decreased from 69 per cent in elections for the Sixth Majlis to 51 per cent for the Seventh (see Tables 3 and 4 in Appendix). As already noted, the regime regards voter turnout as a real barometer of its standing; the lower participation rate was immediately interpreted by some as evidence for the ebbing of public support.[17] The neoconservatives' Majlis election victory was eye-catching, but it also provided the launch pad for an assault on the presidency. The eyes of the neoconservatives were now set on the 'third step' as Haddad Adel, the Speaker of the Majlis, put it. This step was the ninth presidential election, scheduled for June 2005.

NINTH PRESIDENTIAL ELECTIONS:
THE RISE OF AHMADINEJAD

Since the first-term election of President Khatami in 1997, pundits and students of Iranian affairs took for granted that Iranian society was steadily undergoing political transition and was retreating from its revolutionary politics. At the heart of this reform movement, it was believed, lay the easing of social restrictions and a host of secular liberal rights such as freedom of expression, movement and association.[18] Although this reformist agenda remained far from realization, during his two terms President Khatami championed the expansion

41

of the institutions of civil society and the transformation of Iranian political discourse towards democratic pluralism.

However, while he may have succeeded in transforming the political discourse, he ultimately failed to introduce the real changes that might have made the process irreversible. Ultimately, the failure to deliver led to public dissatisfaction and alienation.[19] This was exacerbated by the chronic economic problems facing Iran prior to the oil boom of the mid-2000s. It is worth noting that well before the presidential elections, the reform coalition that had brought Khatami to power concluded that Khatami had lost much of his popular support due to his inability to improve socio-economic conditions, and for failing to stand firm against conservative factions and an antagonistic judiciary.[20]

Ironically, the idea of social and economic reform had become so well entrenched in the Iranian political landscape that, by the time of the 2005 presidential elections, it provided the golden opportunity for potential candidates of the Rightist persuasion to speak to pertinent social and economic issues without surrendering their core beliefs. This election was to be about values and the means to the realization of a good life while remaining committed to the founding principles of the Islamic Revolution. The election itself, sadly, proved to provide another example of a cynical manipulation of the electoral system rather than the politics of values so warmly promised by the messages of potential candidates in the race.

In the end, only eight presidential candidates from the list of over 1,000 registered candidates were authorized to run by the Guardian Council; the vast majority of the candidates had been disqualified by the body. Amongst the list of eight candidates, Mahmoud Ahmadinejad appeared alongside the least competitive and was in fact an unknown political entity to the Iranian electorate.[21] Until a week prior to the election he had barely surfaced in opinion polls and, due to lack of enthusiasm surrounding him, he was continuously denying rumours of his withdrawal from the electoral race. Indeed, even in the last week of campaigning, most surveys were predicting a three-man race between a centrist (former President Hashemi Rafsanjani), a conservative (former National Police Chief Muhammad Bagher Qalibaf) and a reformist (former Minister of Higher Education Mostafa Moin).[22] There was no sign of Ahmadinejad in the national coverage of the electoral debates.

Moreover, every major presidential candidate spoke in terms of the need to enhance social and economic reforms in the country, which not only indicated the success of Khatami's ability to change the discourse of the nation but also showed blanket support for the chosen path of the country by the candidates. Even Mohsen Rezaei, former head of the Revolutionary Guards, and Bagher Qalibaf wrapped themselves in the rhetorical cloak of social and economic reform. Tehran's Police Chief even went as far as sending his advisers to seek guidance from Prime Minister Tony Blair's campaign managers in the UK on how to target the affluent middle classes of Tehran and succeed in repackaging himself as a pro-reform candidate.[23]

Amongst the reformers, media attention focused on Moin, who called for democratization and greater respect for human rights. Moin started slowly but appeared to finish strongly, igniting at least some enthusiasm amongst the young and the more well-to-do reformers alike. Amongst the Right, eyes were on Qalibaf and Ali Larijani (a close adviser to Supreme Leader Ayatollah Khamenei). Weeks prior to the poll itself, newspapers considered close to Khamenei even urged Qalibaf to withdraw in favour of Larijani as a means of strengthening the conservative faction in the race; in conservative strongholds such as Qom, Larijani's presence was the most visible. However most of the focus, domestic and international, was on Rafsanjani. People close to Khamenei signalled a lack of enthusiasm for him, viewing him as a potential counterweight and a threat to the Supreme Leader's authority. Broadly disliked and perceived as corrupt,[24] he nonetheless appeared to be the default of all candidates – a potential bridge between neoconservatives and reformers, and a gateway for the West.

In short, compared with the others, Ahmadinejad was little more than a dark horse, seemingly lacking important financial, institutional and popular support. Few appeared to have given serious thought to his candidacy until shortly before the vote itself. Nor was he noticed as a serious competitor by Rafsanjani, Qalibaf or Moin. Their advisers failed to even mention Ahmadinejad as a serious contender for presidency. With attention on Rafsanjani and Moin, the neoconservatives appeared worried and divided.

The Iranian presidential elections of 2005, the ninth presidential election in Iranian history, took place in two rounds. The first round was held on 17 June 2005, and the second round was held as a run-off on 24 June.[25] This in itself was a new development, forcing the former president Rafsanjani to battle twice in the same race against a little-known foe. The surprise remains that the election led to the victory of Ahmadinejad, the conservative Mayor of Tehran, with 19.48 per cent of the votes in the first round and some 61.69 per cent in the second.[26] The first round of the election was a very close race, with minor differences in the number of votes won by each candidate. Ahmadinejad is believed to have won the second round because of his populist views, especially those regarding the poor people and their economic status. The election saw a turnout of over 60 per cent of eligible voters, seen as a strike back by Iran at the USA's initial allegations that many in Iran would be restricted from voting.

As already noted, this was the first presidential run-off in the history of Iran. Before the run-off took place, it was compared to the French 2002 presidential elections, in which the splintering of the left-wing vote similarly led to a run-off between the moderate Jacques Chirac and the far-right Jean Marie Le Pen. The comparison was made because of the unexpected votes for Ahmadinejad, the very close race and the comparability of the political standings of Rafsanjani and Ahmadinejad to those of Chirac and Le Pen. However after the results for the run-off were out, the comparison was considered void because of the higher standing of Ahmadinejad and the inability of his opponents to form a majority alliance against him.

While pre-voting polls mostly favoured a run-off between Rafsanjani and Mostafa Moin, the actual vote count from the Interior Ministry unexpectedly put Ahmadinejad and Mehdi Karroubi in second and third places. Rafsanjani and Ahmadinejad led with 21.0 per cent and 19.5 per cent of the vote respectively, and were followed by Karroubi (17.3%), Qalibaf (13.9%), Moin (13.8%), Larijani (5.9%) and Mehralizadeh (4.4%).[27] This was the result of 29,317,042 votes, which amounts to a turnout of 62.66 per cent, as there were 46,786,418 eligible voters.[28]

While Rafsanjani had secured the first place in the first round, he failed to win the second round by failing to attract the people who had voted for the reformist candidates and who were expected to support him in the second round. Ahmadinejad won with 61.7 per cent of the vote, while Rafsanjani only secured 35.9 per cent. There was a total of 27,959,253 votes cast in the second round, slightly lower than the first round. Considering that the number of eligible voters was raised by about 150,000, the turnout can be placed at about 59.6 per cent.

The victory of Mahmoud Ahmadinejad was the third step in the neoconservatives' drive towards securing for themselves the highest echelons of executive power. It also came as a new challenge to the traditional conservatives in Iran. His victory has opened the door for more questions about the future of 'Islamic democracy' in Iran, the future of the reform movement itself, and the relationship with the USA and the West in general. Arguably none of the general and pressing concerns of the people of the Islamic Republic were addressed by this election victory.

CONCLUSION

Ahmadinejad represents a new breed of conservatism in Iran. The differences between his neoconservatives and the traditional conservatives lie in the following. First is the prioritization of the needs of the destitute masses, to win back their support for the regime. Second, they differ on their definition of the state, which for the former is to be an interventionist state – a state that will control all the main lifelines of the country, quite unlike the 'privatized' variety of the traditional conservatives. Third, the focus of the neoconservatives is on the discourse of social justice and the welfare of the *mostazafin umma* and on Islamic values and the question of *haq* versus *batil* (right and wrong in religious matters).

Together, these differences mark a major rupture in both policy and conceptual terms between the two strands of conservatism in the country. What is noteworthy is that it was the traditional conservatives who used their residual power base in the institutions of the state to secure for the neoconservatives majority control in the Seventh Majlis and, subsequent to their success there, to capture the presidency (both in the run-up to and in the course of the presidential race). The role of the Guardian Council in particular was crucial in bolstering the neoconservative candidates and at the same disqualifying many of those associated with the reform camp.

Thus, the three victories of the neoconservatives – in the local, Majlis and presidential elections – have shifted the locus of power in Iran away from the old guard and towards a new and fresh political elite. These new political forces have succeeded in these elections because they have focused on the daily and ordinary problems of the average citizen. Using slogans and promises of social justice, and the promise of tackling corruption and corrupted politicians, has endeared this group to a large crust of Iranian society that has in recent years felt helpless in the face of developments in the country.

Ironically, it was the reformists that gave the masses the voice and the tools to articulate their concerns, and it was the movement's failure to deliver on the tangible needs of the people that left the door open for neoconservative forces to present themselves as a new alternative. They also used some of the reformists' slogans to appeal to a wider community and partly to present themselves as moderate. Even their appearance and style is less traditional, particularly when compared with the traditional conservatives. The neoconservatives' social policies, however, do seem to be directed towards forcing the Iranian people to change their lifestyle – but the social freedoms that Iranians gained in the course of the reform era continue to be present, despite the many pressures from the neoconservatives to reimpose strict Islamic codes of conduct and values.

Despite the electoral successes of the neoconservatives, the figures for each election since 2003 show that there is a declining rate of participation in national elections. This of course could be a direct result of dissatisfaction with the Guardian Council's interference in candidate selections, but the figures do nothing to strengthen the legitimizing base of the neoconservatives. Declining participation rates, therefore, can just as easily be seen as a questioning the legitimacy of the regime as a whole. A system which relies on public support cannot afford to run its public offices through minority governments.

As we have noted, the economic policies of the neoconservatives is another area of concern. In both the Seventh Majlis elections and the ninth presidential elections they have promised new economic policies and priorities, but have remained thin on delivery. With oil revenues being as high as they have been since 2004 the government should have sufficient financial reserves to take risks and also to try and advance its populist economic programme. But the big problem will emerge towards the end of Ahmadinejad's first term as inflation is predicted to accelerate from 2007, and this problem is likely to be compounded by the higher oil-related expenditures.

Finally, it has been suggested that the neoconservatives, who apparently aim to follow the so-called 'Chinese model', are trying to show that they can have a coherent economic strategy that will deliver on the economic front without dependence on the West or, more specifically, on the USA. If they, following the Chinese model, can deliver on the economy and open up to the USA, we end up wondering what the fuss was all about! But for the moment we might be just as wise to consider the high price for relations with the USA that the Iranian people will be paying. Ultimately they will be trading in their hard-earned political freedoms for intra-elite contact between Tehran and the USA. This may be good for business, but in the absence of the West's insistence on the implementation of the political reform agenda, it could prove much less healthy for the Iranian people.

More broadly, the success of the Chinese model that the Iranian conservatives favour — a complete separation of political and economic reforms — could, of course, have repercussions far beyond Iran's own borders and directly affect the political discourse in the highly charged post-9/11 political environment throughout the Arab world. Success on the economic front without political reforms could provide the classic antidote to the Arab autocrats resistant to Western pressures for democratization. In the successful implementation of this strategy the Islamic Republic could be providing a model much more problematic for the West than the one being pursued by the Chinese themselves!

III

The Ahmadinejad Phenomenon

It's possible and we can do it.

President Mahmoud Ahmadinejad

You can tell whether a man is clever by his answers. You can tell whether a man is wise by his questions.

Naguib Mahfouz, Egyptian novelist

Introduction

The first round of the 2005 presidential elections in Iran brought with it both shock and surprise, when it emerged that the two candidates facing each other in the run-off were to be the veteran religio-politician Ayatollah Ali-Akbar Hashemi Rafsanjani and the little-known, neoconservative mayor of Tehran, Mahmoud Ahmadinejad. The shock and surprise of the first round was soon forgotten by the much bigger shock of Ahmadinejad defeating the former president and iconic figure in a landslide victory that consolidated power in the hands of the ruling neoconservative faction.

Most of the American mass media followed the lead of the Bush administration in the aftermath of Ahmadinejad's victory by characterizing the election in Iran as an inconsequential 'sham'. For example, in an editorial on 21 June 2005, the *New York Times* called the election 'a race for the mostly meaningless position of the President of Iran'.[1] The *Times*' editorial was written after the first round of the elections, which drew over 63 per cent of eligible voters to the polls. Only if the editors had read the work of their own reporters in Tehran would they have appreciated more fully the enthusiasm that had preceded the voters' engagement in the elections. It is hard to imagine the kind of fervour and energy on display for what was rather unkindly said to be a 'meaningless' position. This was no window dressing to satisfy the West; the poll, rather, represented a real political struggle between the competing forces in Iran.

It also has to be acknowledged that the electoral victory for Ahmadinejad dealt a crushing blow to those Western governments who had banked on the victory of a moderate, with some even openly speaking in support of the reformist candidate Mostafa Moin – an ally of outgoing President Muhammad Khatami – in the first round. Not losing heart, in the second round they pinned their hopes on the 'pragmatic' Ayatollah Ali-Akbar Hashemi Rafsanjani in the run-off.[2] Their positions in the elections were duly noted by the neoconservative camp, of course, which further fuelled their scepticism towards the West.

Accusations of electoral irregularity, which were immediately raised in the aftermath of the elections, increased the underlying tensions between the West and the victorious neoconservatives, as Western governments began to complain that the process had not been a healthy one. However, despite the political tensions following the elections, Ahmadinejad was sworn in as president and the world spotlight descended upon him. What he stood for and what his programme in office was to be, remained a mystery to the outside world. To appreciate the direction of change in Iran today, therefore, it is of paramount importance to understand Ahmadinejad's background. To appreciate fully his impact we propose to contextualize his rise to power, and the influence he has had on politics in Iran, around the major socio-economic and political upheavals that the country went through during the last decade of the twentieth century.

THE FAMILY AND SOCIAL ROOTS OF
PRESIDENT AHMADINEJAD

At the age of 49, Mahmoud Ahmadinejad became the sixth president of the Islamic Republic of Iran. The early childhood home of young Mahmoud Saborjhian, as he was known, sits rundown; the garden is overgrown with weeds appearing from the cracks in the ground. The well where his parents used to store the drinking water they collected from local channels is dry, long since outdated by the economic progress that delivered running water to an arid region. It is a scene reminiscent of Iran's past but, for Iranians, these humble surroundings – in the town of Aradan, about 120 kilometres south-east of Tehran and directly on the path of the ancient Silk Route – have acquired a contemporary significance.[3] This is where the country's sixth president was born, the fourth of seven children. The Saborjhian family rented a two-storey house before leaving their impoverished environment in the late 1950s in search of prosperity in Tehran. That was when the Pahlavi throne had been restored and small rumblings were being heard in Qom about the Shah's new economic policies and his regime's international role.

Ahmadinejad was little more than a year old when they went to the city. It was a move that coincided with changing the family name, a step taken for a mixture of religious and economic reasons. The name change provides an insight into the devoutly Islamic working-class roots of Ahmadinejad's brand of populist politics. The name Saborjhian is derived from 'thread painter' – *sabour* in Farsi – a once common and humble occupation in the carpet industry in the Semnan province, where Aradan is situated. *Ahmad*, by contrast, is a name also used for the Prophet Muhammad and means virtuous; *nejad* means race in Farsi, so Ahmadinejad can mean 'Muhammad's race', or 'virtuous race'. According to Mehdi Shahhosseini, 31, son of one of Ahmadinejad's cousins, still living in Aradan:

> Moving from a village to big cities was so common and widespread
> at that time that perhaps people, not wanting to show their roots,
> would change their names ... Some people were more religious and
> chose names to reflect that.[4]

If the cover-up of the family's origins diminished local pride in
Ahmadinejad, it has certainly not been reflected in the behaviour of
the residents of Aradan towards him. The town – consisting of just
7,000 people sitting in the shadow of the Alborz mountains – had
a street festival to celebrate his landslide victory in the presidential
election. It was an occasion born of surprise as much as joy. 'We never
expected him to be president', Mr Shahhosseini, a relative, said. 'We
could see he was improving and making progress but we thought he
would stay in his area of expertise [the Islamist Mayor of Tehran has
a PhD in traffic management and engineering]'.[5]

About 98 per cent of local voters are believed to have backed
Ahmadinejad in the run-off contest against Hashemi Rafsanjani.
Apparently, Ahmadinejad still makes visits to his birthplace to pay
respect to the memory of a late uncle buried in the local cemetery.
He also keeps in close contact with his cousins, who visit him in
Tehran. Relatives say his professed concern for the poor and Iran's
growing wealth gap stems from his familiarity with this local area,
which has a fragile economy based on sheep and cattle farming.
Mehran Mohseni, the son of another cousin, is reported as saying:

> He has tasted poverty himself. He and his family have had a lot
> of problems ... The family was not poor but they were living very
> simple lives. He had to struggle to get his BSc and his PhD. His life
> is not luxurious at all. There are no sofas in his house in Tehran, only
> cushions and rugs.[6]

The president's solidarity with the poor is also believed to have
been influenced by his father, Ahmad, who became a blacksmith
in Tehran after running a grocery store and then a barber's shop in
Aradan.[7] Ahmadinejad, it is said, refuses to eat at the table of any
host who does not pay *zakat* (the portion of annual income that
Muslims are required to give to the poor). Journalists' interviews with

Ahmadinejad's relatives reveal that they speak approvingly of how Ahmadinejad's father, who now works in a Revolutionary Guards' shop, sold his Tehran house for around $63,000 and bought a smaller home for half the price, giving the proceeds to a charity for the poor. They seem to talk about him with adulation bordering on reverence, and depict his favourite pastimes as football and mountaineering (a recreation favoured by young and old alike as a result of Iran's rugged terrain, particularly around the capital Tehran).[8]

Nevertheless, it is clear from family accounts that he was a committed activist. Hand in hand with the attempts at smoothing the hard edges go expressions of pride in his revolutionary credentials. That background remains under fierce scrutiny from the Bush administration after several former US diplomats held captive in the 1979–81 Tehran embassy takeover alleged that Ahmadinejad was in fact a ringleader of the students.[9] (Of course aides to Ahmadinejad, as well as other hostage-takers, deny the charges.) Before the 1979 revolution Ahmadinejad visited Lebanon during the country's civil war and is said to have been active with Shia groups there. During the reign of the last Shah, he kept a printing press at home, which he used to print leaflets denouncing the monarch. On the eve of the revolution his activities forced the entire Ahmadinejad family to flee Tehran and go into hiding in the north-eastern province of Golestan to avoid arrest by the Savak, the Pahlavi regime's secret police.

It is often said that Ahmadinejad's strong religious beliefs surfaced early. An older cousin to whom he remains close, Maasoumeh Saborjhian, has stated that

> He had an interest in and talent for the Qur'an as a very small child … He liked to go to classes but they threw him out because he was too young. He was only 10 or 11. But he would insist, saying, 'No, no, I know how to read the Qur'an.'[10]

His mother, addressed by friends and relatives as Seiyed Khanom (literally, 'Madam descendent of the Prophet'), dresses in an all-embracing black chador and is said to be very religious.[11] It is an aspect of Dr Ahmadinejad's background that will ring alarm bells for Iran's mostly affluent secular population – the group who supported the modest social liberalization that unfolded during the reformist presidency of Muhammad Khatami. Social groups such as this have feared a return to the early days of the revolution, which Ahmadinejad admires, when Islamist principles and values formed the basis upon which society was constructed. The president's aides have said that public policy is not his first priority, but rather dealing with the economic problems of the average and below-average Iranians. 'Poverty is the real problem' that needs sorting, according to Mr Mohseni, son of Mrs Saborjhian and Ahmadinejad's campaign manager in Aradan.[12]

HIS EARLY POLITICAL CAREER

After finishing high school, Ahmadinejad went to Elm-o Sanaat (Science and Technology) University in 1975, to study engineering. The whirlwind of the Islamic Revolution soon swept him from the classroom into political activism. Student activists in Elm-o Sanaat University at the time of the revolution were dominated by the conservatives. Ahmadinejad soon became one of their leaders and founded the Islamic Students Association in that university soon after the fall of the Shah's regime.

In 1979, Ahmadinejad was the head representative of Iran University of Science and Technology (IUST) to the unofficial student gatherings that occasionally met with Ayatollah Khomeini. These sessions created the foundations of the first Office for Strengthening Unity (OSU) (*Daftar-e Tahkim-e Vahdat*), of which Ahmadinejad became a member. This was the student organization to which several members behind the seizure of the US embassy belonged (the event that was to become the Iran hostage crisis).[13] The OSU was set up by Ayatollah Muhammad Beheshti, who was at the time Khomeini's top confidant and a key figure in the clerical leadership.[14] Beheshti wanted the OSU to organize Islamist students to counter the rapidly rising influence of the opposition Mojahedin-e Khalq (MeK) amongst university students. According to other OSU officials, when the idea of storming the US embassy in Tehran was raised in the OSU central committee by Mirdamadi and Abbas Abdi, Ahmadinejad suggested storming the Soviet embassy at the same time.[15]

A decade later, most OSU leaders regrouped around Khatami but Ahmadinejad remained loyal to the conservative ruling guard in Iran. During the crackdown on universities in 1980, which Khomeini called the 'Islamic Cultural Revolution', Ahmadinejad and the OSU played a critical role in purging dissident lecturers and students, many of whom were arrested. In the early 1980s, Ahmadinejad worked in the 'Internal Security' department of the IRGC and earned notoriety as a strong personality and interrogator. According to the state-run website *Baztab*, allies of outgoing President Muhammad Khatami have revealed that Ahmadinejad worked for some time in the notorious Evin Prison, where thousands of political prisoners were detained during the 1980s.[16] Scores of the Evin prisoners were tortured and executed at the height of the revolution, in the early to mid-1980s.

Ahmadinejad joined the Sepah in 1986 during the Iran–Iraq war.[17] After training at the headquarters, he saw action in extraterritorial covert operations against Kirkuk in Iraq. Later, he also became the head engineer of the Sixth Army of the Sepah and the head of the Corps' staff in the western provinces of Iran. With the formation of the elite Qods (Jerusalem) Force of the IRGC, Ahmadinejad became one of its senior commanders. It is also alleged that he directed assassinations in the Middle East and Europe, including the assassination of Iranian Kurdish leader Abdorrahman Qassemlou, who was shot dead by senior officers of the IRGC in a Vienna flat in July 1989 – it is claimed that Ahmadinejad was a key planner of the attack. He was also reported to have been involved in planning an attempt on the life of Salman Rushdie but, again, without much evidence.[18]

He served as governor of Maku and Khoy cities in the West Azarbaijan province for four years in the 1980s and as an adviser to the governor general of the western province of Kurdestan for two years.[19] While serving as the cultural adviser to then Ministry of Culture and Higher Education in 1993, he was appointed as governor general of the newly established north-western province of Ardebil. He was elected as the exemplary governor general for three consecutive years. However in 1997 the newly installed Khatami administration removed Ahmadinejad from his post as Ardebil governor general.

Ahmadinejad returned to Elm-o Sanaat University to teach in 1997 and became a member of the scientific board of the Civil Engineering College. He is said to have carried out several scientific, cultural, political and social activities and to have worked with Ansar-e Hezbollah, a revolutionary group. In April 2003 Ahmadinejad was appointed Mayor of Tehran by the capital's municipal council, which is dominated by the conservative Islamic Iran Developers Coalition (Abadgaran).[20] Working in close conjunction with the Sepah, the Abadgaran were able to win both the municipal elections of 2003 and the Majlis elections of 2004. Abadgaran bills itself as a group of young politicians who want to revive the ideals and policies of the founder of the Islamic Republic, Ayatollah Khomeini. It was one of several groups that were set up on the orders of Ayatollah Khamenei in order to defeat President Muhammad Khatami's faction after the Majlis elections of February 2000.

In some of Ahmadinejad's public statements, he has appeared to identify himself as a Developer. As already noted, he expresses a preference for a very spartan lifestyle and is keen to project this image. As mayor, he used his position to build up a strong network of grass roots support. He reversed many of the policies of previous moderate and reformist mayors, placing serious religious emphasis on the activities of the cultural centres by turning them into prayer halls during the Islamic holy month of Ramadan. He also suggested the burial of the bodies of martyrs of the Iran–Iraq war in major city squares of Tehran.

As the mayor of Tehran, Ahmadinejad also became the manager in charge of the daily newspaper *Hamshahri*, replacing Editor Muhammad Atrianfar with Alireza Sheikh-Attar. Ahmadinejad subsequently fired Sheikh-Attar on 13 June 2005, a few days before the presidential elections, for not supporting him for the post – replacing Sheikh-Attar with Ali Asghar Ash'ari, a previous vice minister of culture and Islamic guidance during the ministership of Mostafa Mirsalim. He fired Nafiseh Kouhnavard, one of *Hamshahri*'s journalists, for asking Khatami about the so-called 'red lines' of the regime and illegal parallel intelligence agencies – a question that Ahmadinejad did not consider appropriate, it seems. Kouhnavard was later accused by the conservative faction of spying for Turkey and the Republic of Azerbaijan.

Ahmadinejad is known to have quarrelled with Khatami, who then barred him from attending meetings of the Council of Ministers, a privilege usually extended to mayors of Tehran. He has publicly criticized Khatami for wilfully ignoring the daily problems of the general public. After two years as Tehran mayor, Ahmadinejad was short-listed in a list of 65 finalists for World Mayor 2005. Out of the 550 nominated mayors, only nine were from Asia. While he did not win this contest and soon after resigned from his post as the mayor of Tehran, the nomination did help his standing amongst the voters as he prepared to take up the office of president. His resignation as mayor was accepted on 28 June 2005 and, in September 2005, the Tehran City Council elected another neoconservative, Muhammad Bagher Qalibaf (another 2005 presidential candidate) as the twelfth mayor of Tehran, with 8 out of 15 votes.

ELECTORAL SUCCESS: FACTORS AND CAUSES

As already noted, Ahmadinejad's electoral victory was unexpected, and was seen as a major political earthquake in the context of Iranian politics. Clearly, Ahmadinejad's credentials of being an activist in the revolution and his close relations with the ruling conservative faction did ring alarm bells in the West. This was particularly so in the context of Iran's fast-developing nuclear programme and its increasingly tense relations with the Arab world both following the 2003 Iraq war and over the safety of access of oil to feed the international economy. What we must establish are the reasons for his rise to power.

Failure of reformists

Ahmadinejad's electoral victory came about, in part, due to the voting pattern of the supporters of reform over the previous two years – that is, the boycotting of elections to protest against the reform movement's failure to make good on their promises in the sphere of individual and political freedoms.[21] Conservative restrictions are usually highlighted to explain the lack of progress by the reformist movement but it is important to note that not all of the reformist misfortunes can be blamed on conservative resistance. The reformist coalition also suffered from its own disorganization and lack of support from a solid social base.

For instance, in the 2002 municipal elections the constitutive parties of the reformist front were unable to reach agreement on a common list of candidates in large cities. A more striking example of reformist disorganization was the May 2003 election in the House of Parties (Khane-ye Ahzab-e Iran).[22] Although 70 per cent of the House of Parties can be considered reformists, they did nothing to consolidate their power base and reduce conflict amongst themselves. As a result, the conservatives wrestled control of the governing board from the reformists, eventually managing to win a majority of seats on the governing board. Today, as a consequence, two prominent conservative figures, Hassan Ghafuri-fard and Assadollah Badamchian, head the House of Parties.[23]

Along with electorate's political protests in the form of boycotting elections, it appeared that the reform-supporting electorate was disappointed, alienated and somewhat indifferent to the state of Iranian politics.[24] For example, state actions such as closing some 100 reformist newspapers over the previous eight years, imprisoning journalists and bloggers for criticizing the regime, charging reformists who called for the renewal of relations with the USA with treason, and disqualifying reformist candidates – some in office at the time – from contesting elections contributed collectively to the negative political culture that pervaded Iranian society. This had a key role to play in the outcome of the 2005 presidential elections. As a result of these developments, the various student and intellectual organizations announced that they would boycott the presidential elections.[25]

Indeed, even a cursory survey of Iranian electoral behaviour before the 2005 presidential elections would have shown that the attitudes and responses of the Iranian people were in flux and hardening towards the reformists. In the February 2003 municipal elections, and in the February 2004 elections for the Seventh Majlis, voter turnout had been as low as around 50 per cent – providing an early indicator of what could happen in the presidential race. As we know, this was largely due to the fact that reform-minded voters had stayed away from the polls because of the Guardian Council's mass disqualification of reformist candidates, and also following the conservatives' judicial measures against Tehran's previous mayors. Therefore the combined effect of disappointment in the achievements of the reformist movement, lack of organization and conservative state actions contributed to loss of interest in electoral politics.

Economic populism

A further element of electoral protest in 2005 was to be found in the voting behaviour of the poorer classes of society, who apparently refused to support Rafsanjani's candidacy despite mass public support for him from the reformist political camp and from the reformist press following the first round of voting. It is noteworthy that the following groups all called unanimously for the support of Rafsanjani against the Right's champion, Ahmadinejad: reformist politicians such as Hojjatoleslam Mehdi Karroubi and Dr Mostafa Moin (who dropped out in the first round along with Muhammad Bagher Qalibaf); members of reformist movements such as Iran's Islamic Participation Front, the Islamic Republic Mojahedin Organization, the Association of Combatant Clerics and the Qom Seminary Teachers; ayatollahs such as Ayatollah Taheri Esfahani; intellectuals; journalists; and artists.[26] As the final result suggests, the poor decided not to follow the rising tide of support for Rafsanjani and voted overwhelmingly for Ahmadinejad.

Rafsanjani, an ally of the father of the Islamic Revolution, Ayatollah Khomeini, is also a billionaire and a highly influential senior politician, and is apparently identified by the poorer classes in Iran with the current corruption plaguing Iranian society. Despite his campaign promises to provide unemployment benefits of between $100 and $135 a month to every unemployed person in Iran,[27] and despite his commitment to advancing reforms in Iran, he could not persuade the have-nots, the unemployed and the supporters of reform to vote for him in large enough numbers to secure victory.[28] Ironically, his campaign seemed to make matters worse, for he virtually refused to go out and conduct a public campaign, calculating that people would choose him over the uncertainty represented by others.

His elitism only appeared to validate what had turned Iranians off from the start, reminding them of the dishonesty and cronyism that had been associated with his presidency. In 2005 there was no real connection between Rafsanjani and the Iranian electorate; his lifestyle had no resemblance to that of an average Iranian. In addition, in the first round, Bagher Qalibaf's flashy electoral campaign stole the thunder from Rafsanjani's rather low-key affair. Thus, Rafsanjani failed to inspire liberal and secular forces and at the same time put off the traditional voters. In particular lack of appeal to the urban youth, who had been Khatami's mainstay, was a big blow to his chances.[29] The campaign materials he did produce included colourful, Western-style electoral posters and his campaign videos showed him in action, flying around the country. However in the end his campaign slogans were geared towards the urban middle and upper classes, lacking mass appeal.

In contrast, the neoconservative Ahmadinejad's electoral campaign was focused on the day-to-day social and economic problems that the Iranian people faced, such as unemployment, poverty, inflation and corruption. The way he presented himself to the electorate was comprehensively different to the flashy and expensive electoral campaigns of Bagher Qalibaf and Rafsanjani. Ahmadinejad used black and white posters, he showed pride in his spartan home and frugal lifestyle and came across as a man of the people, in touch with their everyday concerns.[30] He toured regions in a small bus and spoke to the Iranian people in places of significance such as mosques and prayer halls – he used the network of mosques across Iran by having Friday prayer leaders give calls to vote for him.[31] His focus on the poor, emphasizing his own humble background and simple lifestyle in contrast to the other electoral candidates, won him a great deal of support and sympathy, depicting him as a populist candidate and a man of the people. Ahmadinejad presented himself to the public as 'a conservative with clean hands' who would fight the corruption that had spread throughout Iran's government institutions and apparatuses. In addition to this was his socio-economic platform, which underlined the values of justice and Islamic morality, social justice, fairness, integrity and modesty[32] – all in accordance with the principles of the Islamic Revolution.

A key aspect of Ahmadinejad's election platform was his presentation of himself as being in touch with the people. One example of this was a verbal clash between him and the outgoing President Muhammad Khatami, in late April 2005 when Ahmadinejad was mayor of Tehran. Arriving late at the degree awarding ceremony at Tehran University, where he was to receive an honorary PhD, President Khatami blamed Tehran traffic jams and told the audience, 'Those in charge of running the city are unable to fulfil their obligation properly... I apologize to you on behalf of those who are incapable of running this city.'[33] In response, Ahmadinejad advised Khatami to 'take a bus', saying that had Khatami remained in his downtown office instead of moving to a complex in the fashionable and wealthy northern part of the city, he would be more in touch with the people's everyday problems. He pronounced himself 'delighted to see that the President got stuck in Tehran traffic at least once, in order to experience up close what it feels like'.[34]

A populist platform rather than a social–political masterplan was vital to Ahmadinejad's electoral victory. He gave the people what they wanted to hear and was able to touch on virtually every issue and problem that they were facing. An aura of a champion of the poor surrounded Ahmadinejad in his electoral campaign, and he portrayed himself as an outsider determined to fight the cronyism and corruption widely associated with the political elite – none more so than Rafsanjani.

The first policy of Ahmadinejad's presidency to emerge was a 12 trillion Rial ($1.3 billion) 'Reza Love Fund',[35] which was named after one of the Shia Imams. By tapping into Iran's huge oil revenues, Ahmadinejad unrolled plans for the use of this fund for helping young people to get jobs, get married and afford homes. The fund also sought charitable donations, and has boards of trustees in each of Iran's 30 provinces. Although the fund has been frozen and it has never taken off, the fact that Ahmadinejad mooted it brought him the support of a large number of young voters who were unable to make ends meet. The fund, after all, was established in response to the cost of housing in urban areas, which was (and is) continuing to push up the national marital age. This was the first example of Ahmadinejad's attempts to fulfil his electoral promises of improving the social and economic living of the Iranian people.

Ultimately, the roots of his victory can be traced to the persistence of social and economic inequalities in Iran and the failure of previous leaders to address them.

Support from state institutions

The two factors just identified played a key role in Ahmadinejad's success, but a further vital link in the chain was the support given to his candidacy by the all-powerful state institutions of the country.[36] No official support for his bid could be detected during the first round of elections, with Larijani seen to be the favourite candidate of the conservative faction in Iran. Ahmadinejad's strong first round show-ing appeared to have reflected a last-minute decision by the Right to throw its resources and institutional weight behind him. That meant that Ahmadinejad not only had populist appeal but also the support of state institutions that would assist in raising his profile around the country. This showing of support for Ahmadinejad by the ruling factions brought accusations from some unsuccessful candidates. Moin, for example, accused the Basij of pressuring voters at the polling stations to vote for Ahmadinejad. He also asserted that people with duplicated or false identity cards were allowed to vote. These claims are of course hard to substantiate,[37] as is the rumour that as many as 5 million votes may have been stuffed in inaccessible ballot boxes in the second round, as those military barracks and similar facilities were not open to public scrutiny.

While finding concrete evidence for vote rigging may be hard, it is not in dispute by the parties involved that the Revolutionary Guards and Basij members actively mobilized their constituencies for Ahmadinejad. At the Friday prayer session on election day, when campaigning officially was banned, Ahmadinejad's supporters were urging attendees and their families to vote for him. To what extent encouragement became pressure and pressure became intimidation is a difficult question to answer. However, there is no doubt that institutional support had a key role to play in the victory of Ahmadinejad.

Mahmoud Ahmadinejad and the 'Third Revolution'

As Mahmoud Ahmadinejad took office, the question of how this unknown academic would want to run a complex country like Iran remained unanswered. There were also a number of questions being asked about his leadership abilities and his ability to act independently when in office.

Mahmoud Ahmadinejad's key characteristics as president can be summarized by the following:

- Ahmadinejad, as a leader who has been elected and supported by the people, does not believe that he needs to change his lifestyle.

- Ahmadinejad's main concern is the internal conditions of Iran. In other words, he is focused on fighting poverty and corruption, and ensuring social adherence to Islamic values. He also believes that Iran's status as an Islamic state should be protected by all in charge.

- Ahmadinejad does not have a positive impression of the West in general and the USA in particular, and therefore views the Western world with doubt and great suspicion.

In a ceremony for the confirmation of his presidency by the Supreme Leader Ayatollah Seyed Ali Khamenei, Mahmoud Ahmadinejad said:

> the new government will stress four principles including promotion of justice, attention to the needs of the people, serving all the masses, and material and moral progress of the country. By following the pure Islamic culture and paying due attention to the people's needs, the new government will put promotion of justice in all areas, fairness in distribution of opportunities and facilities, eradication of poverty and struggle against administrative discrimination and corruption on top of its agenda.[38]

Ahmadinejad again reconfirmed these principles when he outlined his first budget bill for Iranian year 1385 (2006–7): 'his government started its work on the basis of four principles of justice promotion, kindness, serving the nation and all-out development of the country'.[39] From the outset, he was reinforcing his Islamic populist credentials, using every major occasion to emphasize his populist agenda.

There may be profound religious reasons for this, for it has been reported that Ahmadinejad's emphasis on the importance of development and justice is for encouraging the return of the Shia's (12th) Hidden Imam, the Mahdi. The theme of the return of the Mahdi has become a feature of his presidency, reinforced by his own links with the conservative clerical forces based in Qom. Another element of his religious thinking is that which has been inspired by the Hojjatiyeh Society. His relation with Hojjatiyeh, the founder of

Haqqaniya theological school in Qom, was highlighted after he won the presidency. Ayatollah Muhammad-Taqi Mesbah-Yazdi, who has strong ties with the Haqqaniya School, has been described as a spiritual father of Ahmadinejad.[40] Haqqaniya School was established by Ayatollah Mesbah-Yazdi, Ayatollah Dr Beheshti, Ayatollah Jannati and Ayatollah Sadoughi. The reason behind establishing such a school was to train clerics with both a traditional and modern curriculum, including a secular education such as medicine, politics, and Western and non-Islamic philosophy. Many of the influential figures in Iranian politics today have graduated from Haqqaniya School.[41]

It has been argued that all of Ahmadinejad's policies have been influenced by Hojjatiyeh thought. Not only that, but it is also said the hardliner wing that supported Ahmadinejad was itself following Hojjatiyeh. Hojjatiyeh, in fact, has a domestic agenda and very limited space to manoeuvre. It is likely that there has been an exaggeration, since the presidential race of 2005, of the impact of the role of Hojjatiyeh, since it would previously have been unthinkable to suggest that such a group could dominate Iranian politics. Nonetheless, it is possible to suggest that its ideology is more influential today than in the past and that it is very popular amongst the new neoconservative forces and is enjoying a renaissance.

By way of a general comparison, while the reformists were trying to bring back concepts such as Islamic democracy, political rights of the nation and building civil society based on Islamic roles, Ahmadinejad has been more interested in the battle of populist ideals. In addition, the audiences are also different. Khatami's followers were intellectuals, academics or, in one word, moderates. Ahmadinejad's followers, on the other hand, are more religious, traditional and idealistic in terms of the lofty goals of the Islamic Revolution.

President Ahmadinejad's immediate concerns therefore are not political justice, political rights, freedom of speech and modernization of the Iranian state, but rather what he calls social justice for the Iranian people. The theme of social justice has been informing the neoconservatives' strategy since the local elections in 2003 and the Seventh Majlis elections in 2004. They also recognize readily that social justice is the magic term that can mobilize ordinary people. More can be learned of Ahmadinejad's style of leadership, his priorities and also his relationship with other institutions of power via a brief glance at the make-up of his proposed cabinet in September 2005 and its treatment by the Majlis.

President Ahmadinejad in his speech before the Majlis introduced his cabinet by describing them as both faithful and specialized in their respective areas. The new Minister of Health, Treatment and Medical Education, Kamran Baqeri Lankarani, was described as a faithful and specialized young administrator; Muhammad-Hossein Saffar-Harandi, the new Minister of Culture and Islamic Guidance, was justified as having long experience within the press, media and cultural affairs. He suggested Gholam-Hossein Mohseni-Ejehei as Information Minister; Mostafa Pour Muhammadi as Interior Minister and Mostafa Najjar as Defence Minister. He named a campaign against narcotic drugs and the smuggling of goods, the promotion of national solidarity and the provision of a cheerful atmosphere for public participation in political, economic and cultural affairs as some of his other priorities. He presented Ejehei as a specialist in international law and described him as a concerned administrator who is quite familiar with the procedure of affairs in the Ministry of Information, which requires precision given its sensitive nature. Ahmadinejad also introduced Pour Muhammadi as a 'multifariousness and sincere individual of high spirit'. The chief executive pointed to the promotion of national security as the most significant duty of the Interior Ministry. Concerning his Foreign Minister, Ahmadinejad presented Manouchehr Mottaki, whom he described as having more than 20 years of experience in international affairs 'given his two terms as a Member of Parliament and commitment to the principles of the Islamic Republic of Iran and familiarity with diplomatic rules'. Ahmadinejad proposed for Oil Minister Ali Saeedlu, who, he said, is familiar with the national potential in this vital area.[42]

The prevailing view had been that a neoconservative-dominated Majlis would merely rubber-stamp his nominees, but in practice the MPs did nothing of the sort as they started questioning some of his nominees. This was the first gesture to the new president that he had a long way to go before his ministerial list would be approved. The president's approach had been to bring in what he called 'clean hands' and those 'people who are not living in a palace'. His priority, he had repeatedly said, is to find people who can serve the nation. For the MPs, however, qualifications and experience were more important criteria than piety. It took some 10 days of deliberations and public wrangling before the new cabinet was approved by the Majlis. Four ministerial nominees however – those for petroleum, cooperatives, education, and welfare and social security – were not approved. Interestingly, all four rejected nominees had been Ahmadinejad's close colleagues in the Municipality of Tehran!

After the political wrangling over Ahmadinejad's candidates, his cabinet was finally approved. The cabinet included:

- Muhammad Reza Eskandari[43] (Ministry of Agriculture).

- Masoud Mirkazemi[44] (Ministry of Commerce).

- Muhammad Hossein Saffar Harandi[45] (Ministry of Culture and Islamic Guidance).

- Mostafa Muhammad Najjar[46] (Ministry of Defence and Logistics).

- Davoud Danesh Jafari[47] (Ministry of Economy and Financial Affairs).

- Parviz Fattah[48] (Ministry of Energy).

- Manouchehr Mottaki[49] (Ministry of Foreign Affairs).

- Kamaran Bagheri Lankarani[50] (Ministry of Health and Medical Education).

- Muhammad Saeedikia[51] (Ministry of Housing and Urban Development).

- Alireza Tahmasbi[52] (Ministry of Industries and Mines).

- Gholam Hossein Mohseni-Ejehei[53] (Ministry of Intelligence).

- Mostafa Pour Muhammadi[54] (Interior Ministry).

- Jamal Karimi Rad[55] (Ministry of Justice).

- Muhammad Jahromi[56] (Ministry of Labour and Social Affairs).

- Muhammad Rahmati[57] (Ministry of Roads and Transportation).

- Muhammad Mehdi Zahedi[58] (Ministry of Science Research and Technology).

- Ali Saeedlou (first choice: Ministry of Petroleum).

- Mohsen Tasallot (second choice: Ministry of Petroleum).

- Kazem Vaziri Hamaneh[59] (approved minister for Ministry of Petroleum).

- Alireza Ali-Ahmadi (first choice: Ministry of Cooperatives).

- Muhammad Nazim-Ardakani[60] (approved minister: Ministry of Cooperatives).

- Ali Akbar Ash'ari (first choice: Ministry of Education).

- Mahmoud Farshedi[61] (approved minister: Ministry of Education).

- Mehdi Hashmi (first choice: Ministry of Welfare and Social Security).

- Parviz Kazemi[62] (approved minister: Ministry of Welfare and Social Security).

In the end though, and despite the rough ride through the Majlis, the cabinet of Ahmadinejad included many of the individuals that he wanted as his first-choice ministers, inevitably leading to the creation of a largely neoconservative cabinet.[63] President Ahmadinejad described his cabinet as the government of 70 million people, portraying it as representative of the entire Iranian nation. Looking at Ahmadinejad's cabinet, it is clear that at least ten ministers (Manouchehr Mottaki, Mostafa Muhammad-Najjar, Muhammad Hossein Saffar Harandi, Gholam-Hossein Mohseni-Ejehei, Mostafa Pour Muhammadi, Masoud Mirkazemi, Muhammad Reza Eskandari, Muhammad Rahmati, Alireza Tahmasbi and Parviz Fattah) served with or affiliated themselves with the Sepah. Several others were also veterans of the 1980–8 Iran–Iraq war. Their presence and their role in the national political arena has prompted commentators to suggest that a general militarization of Iranian politics has been taking place. Moreover, two of the ministerial nominees (Gholam-Hossein Mohseni-Ejei and Mostafa Pour Muhammadi) also had Hojjatieyah backgrounds, fuelling speculation about the growing role of the Hojjatiiyah in government.

President Ahmadinejad's first cabinet meeting was held on 25 August 2005 in Mashhad. The choice of Mashhad as the location had its own symbolism. This is a holy city to the Shia, as the city in which the eighth Shia Imam Reza is buried. In a statement made by the president before he chaired the first cabinet session, he said:

> We [the cabinet] have come to such a holy place to be inspired before rendering services to the nation … Once again and in presence of Imam Reza … we [cabinet ministers] renew our allegiance to the administration of social justice and serving the masses and development of the country.[64]

In that meeting, the cabinet approved the president's suggestion of holding cabinet meetings outside of Tehran 'to bring the government closer to the people'. Thus, in approximately 10 months of his presidency, Ahmadinejad's cabinet had visited 11 provinces (Kohgilouyeh and Boyer Ahmad, South Khorasan, Sistan–Baluchestan, Ilam, Qom, Hormuzgan, Bushehr, Chahar Mahal and Bakhtiari, Lorestan and Golestan).[65] The issue of communication has been considered a priority for Ahmadinejad's government, and his agenda has highlighted the need to be close to the people and reflect their concerns.

In the first 12 months of his presidency, Mahmoud Ahmadinejad delivered more than 166 speeches inside Iran. In them he tended to reinforce the same message of subservience of the government to the people and the need to realize social justice. Recurring themes are:

1. The government is to improve people's lives.
2. Justice is inevitable in Islamic society.
3. The need to fight corruption.
4. The promotion of Islamic values and 'Quranic culture'.
5. Iran has a glorious cultural history and is therefore in a position to offer the modern world its 'message of hope'.
6. The future of Iran should be built on the glory of the past.[66]

These six themes affirm the four main principles guiding his presidency, of which he spoke at his inauguration. To repeat, these principles have bunched around: the promotion of justice, attention to the needs of the people, serving all the masses, and the material and moral progress of the country.

Ahmadinejad's strategy appears to be based on a sophisticated projection of himself and his administration as not interested in politics for the sake of power, but to take power in order to improve the lives of ordinary people. He regards this commitment to be central to the vitality of the Islamic Republic and as one of the main principles of the revolution itself. Thus the whole manner of his leadership, from the way he dresses and lives to how he receives guests and visiting dignitaries, are throwbacks to the early days of the revolution. His personal and professional life set him apart from the previous generation of politicians and policymakers of the country.

CONCLUSION

As already mentioned, Mahmoud Ahmadinejad has presented himself as a politician who wants to serve the Iranian nation, in particular those who have been forgotten by previous governments. There is no doubt that his social and religious background are behind every move or statement. Using religious phrases about the hidden Shia Imam, speaking extensively about social justice, redistributing wealth, bringing new but inexperienced faces to politics, ignoring the political role of women and limiting it to family affairs and, lastly, presenting the government as a representative of the people rather than their master, continue to dominate his strategy. It is for this combination of religion and new-style politics that Ahmadinejad is being referred to as a real phenomenon in modern Iran.

He does, however, represent a far more radical shift in the social structure of the country's elite than is immediately apparent, and his agenda seems more radical even when compared with the first revolutionary generation. He hails from those who inherited the country from the Pahlavis and thus formed the new, emerging urban-based social classes. The bulk of this group had emigrated from different Iranian cities to the capital, swelling its population to the 12 million that it is today. The interests of these internal migrants were inextricably linked to that of the Islamic regime and many of them joined the Sepah for ideological reasons, and also for defending their new power base. They are religious to the extent that religion dominates their lives. Mahmoud Ahmadinejad is a child of this same social environment and his presidency reflects the same.

Those social groups associated with the revolution were adversely affected by the reform policies of President Muhammad Khatami, and they felt that their hard-fought-for revolutionary aims had been undermined by Khatami's reforms. They felt a real sense of isolation and alienation in what they regarded to be 'their' Islamic Republic. The reform movement – in their eyes – focused on political change, forgetting the role of these social groups in establishing the Islamic state and in protecting its ruling regime. They felt that they had been betrayed, and that the regime had been 'kidnapped' by liberals, intellectuals and unreligious people. Perceptions of the reform movement amongst various social classes has played an important part in the divisions emerging between the political elite itself. In the last analysis, fear of the reforms helped in mobilizing the traditional urban masses in support of the neoconservatives, especially Mahmoud Ahmadinejad.

The Iranian neoconservatives are in power precisely because they 'rediscovered' the traditional lower and middle classes and also because they separated themselves from the traditional conservatives, who were seen as not having done enough to protect the masses. The masses were also angered by the level of corruption of Iranian politicians who were busy protecting their own interests and using their political vantage point for personal gain. Ahmadinejad used hatred of corruption to great effect in his election campaign, arguing that such individuals were not only unclean morally but also untrustworthy, for they had also abused the religion of the people. Only he, Ahmadinejad claimed, could rid the Republic of these unworthy politicians. He was, he said, 'the people's man', and the only man who could lead Iran's 'third revolution'.

IV

DOMESTIC POLITICS AND INTERNAL CHALLENGES UNDER AHMADINEJAD

Extremism does not have a place in the popular government. It will be dealt with. All powers and abilities, all opportunities and all competencies, will be used in the popular government. The focus will be on national interests, national honour, and progress for all.

Mahmoud Ahmadinejad, 26 June 2005

With the forming of the ninth government (Ahmadinejad's government) the death knell of intellectualism was sounded.

Emad Afroogh, head of Majlis Commission for Cultural Affairs, 29 April 2006

INTRODUCTION

Iranian politics entered a new era after the election of Mahmoud Ahmadinejad as the sixth president of the Islamic Republic of Iran. The victory of Ahmadinejad did not simply imply a defeat for the reformists, but it also indicated the rise of a new political elite of 'neoconservatives' with a new political discourse and a new agenda. This new political elite is directing its new political discourse towards those in society who are in need of economic and social justice rather than purely political rights. The return of religion and its values to the public arena forms the ideological basis of this new political discourse.

The rise of the new political elite has added a new element to the dynamics of politics in Iran. After eight years of attempts at reform, through the opening up of debates on political rights, civil society, Islamic democracy, freedom of speech, freedom of the press and women's rights, these new Iranian neoconservatives have by-passed reform issues and have created for themselves a new agenda. This populist new agenda focuses more on meeting the so-called basic needs of the Iranian people, which they believe is the responsibility of every administration.

The unique Iranian 'nanny' state that is being forged by the neo-conservatives represents an attempt by the new elite to build a new relationship with those forces in society who were ignored during the reform period. President Ahmadinejad himself has promoted the new administration's populism in the context of his four principles of governance, with such statements as 'the new government will stress [...] [the] promotion of justice, attention to the needs of the people, serving all the masses, and material and moral progress of the country'[1] and 'The tools to do so are Islamic values.'[2] The rise of the neo-conservatives has reopened the door to the debate about the nature of the Iranian Islamic state, and has also highlighted the wide gap now emerging between the old and new generations of the country's revolutionary political elite.

THE STRUGGLE FOR POWER

In many ways Ahmadinejad's victory reflects the transformation of the political struggle in Iran from being one between the conservatives and the reformists to one within the powerful conservative faction itself. The new guard represents the rise of the military in Iranian politics. The old guard, however, remains at the heart of power, occupying many of the unelected offices of the system. Such figures as Ayatollah Rafsanjani, representing pragmatic conservatism, remain powerful actors in Iranian politics. In his case this is not only because of his role as head of the Expediency Council but also because of his strong patrimonial network of political support that he has been able to develop over the decades. On the other hand there is Ahmadinejad, a man of humble origins with support amongst the lower classes and strong links to the IRGC, the Basij and to cliques such as the Hojjatieh Society. It has become clear since the election that Ahmadinejad has been manoeuvring to create political space for ideologues close to him and to dominate state institutions with like-minded individuals. Ahmadinejad represents a close-knit network of factions populated by ideologues who display a strong sense of entitlement to power as true sons of the revolution.

The harsh reality of the ongoing power struggle is clearly visible in Iran. Rafsanjani, for example, has on more than one occasion attacked Ahmadinejad openly and accused him of undermining national unity and elevating incompetent cronies to positions of power and influence. Not to be outdone, Ahmadinejad in turn has hinted that he would seek to bring Rafsanjani and those who benefited excessively under his tenure of presidency to trial for corruption.[3] If the president were to actually act on this threat then he would more than likely open a major faultline amongst the elite, perhaps irrevocably ending any pretence of union amongst them.

In the midst of this power struggle, the position of the Supreme Leader Ayatollah Khamenei has remained somewhat ambivalent. Although Ahmadinejad had originally been Ayatollah Khomeini's protégé, there were rumours that Khamenei would have little choice but to realign himself with Rafsanjani to protect the old guard in the midst of its struggle with the new guard. This is an outcome that Ayatollah Khamenei would not relish, given the tense relations between himself and the Rafsanjani camp.[4]

Given the potential gravity of the situation, the victor of this conflict is likely to be the old guard. Ahmadinejad and his advancements are likely to be blocked by the old guard, because Ahmadinejad threatens their political and economic power in Iran. Whatever the outcome of the political struggle, the old guard would still have to deal with the pressing social and economic crisis besetting the country. The reformist movement may have been defeated politically, and it is without the momentum it had during the late 1990s, but those who supported it continue to exist in Iran and the discourse of the reform movement continues to resonate. As the doors to state institutions are locked to them, these individuals have looked to alternative methods of political engagement, whether through the expansion of civil society or through the use of the Internet.[5] The possibility thus exists that the conservative old guard would emerge from its struggle with Ahmadinejad seriously weakened, providing an opportunity for the reformists to re-emerge.

At stake in this political infighting is not only pride but the economic spoils of political power. The formal Iranian economy is worth about $500 billion, but there is also a vast informal economy; much of which is actively encouraged by the political system and managed by religious foundations and other networks that link the market with different parts of the power structure.[6] Despite a number of internal social and economic problems, economic development has occurred and this has been fuelled by oil income. The main beneficiaries have been the elite business factions linked to the old guard. These factions have in turn used their wealth and influence to engage in speculation on the stock market and in real estate, and to reinforce their economic and political power, in particular strengthening their ties within the economic elite.

However, in the first year after the election of Ahmadinejad the economic situation deteriorated. Foreign investors fled to surrounding Arab countries, the stock market plummeted and confidence in the banking system weakened.[7] Most of this was due to a lack of confidence in the economic policies of Ahmadinejad by foreign investors and the appointment of ministers with little known economic and political management experience. The poor handling of the economy is a strong reason for the old guard in combination with the business faction to rein in Ahmadinejad and his followers.

Ahmadinejad's ideological leanings are also a liability for the old guard. Islamist ideology has been exploited by the old guard to entrench their status and power in the hierarchy of politics in Iran; this can explain why they have maintained and consolidated their strength – even not reversing Khatami's policy of liberalism. However, Ahmadinejad has spoken of a necessity to roll back secular liberalism to protect the Islamic identity and principles of Iran. This is likely to be seen as a threat to the old guard's position, adding another source of conflict in the collision between the two camps.

In the last analysis, we can speculate that the nuclear issue and the way it is handled by Ahmadinejad could be the justification that is needed by the old guard to step up their campaign of putting a check on him, if not ousting him – though the latter would be of last resort. It can therefore be seen that a number of factors are responsible for this power struggle. From the militarization of politics to the mishandling of the economy, the struggle is likely to continue.

Ascent of the 'Populist Republic'

Iran is governed by a set of elected and unelected individuals and institutions, including the Supreme Leader, the president, Guardian Council, Assembly of Experts, parliament, Expediency Council and a vast array of security forces. A parallel government is seen to co-exist at the same time as the visible government, acting as a source of adjudication to preserve the unique Iranian Islamic Republic.[8] With Supreme Leadership, presidency and parliament in conservative hands for the first time in years, Khamenei's power certainly has been consolidated and strengthened. The presidency was the last holdout for Iran's reformists, and the victory of Ahmadinejad gave total control of state institutions to the conservative camp. As Ahmadinejad is closely interconnected with the conservative hierarchy, he is unlikely to challenge the Guardian Council or the powers of the conservatives in society.

Ahmadinejad's electoral campaign was fought on the basis of social and economic issues rather than ideology and political opinion.[9] The state's backing of Ahmadinejad began to shed more light on his ideological leanings, however, with further insights into his views and opinions becoming apparent when he presented his proposed cabinet to parliament. The conservative lawmaker Manouchehr Mottaki was nominated as foreign minister and a former conservative deputy intelligence minister, Mostafa Pour Muhammadi, was named as interior minister.[10] Ahmadinejad named as intelligence minister Gholam Hossein Mohseni-Ejehei, a cleric with a strong affiliation to the ruling faction in Iran. The proposed foreign minister, Mottaki, is a conservative who strongly criticized the previous administration's nuclear negotiations with the Europeans, saying the country should adopt a tougher position and not make concessions.[11] Ahmadinejad also replaced Hassan Rohani, Iran's chief nuclear negotiator, with Ali Larijani, a conservative former head of state broadcasting. Ali Larijani has described giving up Iran's right to uranium enrichment in exchange for EU incentives as like swapping 'a pearl for a sweet'.[12]

Ahmadinejad stated he had signed an anti-corruption 'pact' with his ministers, committing them to giving up their own economic activities and against giving family members any benefits. Key ministerial posts were given to conservatives, while technocrats were appointed to head the oil and foreign ministries. Most of the 21 candidates Ahmadinejad introduced were unknown, even to the conservative-dominated Majlis. MPs showed their scepticism by directly questioning Ahmadinejad's agenda and choice of candidates. Emad Afroogh, a conservative parliamentarian who had supported Ahmadinejad before his election, asked,

> Can't we use people who have past experience in the ministries they have been suggested for? … It seems that your plan is full of beautiful words … They are more like ideals than policies. One cannot call certain goals and ideals an agenda.[13]

The candidate who drew the most criticism was Ali Saeedlou, who had been nominated to run the oil ministry.[14] Saeedlou's critics argued that he had no experience in the field and was not capable of handling such a high ministerial position. The Ministry of Oil in Iran is not your average ministry; it is a super-ministry because the country's primary export is oil, which, along with reserves of natural gas, accounts for Iran's international significance. Ahmadinejad presented four nominees for the post who – like himself – were historically affiliated to the Sepah and who lacked requisite professional and administrative knowledge. After much parliamentary debate and public speculation about the president's judgement, finally the fourth nominee, Kazem Vaziri Hamaneh, was accepted by the Majlis.[15]

The jostling that was witnessed between the parliament and Ahmadinejad was indicative of the importance of this ministry to Iran and of a division between the old and new guard in Iranian conservatism. Ultimately the cabinet of the president has been instrumental in strengthening the hold of the conservatives on national affairs and in representing a changing of the guard, with new faces entering mainstream Iranian politics.

THE CHANGING OF THE GUARD – THE RISE OF THE MIDDLE GENERATION

Ahmadinejad, as well as Majlis Chairman Gholam-Ali Haddad-Adel, are amongst the younger members of the 'middle' generation of the Islamic Revolution, who are faithful to the revolution's values and grew up under the establishment apparatuses. Unlike some in the old guard, they are not clerics. As already highlighted, Ahmadinejad is a former Revolutionary Guards commander and had the support of the conservative bloc in the Majlis and of the prominent conservative party, The Islamic Iran Developers Coalition (Abadgaran), throughout his election campaign.[16]

The country's executive positions are now also being held by 'middle generation' conservatives. Despite statements by Khamenei that the regime is based on two 'wings' (that is, the reformist and the conservative), all branches of the government are now in fact in the hands of the conservatives.[17] It seems that the conservative regime prefers the middle generation of non-cleric conservatives – who grew up in the institutions of the regime – over members of the founding generation.[18]

The simmering conflict between the old and new guard in Iranian conservatism entered the public arena immediately after the presidential elections. Ansar-e-Hezbollah, one of the main groups behind Ahmadinejad's campaign, in a harsh and critical article entitled 'The right faction, leave Osoulgaran [Fundamentalists] alone!', wrote against the old guard, specifically naming a few leading conservative figures (such as Nateq-Nouri, Asgarouladi, Asadollah Badamchian and Muhammad Reza Bahonar) and conservative organizations (such as Jam'aiyat Mo'atalefeh Islami (the Society of Islamic Coalition, or JMI), Rouhaniyat Mobarez (the Society of Combatant Clergy), Anjoman Islami Mohandesin (the Society of Engineers) and Shoray-e-Hamahangi (the Council of Co-ordination)).[19] All the individuals and organizations listed were behind Larijani in the presidential elections and had endorsed Nateq-Nouri, former speaker of the Majlis, in his presidential bid in 1997. In addition, almost unanimously, the Ayatollahs of the holy city of Qom had backed Rafsanjani. Ansar-e-Hezbollah accused the former president of being 'the right-wing monopolist' and responsible for what the Osoulgaran suffered after Khatami's election in 1997. The Ansar also criticized those whom, it claimed, had continued to impose their candidates on the conservatives and had tried to force Ahmadinejad to drop out of the presidential race.[20]

The victory of Ahmadinejad built on what some observers viewed as a 'conservative coup' in the parliamentary elections of 2004. The main concern of the West is that a militarized governmental apparatus would engage in the restoration of the revolutionary and religious values ascendant immediately after the 1979 revolution. There is a fear in the international community of the neoconservatives using external crises to forge a new security-driven national consensus of the sort that existed during the Iran–Iraq war. It is feared that under such circumstances, the position of dissidents and reform-oriented forces would be weakened even further, creating a major obstacle (at least in the medium term) for political change in Iran.

The election of Ahmadinejad as linked with the Revolutionary Guards has been contextualized by Iran's relations with other countries, where the nuclear issue is the predominant concern. Suspicion surrounding Iran's nuclear programme has grown with the creeping militarization of politics in Iran.

MILITARIZATION OF IRANIAN POLITICS
UNDER AHMADINEJAD

The failure to achieve Islamic social justice and welfare for the poor (the *mostazafin*) was exemplified in the Rafsanjani administration's economic liberalization strategy. This produced a backlash at both the mass and the elite level. The liberalization strategy led to urban riots and to more direct involvement of the reconstituted security forces in domestic affairs. At the elite level the failures of the Islamic justice programme generated new demands, largely from the neo-conservative factions, for the imposition of stricter cultural norms. This was not an unnatural response to the realities of life in the Islamic Republic of Iran, in which all that remained of the distinction between Islamic Iran and its predecessor was in the cultural realm – to be more precise, in the Islamic–cultural value system introduced by Ayatollah Khomeini. However even in the cultural arena the regime has had to come to terms with the grave shortcomings in its plans to purify society and establish traditional Islamic customs as the norm, particularly as the pace of secularization has continued to accelerate with every passing season.

The neoconservative movement, which first made its organized presence felt in 1993 (after that year's presidential elections), accelerated the pace of its political march in the mid-1990s, and from March 1996 it openly began challenging the pragmatists' grip on power. It did much, in the Majlis and elsewhere, to weaken the Rafsanjani administration's institutional control and its public policy reforms. For a while, the stunning defeat of the New Right's champion (Hojjatoleslam Nateq-Nouri) in the May 1997 presidential elections did help to check their growing influence. But due to the disparate nature of Khatami's coalition, the ideological and political divisions in the ranks of his allies, and, perhaps most important of all, the entrenched position that the New Right had in the key institutions of power, neoconservatism remained a potent force.

For all the public support he enjoyed, it proved very difficult for President Khatami to decisively reverse the balance of power in favour of his own camp. This was driven home in the elections for the Seventh Majlis in February 2004. Through manipulation of the candidates list by the conservative-dominated Guardian Council, the reformists decisively lost control of the Majlis to the Right, and it also ensured that a high proportion of deputies with links to the Sepah or related organizations were to be present in the new Majlis.[21]

As the Iranian political system has matured and settled down to the drum of regular, openly contested elections, it has become easier for the Artesh and the Sepah to stay out of domestic squabbles of the political elite and not compromise their political presence. However when the system itself generates instability and when elections result in the rise of a 'Third Force'[22] – a new and different revolutionary agenda – it is far from clear that the Sepah (or at least its associates) will be disinclined to behave as independent actors. While it is true that the Sepah wants much more to be allowed to shadow, emulate, compete with and complement the work of the Artesh, military intervention of some kind in politics is nonetheless not impossible – particularly if internal divisions continue to deepen at the elite level, and if ideological faultlines widen and the scale of factionalist violence escalates.

Many of the centres of power present in Iran evolve around religious, political, economic and military figures. The IRGC and the security forces have emerged as the most independent, and prevail over all others centres of power in Iran.[23] The US military threats against Iran, nuclear confrontation with the West and the invasion of Iraq are amongst the fundamental causes behind this gain in power. Currently, a group associated with the IRGC controls the major state-sponsored media. After gaining control of numerous city and town councils in 2003, many former members of the IRGC or its associates managed to enter into the legislative branch in the 2004 elections; the group had also set its sights on gaining control of the executive branch in 2005.

Prior to taking on a higher political profile, the IRGC had established itself as an economic force in the country, controlling a vast array of financial and economic enterprises. To a large degree the businesses were seen as needed to finance IRGC security programmes. At the same time, the ventures were intended to build the Sepah's independence; in this, Sepah commanders sought to mimic their military counterparts in Pakistan and Turkey.[24] In both these countries the army has tended to act as far more than an instrument to protect national interests: the armies have high-profile political roles and often define the respective nations' security interests. Since 1997, the Sepah in Iran has had a growing influence on foreign policy, strategic thinking and the economy.[25] This 'Praetorian Guard' has been a cornerstone of the conservatives' survival and comeback strategy since 1997, and has been substantially rewarded by Khamenei. The IRGC also has a strong presence on the Supreme Council for National Security.

Further signs of the ever-growing political clout of the Revolutionary Guards are abundant. For instance, on 18 May 2004 a former Sepah commander, Ezatullah Zarghami, was named for the key post of chief of national television and radio. In addition, in apparent exchange for its help during the parliamentary elections, the Revolutionary Guards were permitted to field their own slate of candidates. Thus, when the new parliament convened later in May, about a dozen legislators were under the effective control of the Revolutionary Guards. Political observers note that this is the first time in the Islamic Republic's history that the Sepah have had such a parliamentary presence.

By far the greatest demonstration of the Revolutionary Guards' political influence occurred in early May 2004, when the military abruptly closed down Tehran's new Imam Khomeini International Airport.[26] In justifying its action, the Guards' representatives said the fact that a Turkish consortium, TAV, was in charge of operating the airport terminal posed a threat to Iran's 'security and dignity' (according to the IRNA, the official Iranian News Agency). Accordingly, the Sepah demanded that the TAV airport deal be voided before the airport reopens. Some observers suspect that an economic motive was behind the Revolutionary Guards' action in the airport row; when TAV won the tender to operate the airport, the losing bidder was reportedly a company with close ties to the Revolutionary Guards.[27]

In these presidential elections the Guardian Council confirmed only six individuals out of 1010 candidates as qualified to participate and contest the elections. Of the six qualified to stand, four were in fact former IRGC commanders and two were clerics.[28] The main candidates of the IRGC were Ali Larijani, a former IRGC commander and ex-director of the highly politicized state television and radio network, and Muhammad Bagher Qalibaf, the former Chief of Tehran's police force, who is also a former IRGC commander. Qalibaf openly declared himself to be a 'religiously' devout Reza Shah.[29] He noted that Iranians were tired of the country's chaotic power relations and were desperate for central rule. Mohsen Rezaei, longtime Commander-in-Chief of the IRGC and present speaker of the Expediency Council, was another military-oriented candidate. Prior to the elections Javad Larijani, older brother of Ali Larijani, argued in an article published in Iran that the former president, Rafsanjani, should not enter the presidential race; for he, according to Javad Larijani, represented the old guard who had paid their dues and should now do little more than attend ceremonial gatherings. Leadership, he said, should be left to new figures.[30] If further sign of the militarization of the political space in Iran were needed, it would be the fact that ten of the new president's cabinet nominees had military or security backgrounds.[31]

Regarding the sudden rise of the military and victory of Ahmadinejad, General Muhammad Baqer Zolqadr, Deputy Commander-in-Chief of the IRGC, made a very revealing statement. In his speech during a gathering of commanders of the Basij forces Zolqadr said, 'in the current complex political situation, in which both foreign pressures and internal forces were trying to prevent us from forming a fundamentalist government, we had to operate with complexity'. He added, 'fundamentalist forces, thank God, won the election thanks to their smart and multi-fold plan and through the massive participation of the Basij'.[32] The plan was known as the military strategy of 'moving with lights off', so as not to be noticed by rivals.[33]

The militarization of Iranian politics has drawn strong criticism from the reformist camp. For example, reformist presidential candidate Mehdi Karroubi stated in a late-March meeting with officials from his election headquarters that in recent years he has been warning of IRGC involvement in political affairs. The daily *Etemad* quoted him as saying, 'I have repeatedly condemned it and have openly criticized them.'[34] He added that it is a mistake to ignore the actions of the IRGC, the Basij, the Guardian Council, the judiciary, the Special Court for the Clergy and agencies affiliated with the Supreme Leader in the 2005 presidential elections. Mehdi Karroubi and Mostafa Moin claimed that Ahmadinejad's electoral victory was backed illegally by well-financed regime elements, including members of the IRGC and the Basij. Muhammad Reza Khatami, Moin's running mate, concluded that they were defeated by what he called 'a garrison party'. He said:

> until three days before the election, everything was fine, then after a military coup was launched, of which we only learned later, an order was given to a specific military organization to support a specific candidate, a person whom all the left-wing and the right-wing pre-election pools had shown to be the least favourite among the seven candidates.[35]

AHMADINEJAD AND THE CHALLENGE OF GOVERNANCE

As has already been discussed, Ahmadinejad faced a major challenge in forming his cabinet. However, this was not the only challenge he would face. Other challenges included the need to deliver on his promise of bringing the benefits of oil revenues to the Iranian people, at the same time as strengthening the country's Islamic and traditional cultural and social values.

Oil revenues to the people's table

The first challenge President Mahmoud Ahmadinejad faced in power started after he outlined the priorities of the draft budget bill for the Iranian fiscal year of 1385 (21 March 2006–20 March 2007). President Ahmadinejad submitted the budget bill to the Majlis during its open session. In so doing, he again repeated the four principles of his government – promotion of justice, attention to the needs of the people, serving all the masses, and material and moral progress of the country.

Ahmadinejad cited dynamism of the administrative system as another priority of the bill: 'the administrative body should implement programs with the highest potentiality'. Regarding the banking system, he said this system was another priority of the bill, stressing that the 'banking system is the driving force of the national economy. This system should move towards the goals of the budget and the 20-Year Development Vision Plan.' Emphasizing the populist underpinnings of his administration, he said that the 'economic growth envisioned in the bill will not be realized without the nation's presence in development fields'. He highlighted the role of government in encouraging internal and foreign investment and also reassured the people that his government was aiming to improve the quality of work and increase efficiency. He affirmed that his government would support exports, low-price facilities and would prepare the ground for export-related activities.[36]

Ahmadinejad stated that his government stressed the need to become self-sufficient in oil, gas and petrochemical industries making optimal use of energy according to the budget bill. He added, 'The government stresses the need for development of indigenous sciences, conduction of useful research, settlement of problems and developing the talents of the youth.' He added, 'The bill pays attention to jobs, housing and marriage of the youth.'[37]

Of an estimated $75 billion in oil revenues, $25 billion was to be used inside the country. The figures reveal that the total budget for the year was to be set at $217 billion, however. Of this, $68 billion was allocated to the public sector and $149 billion to other state enterprises like banks and non-profit organizations.[38] This was to be a budget of huge expenditures without clearly identified income tracks. Upon the publication of the proposed budget, Emad Afroogh, Head of Majlis' Commission for Cultural Affairs, openly criticized the budget bill for its short-sightedness and inflationary pressures. Afroogh insisted that the new budget bill was not in conformity with the Fourth Five-Year Economic Development Plan (2005–10). He questioned the figures and questioned whether they were 'in line with the slogan of social justice, decentralization and removal of deprivation in certain areas', asking 'how this budget helps to create jobs, and reduce the dependence on oil revenue'.[39] Afroogh described the policy of depending on oil revenue as running 'counter with the national strategy to gradually free national economy from oil revenues'.[40] Iraj Nadimi, rapporteur of the Majlis' Economics Commission said that 'the seventh Parliament will not sacrifice its objectives for those of the government when studying the budget bill'.[41] The Iranian lawmakers' position was clear:

> meeting public demands should not be limited to short-term needs and current expenses...parliament, as the main decision-making body, will not turn a blind eye to its obligations under overt and covert pressures... any decision on the budget bill will be within the framework of the Fourth Five-Year Development Plan (2005–10) and the 20-year perspective.[42]

It was very clear that the new budget would not be able to tackle the major problems that the Iranian economy was facing.

According to the neoconservatives, what people in Iran needed was 'focus on growth and jobs'[43] in contrast to Khatami's agenda of political reform. Khatami, however, did unveil a strategy of economic reforms as well. The break-up of economic monopolies, liberalization of imports, encouragement of foreign investment, privatization of hundreds of state companies, unification of the exchange rates, increase in controls on smuggling and calls for central control of the budgets of such entities as the Bonyads were the main planks of his economic reform strategy. As Khatami's economic reforms would in fact directly hurt the vested interests of the conservative-leaning forces it is understandable that his plans were under attack by the neoconservatives.[44] Interestingly, despite the harsh criticism that Khatami had faced, he still had the incisive vision that political reform cannot be reached without the introduction of serious economic reforms.

Political debate over political rights, civil society and even Islamic democracy no longer exist in Iran under the neoconservatives. This is understandable, given that they have openly embraced the so-called Chinese model of development.[45] In such a model, Iranian neoconservatives believe, political reform has virtually no role to play. Instead, Ahmadinejad has repeatedly emphasized the desire to focus on meeting the needs of the *mostazafin* (the downtrodden).

Ahmadinejad's policies can be said to be part of the

> new economic policies that followed the death of Ayatollah Ruhollah Khomeini and the transferring of populist elements in the theocracy – the maktabies, whose economic philosophy was based on Iran's economic independence from the West, active state intervention in the economy in favour of low-income and marginal groups in society and redistribution of national income away from the propertied classes and towards the 'mostazafin'.[46]

It is therefore no surprise that the neoconservatives have considered the *mostazafin* to be at the centre of their policies and why liberalization of the economy has not been a major part of their discourse. Liberalizing the economy, as the neoconservatives understand it, would, in their view, adversely affect the *mostazafin*. Liberalization of the economy also has a direct impact on the social values of the country, which has always been a concern for the neoconservatives.

Thus, the victories of the neoconservatives in the Seventh Majlis elections in 2004 and then in the ninth presidential elections in 2005 has changed the whole economic debate in Iran. Any debate about privatization has had to be frozen, or at least priority given to the *mostazafin* to become the main beneficiaries of ownership rights of formerly state-owned corporations.

In this context the president has 'ordered big public banks whose books are full of non-performing loans to lend generously, especially to ordinary citizens'.[47] While such policies could be considered as empowering the poor by pushing them into active economic life through microfinance-oriented projects, the scale of such borrowing would have to be considered carefully in order to evaluate its results. While individuals can be encouraged to contribute to the value of the economy with such financial incentives, the inflationary pressures generated at the same time can quickly remove any short-term benefits derived from financial borrowing for investment or for current expenditure. In this particular case, Iranian people most probably will use these extra finances for current consumption, thus further fuelling double-digit inflation.

This indicates the incoherence and short-termism in economic policymaking for the sake of political popularity. This was the impression that some lawmakers got when they stated that 'meeting public demands should not be limited to short-term needs and current expenses'.[48] The budget debate, thus, was a reflection of the unease about the entire economic premises and policies of Ahmadinejad regarding social justices. His call for the government to become a 'nanny state' in caring for its people met a wall of protest when set against the financial costs of realizing this ambition.

Another of the major challenges facing Ahmadinejad's government is economic corruption. The roots of this, it is widely unacknowledged, are to be found in the state's formal and informal institutions – some of which form the very foundations of Ahmadinejad's presidency. The Transparency Organization, dealing with corruption issues internationally, has confirmed that Iran's Corruptions Perceptions Index (CPI) for 2005 was 2.9 (with 10 being 'highly clean' and 0 'highly corrupt)'.[49] Looking back to the CPI 2003, the index for Iran was 3.0,[50] showing that the situation had been getting worse and corruption had increased during the Khatami period. The question of corruption has its own particular sensitivity in a country like Iran, which claims that its task is to promote Islamic justice, equality and Islamic values.

The debate about this matter was part of Ahmadinejad's election propaganda, and later formed part of his economic strategy as well. Be that as it may, there was to be much resistance to the fight against corruption. The Director of the Centre for Combating Economic Corruption, for one, made it clear that he 'will not be able to release the names or organizations involved in economic corruption, unless he receives permission from higher authorities'.[51] This was to prove a difficult challenge for the new anti-corruption president to manage.

Cultural and social challenges

If there is to be a description of Ahmadinejad's presidency to date, it can be summed up in the 'disappearance of the intellectual elite'. Emad Afroogh, Head of Majlis Commission for Cultural Affairs, had confirmed that 'with the forming of the ninth government [Ahmadinejad's administration] the death knell of intellectualism was sounded'.[52] The image of the intellectual elite presented by the conservatives – as liberal-leaning and ideologically Westernized – led to the creation of a wide gap between those intellectuals and the *mostazafin*. For the *mostazafin*, claimed the neoconservatives, such matters as civil society, democracy, economic reform, women's rights and human rights were irrelevant. When justice and economic well-being were needed, there would be no room for intellectuals who want to give the masses Western civil society.

The marginalization of the intellectual elite has created a new and illiberal political atmosphere in the country, which has been further compounded by removal from the public space of academics, senior officials associated with previous administrations, former ambassadors, and those individuals who had played a part in formulating decisions and policy priorities for the Khatami administration. According to Hojjatolislam Mehdi Karroubi, many of the senior officials, decision makers and the 2nd Khordad activists are now 'street-corner managers'.[53] The limitations imposed by President Ahmadinejad have made it impossible for these individuals to work with him. Some of them in fact decided to withdraw from public life in response to his victory in the elections. However, the majority were 'encouraged' to resign their posts before being considered for dismissal.

The failure to reappoint well-qualified senior officials or diplomats has been considered as part of Ahmadinejad's agenda to clean the state of the so-called 'liberals' who had not paid enough attention to the values of religion and the revolution. Removing key figures from office, around 600 in total, has had a direct bearing on the perform-ance of the government in general and the realization of its own priorities in particular. A gap has been created between the previous senior officials and the new government. Even the performance of foreign policy has been affected, where embassies in such important capitals as London and Paris were kept without ambassadors for nearly the entire first year of his government.[54]

On the social front, questions have been asked about the neocon-servative elite's approach towards such issues as the *hijab* (the head covering worn by some Muslim women) and Islamic values in gen-eral. According to authorities, the objective is to target the women and girls who 'pay no attention to the Islamic social values by the way they dress, those women and girls who wear shorter, tight-fit-ting coats, Capri pants, smaller scarves, and light-coloured dresses'.[55] Such issues were not on the agenda during former reformist Presi-dent Muhammad Khatami's era, when Iranian women had many choices beside the traditional long, dark-coloured *chadour*.

Responding to the president's cultural concerns, the Majlis put the issue of the Islamic dress code at the top of its own agenda. The new Islamic dress code legislation was approved by the Majlis, with 137 MPs voting in favour of it, and there has been a suggestion to encourage factories and manufactures to work on designing a new national attire for both genders, taking women as its primary focus. The new law has 113 articles identifying the necessity for such a law, demanding that the government, private sector and Iranian society in general work together to uphold Islamic morals. It also deals with designs and clothes in general, even for men. Emad Afroogh made it clear that the new legislation should not be imposed by the authori-ties. Ismaeil Gramie Mogadam, MP of Bojounord province, voted against the new law. He considered such a law to be interference in people's private affairs: 'now we decide what people should wear, next time we have to decide what they have to drink or eat!' He also highlighted the likely economic costs of such legislation to the fashion industry, where Iranians would more than likely end up boycotting such imposed dress codes.[56]

Nevertheless, the new government started a moral code campaign immediately after the adoption of this law, reminding women that they should watch what they are wearing outdoors. It also began a campaign of pressure on those manufactures and stores that were selling 'fashionable' clothes.[57] In addition, more than 200 police men and women were deployed on the streets of Tehran, charged with challenging women who showed disrespect to Islamic values by wearing short overalls, tight jackets, thin headscarves or by revealing their ankles.

The backlash of the 'moral crusade' was so great that the president had to backpeddle and state that it was 'unfair to claim that women lie at the root of any social problem you care to discuss'. He went further and insisted that as Iranian women 'respect the Islamic headscarf … there is no need for authoritarian action to spread the culture of the headscarf'.[58] Moreover, he went on to emphasize the important role of women in society. In an unexpected and unprecedented move the president ordered that suitable sections of football stadiums be considered for putting aside for female spectators and their families: 'the best stands should be allocated to women and families in the stadiums in which national and important matches are being held'.[59] He also asked the interior minister to be involved in implementing his order.

However the campaign to reinforce the *hijab* and Ahmadinejad's letter about women's presence in stadiums exposed the government to attack from more than one front. The Iranian public showed its own concern about the so-called 'Talibanization' of society, forcing the president to try and calm the situation by arguing that the *hijab* issue was a cultural one, and should be dealt with through cultural tools and not through legal enforcement. On the other hand, his move to allow women to attend sporting events incurred the wrath of several ayatollahs and MPs.[60] For the clerics, he was interfering in doctrinal matters of religion and thus stepping beyond the boundaries of his office. The fact that many of them so publicly censured him put Ahmadinejad personally in the firing line, generating opposition from the powerful clerical establishment and conservatives in charge. The final blow for Ahmadinejad was the Supreme Leader's veto of this policy, indicating to all that it was he who had the final word on such matters.[61]

The *hijab* issue and the campaigns against people being able to walk their pets in the street or for men to sport outlandish hairstyles, with penalties of up to $55 (£31)[62] for offenders, are indicative of how the relationship between the Iranian public and the government had changed very soon after the election. But it is worth noting that these cultural initiatives are nothing new and Ahmadinejad has been following a well-trodden path of social control that has existed since the early days of the revolution. Social themes were one of those challenges that always faced Khatami's government as well and it is interesting that within months of Ahmadinejad taking office they had emerged to directly affect his government. It is also worth noting that during the Khatami period, the president's 'liberal' social policies were under constant scrutiny for political gain. The Baztab website (*www.baztab.ir*), for example, which is close to Mohsen Rezaei (Secretary of the Expediency Council), has been active in blaming Iranian administrations for their failure to enforce the *hijab*. Thus far there have been more than 15 campaigns to implement a *hijab* policy, but all have failed because no one believes that the government is able to impose its will on the population.[63]

CONCLUSION

The election of Ahmadinejad represents a major turning point in Iranian politics. First and foremost, we may look back in five years' time and see his success as marking the twilight of Hashmi Rafsanjani's political influence in the country. The reasons for Rafsanjani's defeat, and Ahmadinejad's success, are complex but on the whole they fall into two categories; namely, Rafsanjani's failure to gain the support of Khamenei and his coterie of advisers, and Rafsanjani's failure to convince the people of his sincerity and the soundness of his policies.[64]

At a broader level, the reformists and even dissidents failed to understand the possibility of a regressive revolution in the country. They assumed that their slogans in support of political development, multi-party politics and integrating Iran into the international system would guarantee their victory. More than anything, Ahmadinejad's victory demonstrated that Iran remains a deeply polarized society 26 years after the victory of the revolution. In the same way that Khatami's victory in 1997 and 2001 demonstrated that there was grass roots support for reform and Iran's integration into the international community, Ahmadinejad's victory has shown that a large number of Iranians strongly support the conservatives and believe in their slogans regarding the redistribution of wealth, eliminating poverty and rooting out corruption.[65]

Time will tell whether Ahmadinejad can deliver on the promises[66] he made during his electoral campaign and convert his election slogans into tangible outcomes. However, what is for certain is that Ahmadinejad is in the process of revolutionizing Iranian politics by introducing the middle-generation conservatives into the mainstream. With them has come a military baggage, resulting in the militarization of Iranian politics. Three of Ahmadinejad's ministers, Intelligence Minister Gholamhoseyn Mohseni-Ejehei, Interior Minister Mostafa Pour Muhammadi and Culture and Islamic Guidance Minister Hoseyn Saffar-Harandi, are close to the conservative hierarchy and are openly accelerating this process.

These innovations by Ahmadinejad have not gone unnoticed, internally and externally. Internally the old guard are fearful of the road down which Ahmadinejad may be leading Iran – with fear of their economic and political status being diminished by a new revolution launched by Ahmadinejad. Externally the military character of the Iranian regime has raised alarm bells and has intensified the nuclear stand-off between Iran and the West.[67]

Internal challenges to Ahmadinejad have begun not from the reformists but from the old faction of the conservatives who feel that they are being pushed aside by the ascent of the new guard in Iranian conservatism. This power contestation is likely to be the defining feature of Iranian politics into the future, in addition to the external pressure being imposed upon Iran over suspicion of its nuclear ambitions. The manner in which Ahmadinejad handles and manages both challenges will determine his support base in society and, importantly, his longevity in power. It seems that the division within the ruling neoconservatives is also serious and this division is likely to increase in time over Ahmadinejad's economic and social policies. We have already seen a clerical backlash over his populist measure to allow women's presence in football stadiums and in tackling social corruption. He has been also accused of following a populist agenda for short-term political gain.[68] What the consequences of these tensions might be for the remainder of his presidency remain to be seen, but an early indicator might be the Majlis elections of 2008, which will bring about an open struggle between the neoconservatives and the reconstituted 'neoreformers'.

V

IRAN'S REGIONAL ROLE UNDER THE NEOCONSERVATIVES: CHALLENGES AND PROSPECTS

What do they [the USA and EU] want to do, place us under sanction? What were they giving us in the first place? For more than 27 years, against all in black and white international laws they have deprived us of airplane parts.

Mahmoud Ahmadinejad, 7 May 2006

...they [international Zionist and Expansionist Policies of the world Arrogance, i.e. United Sates and Israel] are cheeky humans, and think that the entire world should obey them. They destroy Palestinian families and expect nobody to object to them.

Mahmoud Ahmadinejad, 28 October 2005

It is not just for a few states to sit and veto global approvals. Should such a privilege continue to exist, the Muslim world with a population of nearly 1.5 billion should be extended the same privilege.

Mahmoud Ahmadinejad, 19 June 2005

INTRODUCTION

By the late 1980s military and political developments in the region, in particular the costly Iran–Iraq war, had forced a re-assessment of the 'rejectionist' strategy of the Iranian Republic. This critical stage in Iran's foreign relations can best be termed as the reorientation phase, which is characterized by the transition from the Khomeini-inspired radicalism to accommodation with the West and regional actors. This period started in earnest in June 1988 and lasted until August 1990, by which time we see the end of the Iranian transition to pragmatism and the establishment of the pragmatist line in Iran's foreign policy. The pragmatic trend that was firmly established in the 1990s broke down in 2001, however, and was again tested in 2003 with the military campaign in Iraq and the unrelated revelations about Iran's nuclear activities.

First, 9/11 posed a serious challenge to Iran's revolutionary profile as a defender of political Islam, but it did not prove too difficult for Tehran to overcome this as it was able to draw a clear distinction between its own system of governance and the violence unleashed by Al Qaeda. Without hesitation Iran cooperated with the West in the removal of the Taliban regime from Afghanistan, and did what it could to assist the USA in the rebuilding of its impoverished eastern neighbour.

Despite their collaboration in the Afghanistan war, the biggest direct fallout for Tehran was in fact the 2002 'Axis of Evil' pronouncement from Washington (delivered in President Bush's State of the Union Address in January), which inevitably resulted in mounting pressure on the Iranian establishment. The pronouncement by Washington was followed by new and startling revelations about Iran's nuclear programme from the USA and the International Atomic Energy Agency (IAEA), adding further fuel to tensions between Iran and the USA. Iran's sense of injury over the American president's speech, combined with the USA's fears of the Islamic Republic's nuclear activities, helped in making Khatami's second term much more diplomatically tense than his administration had expected – at least in comparison to his first term, which was characterized by the continuation of a pragmatic line that involved accommodation and cooperation with the West and regional actors. Indeed, the nuclear debate not only dogged his administration to its final days until the summer of 2005, it also directly fed into the intense internal political wrangling of the time between the different Iranian political factions, enabling the neoconservatives to adopt a much harder foreign policy line in national debates concerning the country's nuclear programme and its security dimensions as a means of winning favour with a disgruntled electorate as the state was coming under severe international pressure. The neoconservatives were able to use the nuclear stand-off as the best opportunity to show off their patriotism and commitment to the nation.

Beyond the crisis following Iran's nuclear activities, the other dramatic transformation in Iran's regional environment occurred in the context of the fall of Baghdad in March–April 2003. Thanks to the USA's military intervention Iran's most immediate geopolitical and ideological challenger, in the shape of Saddam's regime in Iraq, was obliterated in one fell swoop. The removal of the Baathist regime gave real political sustenance to the Shia of Iraq, who had for years been dependent on the generosity, support and protection of their Iranian brethren for their survival. Post-2003 the Shia-dominated state in Iraq began to look to Iran for economic, social and eventually military support. Iran's growing influence has become a double-edged sword for the US-led occupying forces however, for without question Iran is instrumental in the influence and stabilization of the Shia in Iraq and also has a hand to play in relation to the Kurds – all of which has given the Iranians a strong political hand in Iraqi politics.

At the same time as Iran's influence has grown in Iraq relative to other players, concerns have been raised in the West and amongst Iraq's Arab neighbours that Iran will more than likely stand to reap the benefits of the fall of the Baath regime. There now exists real fear of Arab Shia resurgence, strongly supported by Iran, taking place in the region, which is providing fresh reminders of the security chaos of the 1980s following the success of the Iranian revolution. The political resurgence of Shia communities is a fear that plagues many of the Arab monarchies of the Persian Gulf, many of which have substantial Shia populations of their own to manage. Iranian-supported Shia activism post-2003 has played a key role in adding to these regimes' concerns about their own political survival in an age of growing internal and external demands.

However, while growing ties between Tehran and Baghdad sit uncomfortably with Washington as well as Iraq's Arab neighbours, it is indisputable that Tehran and Washington need each other in the pursuit of their own interests in Iraq; in particular for bringing about stability and normality there. But the uneasy relationship between the two countries inevitably soured their understanding over Iraq. So much so that by early 2005 Tehran was being depicted in both the USA and the UK as a meddler and interferer in Iraq, instead of the stabilizing power it had wanted to be seen as both regionally and internationally.

Returning for a moment to the pre-Ahmadinejad period, it is fair to say that Khatami himself was so bogged down domestically after the loss of the Majlis in 2004, and was under so much pressure internationally over Iran's nuclear programme and its role in Iraq (amongst other factors), that he effectively became hostage to the factional power struggles of the Republic. Being little more than a lame-duck president for much of his second term in office, it can be argued that he was unable to create a sustainable basis for the advancement of his accommodationist foreign policy agenda beyond his own tenure. Indeed, towards the end of his presidency he may have gone a long way towards undoing much of his own legacy, based on short-term political manoeuvring as a result of the pragmatic line he had adopted in foreign policy. His parting shots in the nuclear discussions with the EU3 (in which he raised the negotiating stakes just before handing over power to the new administration) and over Iraq (in which Iran openly demonstrated its security presence there), for instance, were so aggressive as to prepare the ground for the much harsher and more confrontational line that followed the election victory of neoconservative Ahmadinejad and his new administration.

Effectively, therefore, Khatami had upped the stakes in relation to Iranian foreign policy towards the West, allowing this momentum to be fully utilized by the incoming president. The 'radicalization' of Khatami was an important factor contributing to the change of tone, if nothing else, in Iran's foreign relations that one witnessed under the new president. But it is also fair to say that the extent of revolutionary politics was always likely to escalate under Ahmadinejad, and that this would inevitably lead to a face-off between Iran and the West.

New Directions in Foreign Policy

Thus, even without Ahmadinejad as president, the year 2005 was going to be testing for Iran and the region as a whole, but the extent
of the upheaval only emerged as 2005 gave way to 2006 and beyond.
While most observers were eagerly awaiting Iran's presidential poll
of June 2005 for new policy directions from Tehran, by early 2005
external developments were already making their mark on Iran's relations with the rest of the region. Chief amongst these were Iraq's first
free elections of the year, which took place in January 2005. These in
effect consolidated the political presence of Iraqi Shia and Kurds at
the centre of power in that country, which had previously been dominated by the Saddam-led Sunni alliance. As a direct consequence of
the changing political map of Iraq, Iran was now, more emphatically
than at any time since the founding of modern Iraq, a close partner
of the new Iraqi political establishment. However the enhancement
of Iran's influence in Iraqi politics, as a natural extension of its long-
standing links with the anti-Saddam Iraqi forces, would sooner or
later become a source of confrontation with the West.

Of further concern in terms of Iran's regional profile was its apparently underhand nuclear programme, which added to pre-exist-
ing fears of the Islamic Republic's geopolitical resurgence along with
domination of the Persian Gulf subregion and an active presence in
the Levant (as exemplified in the '34-Day War' between Hezbollah
and Israel in the summer of 2006, in which Hezbollah is said to have
received substantial Iranian support). Within a month of the ceasefire
Tehran had committed $50 million in reconstruction aid for Lebanon
as its first phase of support, promising to rebuild mosques, schools,
Shia Husseiniehs, hospitals, roads and bridges.[1] In response, the USA
pressed its own Arab allies to commit themselves to the reconstruction of Lebanon, in the process trying to prevent Iran's emergence as
both the dominant and the victorious party of the 34-Day War.

In the Persian Gulf itself, the continuing 'cold war' between Iran
and the Gulf Cooperation Council (GCC) states over the correct
name of the waterway carries certain political baggage that needs to

be managed if relations between the two sides are to reach a higher level. The dispute, which continues to affect relations, is symptomatic of a bigger problem, we suggest, and has much to do with role perception as well as the prevailing balance of power in the region. For the Arab side, the name 'Persian' continues to emphasize Iran's dominance of the area, and its own mark of submission to this imperial heritage. In the post-1945 period, national pride has come with Arab national independence and economic power, which has manifested itself in the unilateral name change of the waterway. The seed for this unilateral name change was at Nasser's behest, when in 1968 the Egyptian president began a global campaign to change the name 'Persian Gulf' to 'Arabian Gulf', and handed the running of the campaign to the Baath regime in Iraq (who at the time had the financial backing of United Arab Emirates (UAE) due to a close alliance with Abu Dhabi). The name 'Arab Gulf' today is meant to underline the Arab character of the area and, for the GCC countries in particular, it is a measure of their contribution to the Arab world. The GCC also use the 'Arab' prefix as a means of distancing themselves from Iran as the dominant actor of the subregion.

For Iran, on the other hand, the issue has had two important aspects to it. First, there is a real concern that unilateral name change of an international strategic waterway can easily lead to future threats to Iran's national sovereignty, identity and international legal rights if left unchallenged. Iran, therefore, sees the name change in strategic terms, and as a potential prelude for future attacks on its cultural presence in an area that it has long dominated. Second, for a multinational state such as Iran, the change from the Persian Gulf to the Arab Gulf implies an Arabization of the neighbourhood and a deliberate attack on Iran's multicultural identity.

Importantly, continuous Iranian concerns over the role of the Arab minority in its Khuzestan province and their demands for autonomy provide additional reason for it to try and correct the perception of Arabization. The continuing tensions over the three islands (Greater and Lesser Tunbs and Abu Musa at the mouth of the strategic Hormuz Strait have both been claimed by the UAE and Iran) merely add to misperceptions, of course – as they did when the Arab–South American summit of May 2005 made direct reference to the islands dispute in its final communiqué. Iran's rebuke of the host (Brazil) for placing this issue on the agenda of the summit was an indirect rebuke of the UAE for seeking, from Tehran's perspective, to internationalize the islands dispute at every opportunity – thus threatening Iran's interests in the subregion. Foreign Ministry spokesman Hamid Reza Asefi denounced as 'irrelevant' the Arab–South American summit's focus on the row over the islands dispute, adding that the 'three islands of Abu Musa and the Greater and Lesser Tunbs are inseparable parts of the Iranian territory and any claim in this regard is rejected'.[2] Iran has continuously told the international community not to interfere in the dispute. For example, Iran has already rejected the settling of the issue at the International Court of Justice, contending that it is a closed case. In addition, in May 2004 the Islamic Republic warned the EU to stay clear of the issue following a joint meeting between the EU and the GCC in Brussels.[3]

The name of the waterway and the continuing dispute over the three islands help to fuel mutual suspicions across the waterway, which is of course heightened when Tehran is dominated by a neoconservative bent on either demonstrating or actually projecting Iran's power beyond its borders. While the name dispute may be a minor matter in the great scheme of things, fears of Iran's nuclear programme and related surface-to-surface missile (SSM) developments cast a longer shadow over relations. As will be discussed presently the GCC side (for all its diplomatic exchanges with Tehran since the election of Ahmadinejad) failed, at the height of the dispute with the West, to publicly articulate its concerns about a nuclear Iran (though it did begin to show signs of willing to do so after the matter was finally referred to the UN Security Council). Iran, for its part, systematically failed to communicate fully and effectively to its Arab neighbours the essence of its nuclear ambitions, and had not entirely assured them of the extent of its programme and the programme's environmental, technical and security dimensions. These shortcomings merely added to the sense of mistrust pervading relations.

Beyond its immediate neighbourhood Iran's active pursuit of partnerships first built in the early days of the revolution, in Lebanon and with Syria, emphasized its reorientation and its determination to build influence in the wider Middle East. Iran's interests in the Levant have been achieved historically via Hezbollah and the Islamic Hizb al Amal that have acted as Iranian proxies in the region, being supplied, funded and trained by Iran. This has allowed Iran to play a key role in Lebanese politics, although it has been careful not to upset Syria by not undermining Syria's overwhelming presence in Lebanon. Shaikh Fadallah of Hezbollah and Shaikh Musawi of Islamic Hizb al Amal have on many occasions expressed their support for the Iranian regime and for the principles of the Iranian revolution, further adding to Iranian prowess in the Levant. The pursuit of these 'rejectionist' partners thus became more central, with closer association than at any time since the late 1980s with the Palestinian Islamist organizations, notably Hamas and Islamic Jihad.

During the 1990s Iran strengthened its relations with Hamas when it invited representatives of Hamas to attend the Institute for Political and International Studies (IPIS, the Foreign Ministry's think-tank that studies international and political affairs) meetings and gatherings, with the Leader himself receiving them as Palestinian heroes in Tehran. Iran had taken some tentative steps towards establishing proximity with Hamas, therefore, well before their electoral rise. Relations were boosted and acquired a whole new political and strategic dimension upon the victory of Hamas in the January 2006 Palestinian parliamentary elections. The fact that the newly elected Hamas government's first foreign trip was in fact to Tehran underlined the importance of these links and the strengthening of relations between the two since the 1990s. This demonstrated to the Arabs and the Israelis alike the significant geopolitical role that Iran had been able to carve for itself in the Levant, especially in the context of the Israeli–Palestinian conflict.

From 2006 Iran's neoconservative government was not only on Israel's doorstep but also charting a direct path for itself at the heart of the Arab world and in a key Arab matter, notably the politics of Palestine. The close relationship between the two was indicated via Khaled Meshal's statement on 15 December 2005, in which the Hamas political chief said during a visit to the Iranian capital that his group would step up attacks against Israel if the Jewish state took military action against Iran over its disputed nuclear programme. He said at the time that

> Just as Islamic Iran defends the rights of the Palestinians, we defend the rights of Islamic Iran. We [Hamas] are part of a united front against the enemies of Islam. Each member of this front defends itself with its own means in its region. We carry the battle in Palestine. If Israel launches an attack against Iran, we will expand the battlefield in Palestine.[4]

He added that, 'We are part of a united front, and if one member of this front is attacked it is our duty to support them', at the same time also praising Mahmoud Ahmadinejad for his 'courageous' anti-Israel stance.[5]

Thus a combination of the above factors leads us to conclude that the Islamic Republic has indeed entered a new stage in its evolution, in which personnel changes at the top have not only brought to the fore new priorities but have at the same time underlined the force of revolutionary values and ideology in the Iranian system. What is clear is that the rhetoric of President Ahmadinejad sets him apart from many of his predecessors, even Khamenei when he was president in the 1980s, and he is now building on his populist rhetoric to advance his neoconservative-inspired hard line at home and abroad. It is for this reason that from spring of 2006 many commentators and analysts of Iran began to see a confrontation between Iran and a US-led military force as almost inevitable.[6]

IRAN: ENTERING A NEW ERA?

With Ahmadinejad's presidential victory, it can be argued, Iran has been entering new and uncharted waters in both its domestic politics and foreign relations. Elected on an anti-corruption platform,

Ahmadinejad's second-round success in the ballot enabled him to take office on 3 August 2005 as the clear champion of the conservative tendencies in Iran – indeed as articulating a neoconservative position. It is never wise to generalize about Iranian politics, but it is safe to assume that in keeping with the tenets of the conservative bloc, which is itself divided into several camps, President Ahmadinejad has shown that his administration is willing to follow policies that can meet their priorities. However evidence also suggests that despite the rhetoric he will, wherever he can, still try and balance these against the interests of the state as drawn by the two previous administrations of Rafsanjani and Khatami, and as still defined by the Leader, Ayatollah Khamenei.

Slowly but surely though a clearer picture of President Ahmadinejad's foreign policy agenda and his administration's policies towards its Arab and non-Arab neighbours has been emerging, and this suggests a comprehensive changing of the agenda that is taking place. By way of illustration, one can point to the following for concrete examples of the newly emerging trends in Iranian foreign policy: the focus of Ahmadinejad's foreign trips (of which there have been many); meetings and the exchanging of messages with other international figures and heads of state; his speech at the UN General Assembly on 15 September 2005; his pronouncements on Israel in October and December 2005 and again in April 2006; his position with regard to the EU3 negotiations over Iran's nuclear activities since taking office; and his administration's slowly changing policies towards Iraq and the Gulf more broadly.

At the time of writing, since coming to office Ahmadinejad has visited seven countries, all of them being Muslim-dominated. In addition, he has held more than 45 foreign meetings, again predominately with representatives from Muslim countries or states that are seen to be rogue, anti-American or anti-Western on the international arena (such as Venezuela and Cuba). Also he has communicated with over 52 leaders – mainly in the Muslim world but also with leaders in Latin America and Africa. His trips, foreign meetings and messages sent shed some light on the foreign policy direction in which

Ahmadinejad plans to take Iran, which entails a progressive shift towards the Muslim world in the Middle East and beyond but also the forming of alliances with Asian countries (and even 'rogue' states), assisting in their rehabilitation in the international arena.

This could be seen in the context of a potential attempt by Ahmadinejad to mobilize the Muslim world to strengthen it politically on the international stage and, in order to thwart any US aggression against Iran, to build alliances with the Muslim world (Iran being the first port of call by the USA in looking for support to attack a country in the Middle East). This of course was the case in the war against Iraq in 1991 and also 2003, thus giving Ahmadinejad sufficient impetus to forge and build alliances with the Muslim world to prevent collusion in any future conflict led by the Americans. The meetings with representatives from Venezuela and Cuba are interesting indeed, given the contrasting ideological differences between these countries and Iran. Ahmadinejad's decision to make contact indicates signs of pragmatism in the armoury of his revolutionary principles. Importantly, these exchanges would inevitably act as a source of conflict with the USA, further intensifying the confrontation between the two given the USA's poor relations with Venezuela and Cuba. Recently the visit of Omar al-Bashir, the president of Sudan, is further indication of Ahmadinejad's forays into the Muslim world and the positioning of Iran as a premier player in fields as diverse as the Middle East, the Far East, Latin America and sub-Saharan Africa.

The conduct of Iran's foreign relations represents a picture far from the idea of Ahmadinejad leading Iran down a path of isolation and painful retraction. Nor does his foreign policy provide evidence of his naivety in designing a strategy or misunderstanding international politics. Importantly, the trips and meetings he has had so far have been mostly with countries that have suffered a sense of injustice, such as historical colonialism and economic exploitation, and his constant references to the need for justice in international diplomacy, particularly with the problems of Palestine, US imperialism and Zionism in the Middle East, reinforce his position as a strong spokesman for the developing and Muslim world. His 'populism international' has fallen on receptive ears across Asia, Latin America and Africa, it has to be said, carving Ahmadinejad as the figure of an anti-imperialist hero of a bygone era who is committed to redressing the imbalance in the international system in favour of the long-suffering Third World.

The speech that Ahmadinejad gave at the UN in September 2005 provided an insight into his mindset and the actions he has taken and adopted in relation to foreign policy. In the speech he emphasized on many occasions the need for justice, peace, ethics, a balance of power, non-discrimination and equality in the world. He said:

> Justice must reign supreme in the Organization, and in accordance with its Charter, all Member-states must have equal rights. Greater power or wealth should not accord expanded rights to any member. The principles of democracy and ethics should prevail in all organs and functions of the United Nations, so that the Organization could become a manifestation of the prevalence of these two commonly shared values. The United Nations should endeavour to fulfil its responsibility to promote and institutionalize justice at the international level. The host country should not enjoy any right or privilege over the rest of the membership and the Organization and its headquarters must be easily accessible for all.[7]

He further added:

> in our view, these concerns can only be met if the prevailing discourse in international relations is transformed from one based on violence, discrimination and domination to a discourse of peace and global stability based on justice and spirituality through dialogue, compassion and respect for human beings.[8]

A real concern for humanity could be detected from Ahmadinejad's speech, which puts into context his continual reference to the suffering of the Palestinian people and the occupation of Palestinian lands. This is an issue that he has addressed on many occasions since taking office. More significantly, his public support for the Palestinian cause places Iran in the Arab heartland, an area Iran had not fully accessed in the past. In a region that requires leadership and a solution to the conflict in Palestine Ahmadinejad, through his invocations of justice and connections with Palestinian groups, was creating a role for himself – though clearly at the expense of other Arab leaders, who had failed to address the Palestinian issue.

With regard to Israel, the president's speech at the 'World without Zionism' conference was to initiate a process of open hostility towards Israel that has been in evidence ever since, and it signalled a very different approach to the Arab–Israeli conflict to that established as state policy in the early 1990s by President Rafsanjani. Ahmadinejad stated:

> Our dear Imam [Ayatollah Khomeini] said that the occupying regime [Israel] must be wiped off the map and this was a very wise statement. We cannot compromise over the issue of Palestine. Is it possible to create a new front in the heart of an old front? This would be a defeat and whoever accepts the legitimacy of this regime has, in fact, signed the defeat of the Islamic world. Our dear Imam targeted the heart of the world oppressor in his struggle, meaning the occupying regime. I have no doubt that the new wave that has started in Palestine, and we witness it in the Islamic world too, will eliminate this disgraceful stain from the Islamic world. But we must be aware of tricks.[9]

The issue with Palestine would be over, he mused, 'the day that all refugees return to their homes [and] a democratic government elected by the people comes to power'.[10] Also in the speech Ahmadinejad denounced attempts to normalize relations with Israel and condemned all Muslim leaders who accept the existence of Israel as 'acknowledging a surrender and defeat of the Islamic world'. This criticism was not only a criticism of Egypt and Jordan (and Turkey) but was also a less than discreet attack on nearby Muslim countries such as Qatar, Bahrain and Pakistan, which had taken steps towards improving relations with Israel. Clearly the policies of non-provocation of Israel followed in the 1990s and that of 'not being more Palestinian that the Palestinians themselves' were now being eroded.

This provocative speech was followed by two more in December in which the president raised doubts about the validity of the Holocaust and made a call for Western countries to carry the burden of their anti-Jewish policies themselves by finding a state for the Jews on their own lands. On 8 December 2005 Ahmadinejad gave an interview with Iran's Arabic channel Al-Alam during a summit of Muslim nations in Islam's holy city of Mecca, stating:

> Some European countries insist on saying that during the Second World War Hitler burned millions of Jews and put them in concentration camps ... Any historian, commentator or scientist who doubts that [this has] taken [place goes] to prison or gets condemned. Although we don't accept this claim, if we suppose it is true, if the Europeans are honest they should give some of their provinces in Europe – like in Germany, Austria or other countries – to the Zionists and the Zionists can establish their state in Europe. You offer part of Europe and we will support it.

Using the examples of Iran under the Shah, the Soviet Union and Saddam Hussein's regime in Iraq as apparently invincible regimes, Ahmadinejad articulated the position that the USA and Israel can also be defeated, ending his point by saying: 'they say it is not possible to have a world without the United States and Zionism. But you know that this is a possible goal and slogan'.[11]

These remarks were, naturally, condemned by Israeli, European and American politicians. Kofi Annan 'was shocked', and Saudi officials sharply criticized Ahmadinejad's remarks for marring 'a Mecca summit dedicated to showing Islam's moderate face'.[12] Indeed, in his presentation in December 2005 to the extraordinary summit of the OIC in the holy city of Mecca, the president made a formal submission to his peers of the need to remove the oppression of 'the usurper regime' for the sake of Islam. He referred to the 'Israeli regime in the occupied Palestine' as the main obstacle in the way of the Muslim world and said wise removal of this 'anxiety' will give Islam a strong share in administration of global affairs. He added that accepting a usurper government meant making mankind disappointed in the restoration of a lasting peace and calm, and would lead to legitimizing tyranny, arrogance and domination. He stated, 'The only wise breakthrough, which would be based on the international regulations, is return of all the Palestinian refugees, and holding a broad-based referendum on the type of government in the Palestinian lands with Qods being its capital',[13] calling on the OIC to assign a team on behalf of Muslim states to probe into the full implementation of his proposal. Despite this call from Ahmadinejad the OIC failed to adopt a formal position on this proposal and was anxious to deflect criticism that it was pursuing an anti-Jewish line. Needless to say, Tehran's new proposal did not sit well with the other members of the OIC.

Three senior Saudi officials complained in private that the comments completely contradicted and diverted attention from the message of tolerance the summit was trying to project. One Saudi official compared Ahmadinejad to ousted Iraqi President Saddam Hussein and Libyan leader Moammar Gadhafi, whose renegade statements frequently infuriated other Arab leaders and deliberately targeted the Saudis. 'The Iranian president seems to have lost his direction', said Gilan al-Ghamidi, a prominent commentator in Saudi media: 'Iran should be logical if it wants to receive the support of the world. The president didn't score any points. He lost points.'[14] Turkey also denounced the remarks, warning against escalating international tensions and mistrust between nations. A Turkish Foreign Ministry spokesman said, 'It is impossible to approve of such statements of bellicose nature at a time when dialogue, reconciliation and cooperation are needed.'[15]

Even some of Ahmadinejad's allies in Iran were taken aback by the ferocity of his comments, fearing that his comments had hurt the country. According to Hamid Reza Taraqi (leader of a hard-line party, the Islamic Coalition Society): 'The president has to choose his words carefully. He can convey his message to the world in better language [and] tone.'[16] Moderates were calling for the ruling clerics to act: 'The ruling establishment should do something about this man', said prominent Iranian analyst Davoud Hermidas Bavand, 'Ahmadinejad speaks as if he is spokesman of a hard-line vigilante group. His words don't fit with those of a responsible president.'[17] Interestingly, shortly after the domestic reaction to his comments,

Iran's Interior Minister Mostafa Pour Muhammadi claimed Ahmadinejad's remarks had been misunderstood:

> Actually the case has been misunderstood. [Ahmadinejad] did not mean to raise this matter. [He] wanted to say that if others harmed the Jewish community and created problems for the Jewish community, they have to pay the price themselves. People like the Palestinian people or other nations should not pay the price (for it).[18]

Despite the domestic and the international backlash, in his second speech in December 2005 (carried live on Iranian television), he again questioned the truth of the Holocaust, saying:

> If the Europeans are telling the truth in their claim that they have killed six million Jews in the Holocaust during the Second World War – which seems they are right in their claim because they insist on it and arrest and imprison those who oppose it – why should the Palestinian nation pay for the crime? Why have they come to the very heart of the Islamic world and are committing crimes against the dear Palestine using their bombs, rockets, missiles and sanctions? [...] The same European countries have imposed the illegally established Zionist regime on the oppressed nation of Palestine. If you have committed the crimes so give a piece of your land somewhere in Europe or America and Canada or Alaska to them to set up their own state there. Then the Iranian nation will have no objections, will stage no rallies on the Qods Day and will support your decision.[19]

The latter remarks were condemned immediately by the Israeli government. Mark Regev, spokesman for Israel's Foreign Ministry stated:

> The combination of a regime with a radical agenda, together with a distorted sense of reality that is clearly indicated by the statements we heard today, put together with nuclear weapons – I think that's a dangerous combination that no one in the international community can accept. What the Iranian president has shown us today is that he is clearly outside the international consensus, he is clearly outside international norms and international legitimacy, and in so doing he has shown the Iranian government for what it is – a rogue regime opposed to peace and stability and a threat to all its neighbouring countries.[20]

112

Former president Khatami stated, 'those words have created hundreds of political and economic problems for us in the world'. Khatami went further and accused Ahmadinejad and his supporters of being an Iranian 'Taliban' who were giving the enemies of Iran 'the best excuse to attack Islam and Iran'.[21] Unease at home did not prevent the Iranian Ambassador to the EU, Ali Ahani, calling the tough political reactions in Europe against Ahmadinejad 'unrealistic and premature', complaining about the discriminatory treatment of the international community. His view, which was widely circulated in Europe, was that Iran cannot ignore the threats of Israel and its 'organized campaign to provoke others into attacking Iran's facilities and infrastructure', referring to Israel's support of an American military attack on Iran.[22]

Despite the obvious provocation, in an interview on 14 January 2006 President Ahmadinejad said, 'I've just asked two questions. But I have not received any clear answers' – referring to his previous statements on the Holocaust. He added, 'I will not make any historical argument. European scientists are in a position to answer these questions.' Referring to Europeans, President Ahmadinejad added, 'I want them to offer a clear answer to these questions ... whatever they say I would agree.'[23] Ahmadinejad also defended his speech that had resulted in wide criticism by saying, 'There is no new policy; they created a lot of hue and cry over that. It is clear what we say: let the Palestinians participate in free elections and they will say what they want.'[24]

According to *Aftab News*, Muhammad Ali Ramin, a political analyst and an adviser to President Ahmadinejad, was the person who initiated the idea of the relocation of Israel and also the suggestion that the Holocaust was a myth. He himself accepted full responsibility for this action, as *Aftab News* reported.[25] In an interview with the *Financial Times* Mr Ramin stated that he has also established a Holocaust commission in Iran and he is the founder of the Conference on Holocaust in Tehran. Ramin praised President Ahmadinejad for having voiced his doubts over the Holocaust and the need for relocating the Jews back to Europe if Europeans really did conduct the genocide of the Jewish people during the Second World War.[26] Nevertheless, under severe domestic and international pressure the president's aides had to try hard to moderate his line on the 'Jewish question'. On 20 February 2006 Iran's foreign minister denied that Tehran wanted to see Israel 'wiped off the map', saying Ahmadinejad had been misunderstood. 'Nobody can remove a country from the map. This is a misunderstanding in Europe of what our president mentioned', Manouchehr Mottaki told a news conference, speaking in English, after addressing the European Parliament. He said, 'How is it possible to remove a country from the map? He is talking about the regime. We do not recognize legally this regime.'[27] Ali Larijani, Secretary of Iran's Supreme National Security Council and in charge of Iran's nuclear negotiations, said the speech by Ahmadinejad calling for the destruction of Israel had been subject to 'abusive misinterpretation' by 'certain Western media and certain countries'.[28] He insisted:

> The position of Iran on Palestine has not changed – it is the Palestinians who should defend their own rights and decide on their own fate ... It is a psychological war orchestrated by media who want to weaken Iran in international institutions.[29]

Ahmadinejad's former presidential rival Ayatollah Akbar Hashemi Rafsanjani also entered the debate, insisting that 'We have no problem with the Jews. Our issue is Zionism which is only a limited part of the Jewish society.'[30]

However, arguments defending Ahmadinejad were not helped by the fact that he was not only willingly present at the annual anti-Israel event in Tehran 2005, but was delighted to be giving the keynote address there. These were sufficient reasons to raise serious questions about the longevity of détente as the core of the new administration's foreign policy. Speeches since September 2005, of course, have made the shift in outlook a more concrete reality. On 14 April 2006, he removed all ambiguity by insisting that Israel (the 'rotten, dried tree') was 'heading towards annihilation' and 'will be eliminated by one storm'.[31] In a characteristically confrontational line, Ahmadinejad added:

How long can this situation last and be tolerated? When Imam Ali, Commander of the Faithful, heard that an anklet was forcefully removed from the feet of a Jewish woman by the invaders in one of the frontier cities under his rule, he said, 'If a man dies from grief because of this act, he should not be reprimanded.' Today, even the children are not spared and are targeted by their bullets. Palestinian men and women are abducted and tortured in their fearsome prisons. People are shot dead in schools, on the streets and at markets.[32]

He continued, describing Israel as a threat to the entire region:

The existence of the Zionist regime is tantamount to imposition of an unending and unrestrained threat so that none of the nations and Islamic countries of the region and beyond can feel secure from its threat. The closer these nations are to the epicentre of this threat, the more threatened they feel. The people of Palestine are at the very core of such a threat. They have not been able to spend a day with peace of mind for the past 60 years. Three generations of sons and daughters of Palestinians have lived and are presently living under these circumstances. The peoples of Egypt, Jordan, Syria, Lebanon and the entire Middle East are essentially under similar situation.[33]

He reiterated an argument he has made previously that while the Western powers admit they have killed a large number of Jews, the Palestinian people should not be made to suffer because of it:

Some Western powers admit that they have killed a large part of the Jewish population in Europe and founded the occupying regime in order to put right the wrong they had committed. With deference to all nations and followers of divine religions, we are asking if this atrocity is true, then why should the people of the region pay for it by occupation of Palestinian lands and unending suppression of Palestinian people, by the homelessness of millions of Palestinians, by destruction of their cities and rural areas and agricultural lands? Why should they pay by fire, bullets and imposition of forces? And why should they pay by tolerating occupation of Islamic lands? Are the consequences of the establishment of this regime less than the Holocaust you are claiming? If there are doubts regarding the Holocaust, there is really no doubt regarding Palestinian disaster and Holocaust. The Holocaust in Palestine has persisted for more than 60 years.[34]

In a much quoted statement, he compared the Palestinian resistance to a young, healthy tree and the regime of the Jewish state of Israel to an old dying tree:

> The young tree of resistance in Palestine is blooming and blooms of faith and desire for freedom are flowering. The Zionist regime is a decaying and crumbling tree that will fall with a storm. Today even the inhabitants of the occupied Palestine, especially the African and Asian settlers, are living in pain, poverty and discontent.[35]

Making this speech in an already charged atmosphere, due to Iran's nuclear stand-off with the rest of the international community, at yet another Palestinian-related conference in Tehran, made sure that Ahmadinejad could not back away from the position he had begun articulating in the early days of his presidency. Indeed, the content of his speeches raised great concern, for they have been widely interpreted as an indication of a hardening of Iran's position towards the peace process and a much broader radicalization of its foreign policy. In embarking on a new effort to lead the rejectionist camp in the region, Iran, arguably, has been moving away from the centre ground deliberately since August 2005.

Indeed, one can claim that Ahmadinejad's quest for Palestinian justice was perhaps his great strategy to lead Iran to construct a confrontational and revolutionary stand-off with Israel and the West in general. His fiery rhetoric and imprudent statements concerning Israel deliberately raised the ante, easing the sense of concern and fear over Iran's nuclear programme and the threat it might cause to the surrounding region. If Ahmadinejad was seeking to change Iran's international role through confrontation, then he was doing all the right things for getting it. A sense of confrontation abroad would of course ease the passage of many unpalatable new initiatives at home, making them more digestible, despite their not being necessarily acceptable in their own right.

Though perhaps nothing new in general terms has been said as far as Israel is concerned in Tehran's post-revolution lexicon, nonetheless Iran's harder line towards Israel and the peace process more generally since the 2005 election has had direct implications for Tehran's relations with the Arab world, and indeed with the Western world and the UN more broadly. The fact that it is the Iranian president himself who has publicly and repeatedly attacked Israel, and that it is he who has openly joined the ranks of the Holocaust deniers, has raised concerns over the greater likelihood of a direct confrontation between Iran and Israel. Such fears have raised the temperature amongst Iran's neighbours, most notably in the GCC countries and Turkey, who worry about the direction of Iran's regional strategy under Ahmadinejad, its nuclear programme and also the strategic consequences of a military exchange between Iran and Israel. Thus, the GCC foreign ministers at their 98th session expressed their concerns regarding Iran's nuclear plans and the ensuing threats to regional stability. According to Shaikh Abdullah Bin Zayed al-Nahyan, the ministers expressed apprehension that the tests, being carried out at Iran's civilian nuclear plant at Bushehr, were not really meant for peaceful purposes. Speaking on behalf of the GCC, he said:

> Hectic talks are underway between Iran and the international community to solve the nuclear impasse. We hope that all parties concerned would be serious in their parleys, and that Iran would take into account the GCC's concern in the true spirit in this respect. Being situated very close to Iran, we have genuine fears about the nuclear plans.[36]

He added that any environmental disaster caused by the nuclear tests would pose great risks to the GCC states.

Prince Saud al-Faisal, the veteran Saudi Foreign Minister, also criticized President Ahmadinejad's administration, urging him to forgo atomic energy, to moderate his foreign policy and resist the temptation of interfering in Iraq. Speaking before a terrorism conference in London on 16 January 2006, Prince Saud reminded his audience of the dangers of a regional arms race. He told the *Times* newspaper:

> We are urging Iran to accept the position that we have taken to make the Gulf, as part of the Middle East, nuclear free and free of

weapons of mass destruction. We hope that they will join us in this policy and assure that no new threat of arms race happens in this region.[37]

However, the Prince was not optimistic that his appeal would be heeded. Although the Saudi government had not yet had the opportunity of working closely with President Ahmadinejad, he said, nonetheless Ahmadinejad's statements were being seen as extreme and he urged him to continue the policies of his moderate predecessor Muhammad Khatami:

> We hope his Administration will be a stabilizing force and not a destabilizing force… If he goes the way that President Khatami went in foreign policy, we think we can work together. But that will have to be tested in time.[38]

Already suspicious of Iran's role in Iraq, many GCC and Turkish officials and commentators have interpreted the president's outbursts as a precursor of further tensions in Iran's regional relations. Naturally Turkey is concerned with Iranian positioning at this juncture, given its ties with Israel and also its own history of difficulties with Iran. The Saudis, especially, have grown weary of Iran's overwhelming influence in Iraq. They also fear that if Iran were to develop a nuclear weapons capability, the balance of power in the region would irreversibly tip away from Saudi Arabia and its Arab partners.

There is also increasing concern amongst Gulf Arab states about the influence of predominantly Shia Iran as a result of the war in Iraq. While the GCC states are ruled by Sunni elites, most also have Shia communities that historically have been marginalized. The prospect of Shia-driven rebellions instigated by a nuclear-armed Iran is a daunting scenario for the GCC states, and as such the diplomatic confrontation over Iran's nuclear programme is an obvious source of concern for the GCC. In addition, Gulf Arab governments are wary of even a peaceful nuclear energy programme in Iran, partly because of the risks of a meltdown accident and the ensuing environmental consequences.

On another front, for such countries as Turkey, Pakistan, Tunisia, Morocco, Bahrain, Qatar, Kuwait and Oman, which are striving to build links with the Jewish state, the Iranian president's call for the destruction of Israel has gone down more like a lead balloon than a recognizable rallying cry for Muslim unity against Israel. The Arab world's collective condemnation of President Ahmadinejad's messages, moreover, has added a new geopolitical twist to an already tense situation in the region.

Moreover, with the call to wipe Israel off the map Tehran managed not only to isolate itself from its Arab hinterland, but actually caused severe disruption in Iran's dealings with its European interlocutors as well, and further strained its relations with the USA. Furthermore, for the first time in many years Tehran was distant from both its Arab and non-Arab Muslim neighbours alike. In security terms the president's comments added to the sense of crisis being generated by Tehran, which was itself an unsettling reality for Iran's neighbours who had become accustomed to the conciliatory line of the previous two presidents (who between them had been in power for 16 consecutive years). The winds of change blowing from Tehran were received with much trepidation.

Another line of confrontation, which, to be fair, was not of Ahmadinejad's making, was also appearing in the context of the nuclear discussions that had dominated Tehran's relations with the West since 2003. A glimpse of the changing balance of the international arguments on the pace of Iran's nuclear programme can be gleaned from the IAEA board of governors' resolution of 13 March 2004 – more than a year before Ahmadinejad's election – in which Iran was criticized for the fact that its October 2003 declarations 'did not amount to the complete and final picture of Iran's past and present nuclear program considered essential by the board's November 2003 resolution'.[39] The IAEA expressed particular concern regarding Iran's advanced centrifuge design, its laser enrichment capabilities, and its hot cells facility at its heavy water research reactor. The Iranian expression of outrage at the resolution at all levels of its leadership and the calls from the leadership of the Sepah for Iran to withdraw from the Non-Proliferation Treaty (NPT) altogether were soon tempered with a more conciliatory line – but they did help in setting the tone for Ahmadinejad.

Ahmadinejad's UN speech in September 2005 and his key personnel changes in Iran's negotiating team provided the most direct examples of the new direction of thinking in Iran. Talks between the EU and Tehran had already been broken off in August when Iran resumed uranium conversion after a nine-month suspension, so there was not much that the new administration needed to do to worsen the crisis. However, its tougher language and more confrontational style did prevent the emergence of a satisfactory compromise between Iran and the West. Although an EU3+1 (Russia) team did begin negotiating with Tehran in December 2005, it was clear by early 2006 that Russia was not able to convince Tehran of becoming the country's sole conduit for its uranium enrichment activities.

The Russian plan to allow Iran to enrich uranium on its territory – backed by the USA and Europe – was devised as a way of providing Iran with civilian nuclear power while easing fears over Tehran's alleged ambitions to acquire atomic weapons. Rather unexpectedly, the head of the Iranian nuclear negotiating team, Ali Hosseinitash, adopted a tough stance in his meeting with the Russians, however. News agencies reported that Mr Hosseinitash rejected any link between the Russian plan and demands for Iran to restore a freeze on uranium enrichment. 'The negotiations with Russia do not foresee any preconditions', he said to reporters, adding that there was 'no link between the moratorium on uranium enrichment and talks on the Russian plan. He stressed that Iran did not intend to renounce its right to have control of the full nuclear cycle.[40] But the issue of concern here was not purely the technical aspects of the discussions; the sad reality was that even closure on the nuclear debate would probably not lead to closer relations between Iran and the West, or an opening of meaningful dialogue with the USA. The element of suspicion would have remained over Iran's commitment to suspend its own enrichment programme, therefore taking no action as a means of de-escalating the tension or sense of confrontation permeating relations between the West and Iran was no longer an option.

Thus, within a year of the new president taking office, Iran was already a far cry from the Paris agreement of November 2004[41] in which Iran and the EU3 had talked optimistically of building closer economic ties with each other and working towards creating a region-wide security structure on the back of a nuclear agreement. With Iran's GCC neighbours highly suspicious of Iran's moves and motives, it is less likely that they will accept Iran's terms for closer security discussions without having a US presence at the talks – something that the neoconservative Iranian administration would probably find hard to accept, even if the USA was prepared to go along with it.

Although the new president's position on Iran's nuclear programme has been tougher than former President Khatami's, it is nonetheless consistent with Iran's broad view that the country's right to peaceful use of nuclear technology, know-how and power are enshrined in the NPT. By way of a brief background, it is useful to reflect on the state of the nuclear debate in Iran and the course it has taken under the Khatami and Ahmadinejad presidencies. While it is true to say that Tehran has been redefining its priorities in the post-Second World War, post-Cold War era, it would be unrealistic to have expected it to forego its strategic (in defence and security terms) and Islamic profile only for the sake of economic gains. It is also true, however, that in practice since the early 1990s Iran had chosen to prioritize the resolution of domestic problems (economic reconstruction and the strengthening of civil society and the rule of law) over long-term ideological foreign policy posturing.[42] Today though, under Ahmadinejad we are seeing real revision of these established priorities.

With regard to security also, Iran's strategic missile development programme and its nuclear-related activities point to the same drive. The nuclear programme itself has become much more public since 2002, when a string of revelations forced the Iranian authorities to acknowledge that they had in fact sought enrichment facilities, separating units and nuclear weapons designs. On 14 August 2002 Ali

Reza Jafarzadeh, a prominent Iranian dissident, revealed the existence of two unknown nuclear sites, a uranium enrichment facility in Natanz (part of which is underground) and a heavy water facility in Arak. It was announced by the Iranian authorities in early 2003 that Iran's nuclear programme aimed 'to complete the circle [cycle] of fuel for plants for peaceful purposes'. The head of the country's atomic energy program declared on 10 of February 2003 that his agency had begun work on a uranium enrichment plant near the city of Kashan (the Natanz site), stating that 'very extensive research [had] already started'.[43] The fuel would come from the brand new uranium conversion facility built in the industrial city of Isfahan. It was announced at the same time that the Isfahan plant was to be complemented with another facility for producing uranium fuel casings.

International concerns about Iran's nuclear ambitions were further heightened by these announcements, particularly as only a day earlier Tehran announced that it had successfully extracted uranium and was planning to process the spent fuel from its nuclear facilities within the country. President Khatami himself appeared on national television on the anniversary of Iran's Islamic Revolution in February to congratulate his countrymen on their nuclear achievements, enumerating their research successes, and then underlining the statements already made by the head of the Iranian atomic energy programme. Khatami declared:

> Iran has discovered reserves and extracted uranium. We are determined to use nuclear technology for civilian purposes ... If we need to produce electricity from our nuclear power plants, we need to complete the circle from discovering uranium to managing remaining spent fuel. The government is determined to complete that circle.[44]

The president elaborated that the uranium was being mined in the Savand area, 200 kilometres (125 miles) from the central city of Yazd, and processing facilities had been set up in the central cities of Isfahan and Kashan. In a separate announcement, Iranian Defence Minister Ali Shamkhani said that Iran had, for the first time, developed the capacity for producing composite solid fuels for its missiles: 'This solid fuel could be used for any kind of missile', he said at the launch of a manufacturing plant.[45] In the minds of many, together these announcements had the unfortunate effect of linking Iran's military programmes with its nuclear ones.

The head of the Iranian parliament's Energy Commission, Hossein Afarideh, stated that the extracted uranium, after being processed, could be used as fuel for the Bushehr power plant. The surprise announcement by the moderate and pragmatic Khatami was certain to alarm the USA, which had already expressed concern over Russia supplying nuclear technology to Iran. The IAEA, of course, which was already under severe pressure for its failures in Iraq and North Korea, immediately entered the debate on invitation of the Iranians. To alleviate international concern over its nuclear programme, Iran invited inspectors from the IAEA to visit the two sites identified by the USA as suspicious (Nantanz and Arak) on 25 February 2003. President Khatami declared, 'We are ready to receive the IAEA inspectors for them to examine our activities and to disprove the lies pronounced by others against the Islamic Republic.'[46]

The sites of Natanz and Arak were of particular concern to the IAEA at this time because the agency had first learned of their existence through intelligence sources and not the Iranian authorities themselves. Iran's late notification of the two sites to the IAEA, though legal under the NPT terms, reached the Vienna-based organization only in September 2002, a month after an opposition group, with the assistance of Western intelligence organizations, had published details of the Natanz and Arak facilities. The revelations showed that the underground site near Natanz would house Iran's main gas centrifuge plant for enriched uranium for use in reactors, while the Arak facility would produce heavy water, an essential ingredient for plutonium production. The IAEA's February 2003 inspection of Natanz revealed that not only had Iran been able to develop and advance the Pakistani-supplied technology to assemble and 'cascade' 160 centrifuge machines, but it had assembled sufficient quantity of parts for installing a further 1,000–5,000 centrifuge machines between 2003 and 2005. Natanz, Iran told the IAEA, had been designed to produce low-enriched uranium for Iran's planned expansion of nuclear power plants, and was therefore unable to generate weapons-grade highly enriched uranium. The scientific community, however, is concerned that the depth and extent of the Natanz plant implies a far more ambitious project.[47] El Baradei in his statement to the IAEA about his visit to Iran said 'my colleagues and I were able to visit a number of facilities – including a gas centrifuge enrichment pilot plant at Natanz that is nearly ready for operation, and a much larger enrichment facility still under construction at the same site'.[48] El Baradei did not mention any findings regarding the Arak site during his statement, though IAEA officials say they have visited the site. Instead, El Baradei reiterated his call to Iran to help dispel doubts about its nuclear ambitions by signing up to the IAEA's Additional Protocol, which would allow inspectors freer access to Iran's nuclear sites with little prior warning. Regardless of these statements by El Baradei, from the USA's perspective Iran's intention to process and complete the nuclear fuel cycle would only have one purpose: to develop nuclear weapons.[49]

We also know that Libya's secret negotiations with London and Washington over the abandoning of all of its weapons of mass destruction (WMD) activities also yielded much valuable information about Iran's secret nuclear programme, shedding more light on the nature of its clandestine links with Pakistan and North Korea and the murky nuclear trade across Asia. The IAEA as mentioned above reported that Iran had established a large uranium enrichment facility using gas centrifuges based on the 'stolen' URENCO (Enrichment Uranium Company) designs, which had been obtained from a foreign intermediary in 1987. The intermediary was not named but many diplomats and analysts pointed to Pakistan and specifically to Dr Abdul Qadeer Khan, who was said to have visited Iran in 1986. The Iranians turned over the names of their suppliers and the international inspectors quickly identified the Iranian gas centrifuges as Pak-1s, the model developed by Dr Khan in the early 1980s. Two senior staff members at the Khan Research Laboratories were subsequently arrested in December 2003 on suspicion of having sold nuclear weapons technology to the Iranians. That same month, on 19 December 2003 Libya made a surprise announcement that it had WMD programmes that it would now abandon. The Libyan government officials were quoted as saying that Libya had bought nuclear components from various black market dealers, including Pakistani nuclear scientists. In particular, the US officials who visited the Libyan uranium enrichment plants shortly afterwards reported that the gas centrifuges used there were very similar to the Iranian ones.

It had thus emerged by late 2003 that Iran had established a multiple programme of research and development (R&D), based around a strategy of flexible acquisition. Prior to Iran's 2003 revelations, it should be noted, it had been surmised that Iran was secretly pursuing the development of a nuclear weapons option in parallel with its IAEA-registered nuclear research and power-generation programme. The argument at the turn of the century, therefore, was about 'when' and not 'if' Iran might be able to acquire and deploy home-grown nuclear weapons. In Tehran itself, however, the inter-elite discussions about Iran's nuclear options entered the public arena much later than in the West, namely in the course of the IAEA's high-profile engagement of Tehran from early 2003. In Iran, the nuclear debate tended to follow the pattern of debates established over Iran's place in the post-Cold War order.[50] These debates cut across factional lines. One hears conservative elements making the argument against the possession of WMDs, while some reformers passionately argue in favour of developing a nuclear weapons option as Iran's right and a national security imperative.

Therefore effectively in Iran there is no consensus upon its direction in relation to its nuclear programme but a multitude of opinions can be detected. However, in broad terms, there are five principle arguments circulating within the country for proceeding with its nuclear programme. The first argument is rooted in the rights and responsibilities of sovereign states who are signatories to the NPT. As a loyal member, some circles argue, Iran has never violated the terms of the NPT, but it nonetheless wishes to take maximum (and legitimate) advantage of the opportunities that the NPT offers the member states to acquire nuclear technology and know-how for peaceful purposes. Iran, the argument goes, should take full advantage of its NPT regime membership and the opportunity that this offers via Articles 1 and 2 of the NPT. These articles state, respectively:

1. Nothing in this Treaty shall be interpreted as affecting the inalienable right of all the Parties to the Treaty to develop research, production and use of nuclear energy for peaceful purposes without discrimination and in conformity with Articles I and II of this Treaty.

2. All the Parties to the Treaty undertake to facilitate, and have the right to participate in, the fullest possible exchange of equipment, materials and scientific and technological information for the peaceful uses of nuclear energy. Parties to the Treaty in a position to do so shall also co-operate in contributing alone or together with other States or international organizations to the further development of the applications of nuclear energy for peaceful purposes, especially in the territories of non-nuclear-weapon States Party to the Treaty, with due consideration for the needs of the developing areas of the world.

Others argue that the economic costs associated with nuclear research is so great that Iran should not even enter this field, or at least not by itself. In addition, there are environmental issues to consider, and the fact that by building nuclear facilities Iran will create more strategic targets for its adversaries to strike in case of war. This would leave Iran exposed to vulnerabilities and the ensuing consequences would be excessive in terms of destruction of property and human life.

The second argument pertains to the prestige of being a nuclear state and balancing Israeli military dominance in the Middle East. The proponents of the nuclear option argue that for Iran to be taken seriously as a dominant regional actor it must be seen as having an extensive nuclear R&D programme, even though in practice it may not be translating its research into practical use. However, the research itself would be sufficient for Iran to be taken seriously and not be overlooked in key economic and security decisions concerning the region. In relation to the examples of North Korea, Pakistan and India, it is said that these countries have become immune from US aggression thanks to their nuclear-weapons capabilities, which have acted as a deterrent and established a counterbalancing mechanism to potential future American threats. Indeed, it is apparent to the proponents of this view that India and Pakistan have even been rewarded for their nuclear misdeeds by the USA. For example, India has become a key strategic state in South East Asia for the USA as it aims to balance the growing economic and military strength of China in the region – which is far from the predicament of India being isolated and classed as a rogue state. The opponents of this view argue that the Soviet and North Korean examples show that not only are the technological spin-offs from nuclear research minimal, but any advances in this field will inevitably occur at the expense of another, probably vital, civilian sector that is important for economic prosperity in order to deal with internal population demands. For middle-income countries such as Iran the means of recouping the costs of nuclear research through technological spin-offs simply do not exist, but, particularly as the majority of Iran's experienced scientific community resides overseas, how are the benefits of such highly sensitive research to have the proposed positive national impact?

The third argument for developing a nuclear option is rooted in Iran's geopolitical security environment. The argument is made by members of various factions that Iran's neighbourhood is insecure and inter-state relations uncertain. With Israel and Pakistan in possession of nuclear weapons, it would make strategic sense for Iran to at least develop the option, if not actually declare itself a state with nuclear weapons capability. In addition, the growing military presence of the USA in the region after the 1990–1 Kuwait crisis and in the aftermath of the removal of Saddam in 2003 has added to this anxiety. However others argue that as Iran does not face any existential threats to itself, and indeed as its borders have only been breached once over the last 200 years (in the 1980–8 Iran–Iraq war), there can be no conceivable justification on security grounds for Iran's possession of such destructive weapons. They argue that with the Iraqi threat now removed, Iran no longer has any natural enemies to warrant the deployment of nuclear weapons.

The fourth argument is closely linked to the above and is found in territorial nationalist debates in Iran. Iran's independence and its sovereignty can only be guaranteed in the post-Cold War, post-9/11 era through the possession of such powerful weapons as nuclear-armed missile systems. Without such a capability, Tehran will always be open to threats from the USA and other states with aggressive intent towards it. The opposite camp argues that there is no evidence to suggest that Iran will be more secure as a consequence of nuclearization, that the USA will moderate its policies towards the Islamic Republic, or that the regional countries themselves will submit to Iran's will. If anything, as even some advisers to President Khatami suggested, the deployment of nuclear weapons by Iran will adversely affect its relations with all of its neighbours, including its main military and nuclear infrastructure provider, Russia. Also, it is further maintained, nuclear weapons deployment could encourage militarization and de-democratization of the Iranian polity (including its civil decision-making structures) and perhaps more unwarranted adventurism in Iran's foreign relations.

The final argument relates to the national resources issue. It is argued by the proponents of total freedom of action for Iran in all fields of nuclear research and technological development that to complete the fuel cycle will allow the construction of several nuclear power stations without complete dependence on outside suppliers. Such action will secure for future generations an endless supply of energy, it is claimed. The opponents of this view point to the start-up costs of such a huge programme, as well as its maintenance and periodical modernization expenses. Also, a country that is endowed with some of the largest untapped gas deposits in the world is going to find it hard to convince the international community that its interest in nuclear technology is to secure badly needed energy supplies.

Although these debates do not seem to have reached a conclusive point, the dramatic shift in the balance of power between the various factions and the nuclear schools of thought has led to a hardening of Iran's position under Ahmadinejad. However, the West's position has made it easier for Tehran to pursue this harder line without losing support at home.[51] So, the new Iranian administration can confidently demand that any agreements that Iran may reach with the IAEA or the EU3 must be based on the demonstration of good will by the negotiating parties and a clear recognition of Iran's rights under the NPT. Ahmadinejad is also comfortable that Iran is meeting all its NPT obligations and therefore is not in breach of IAEA rules. Furthermore, he has gone on the offensive in this regard and has challenged the EU3, the USA and the IAEA to identify breaches in Iran's NPT responsibilities.

His administration has also actively been seeking allies in Russia, China and India in its IAEA negotiations since mid-summer 2005. Ahmadinejad's seeking of support from India can be observed via his meetings with the Indian foreign minister in September 2005 and the Indian ambassador in January 2006. In the first meeting the Indian foreign minister expressed the view that Iran did have the right to access peaceful nuclear technology. He further stated that his country supported the resolution of Iran's nuclear issue within the IAEA framework and that he opposed sending the file to the UN Security Council. However, despite statements by the Indian foreign minister in support of Iran's nuclear programme, Iran's strategy of building an alliance with India in this context was to backfire badly. Iran had its fingers burnt in September when it emerged that Non-Aligned India had voted in favour of the UK's motion to refer Iran to the UN Security Council for non-compliance. Since then Iran has increasingly relied on China and Russia to do its bidding in Vienna and New York.

In broader strategic terms, India's position at the IAEA in September 2005 did hurt Tehran and forced the Ahmadinejad administration to reconsider its slowly emerging 'Asia first' strategy. Today, it can only count on Moscow and Beijing (which in any case carry huge weight as permanent members of the Security Council) to prevent the matter progressing any further at the Security Council, but so far it has failed to offer them a working negotiating position. Thus, the spectre of confrontation has continued to loom large, unsettling the region and also playing havoc with oil prices, which had begun to consistently trade above $70 a barrel from April 2006 through to September/October 2006. Other factors of course have contributed to the oil price rally, including unrest in Nigeria's main oil-producing region and new forecasts of strong growth in demand in 2006 and 2007. But as the confrontation over its nuclear research programme swelled, Iran turned out to be the biggest risk for oil markets. Prices were unlikely to fall significantly as long as the dispute remained, according to analysts.[52]

Iran is highly influential in the hydrocarbons market, of course. With about 10 per cent of the world's reserves it is the second largest producer in the Organization of Petroleum Exporting Countries (OPEC) after Saudi Arabia and helps to shape the cartel's pricing policy. It now exports two-thirds of the four million barrels of oil it pumps each day, mainly to Japan, China and other Asian countries. If for any reason those exports were stopped, other producers could not make up for the loss – unlike in 2003, when Saudi Arabia and Kuwait raised their output to make up for the drop in Iraqi exports. Given the overall tightness in global energy supplies, analysts would not expect Iran's oil exports to be embargoed if the dispute before the UN Security Council escalates. Yet alternatives, like forbidding investments by Western companies in Iran's oil sector or banning technology transfers for that industry, might still prove crippling to the country's struggling petroleum sector.

However, targeting Iran's oil sector would be too costly to consider, according to Muhammad-Ali Zainy, an energy economist at the Centre for Global Energy Studies in London, who argues that

> The best punishment, because it would be the most effective, would be to deprive Iran of its oil exports ... But the problem is that this would create a big shortage on the oil markets and lead to a price explosion. It would be disastrous. It is something no one can afford.[53]

The Iranian government derives about 50 per cent of its revenue and most of its foreign currency earnings from oil sales, and, thanks to high prices, is expected to have earned more than $40 billion from those sales in 2005 alone and to earn about $60 billion in 2007.[54] Tehran is betting that the world cannot afford to live without its oil: while that might prove to be a miscalculation, as oil markets tend to be rather resilient, Iran under Ahmadinejad nonetheless has a stronger 'oil hand' to play than under Khatami.

The wider security fallout from Iran's nuclear ambitions, however, has not, in our view been systematically considered in Tehran, which in the medium-term could have a direct bearing on Iran's defence policy. It is widely known, for instance, that Iran's Arab neighbours (particularly the GCC countries) are getting increasingly nervous about Iran's nuclear programme on the one hand and about the failure of negotiations leading to a new war in the region on the other. They are nervous that they could be dragged into a direct military confrontation between Iran and a US-led coalition, and actually suffer militarily from Iranian retaliation for their lending of their facilities to the US armed forces. With substantial US military presence on their soil, a USA–Iran confrontation would immediately put Bahrain and Qatar on the frontline, and also threaten the security of Kuwait, Oman and the UAE, all of whom have close military relations with the USA. These countries fear the direct military as well as the indirect social, economic and political costs of such a conflict for their own societies. How Tehran may be plotting a response to military attack from the USA also concerns them, for they assume that Iran will try and prevent the flow of oil from the Persian Gulf, will disrupt their trade and will use Iraq as a base from which to undermine their domestic stability.

If Iran is unable to target the USA itself, then the comments of Iran's military commanders and political figures about Iran's military contingencies leads one to conclude that it will have little choice but to unleash a regional war. What remains unclear, however, is whether Iran will escalate the conflict once it starts, or whether it will respond in an escalatory fashion to the challenges posed by the USA. Of course if Israel was to get involved in the military operation against Iran, not only would this make the position of the GCC states as US allies wholly untenable regionally, but it would give Tehran hard-liners the perfect pretext for widening the conflict. The most imponderable aspect of this equation is whether the stand-off between Iran and the USA would ultimately lead to a direct and deadly confrontation between Tehran and Tel Aviv. As things stand, for all the bellicose comments coming out of Iran and Israel, neither would want a war with the other on its hands – particularly when both countries are doing rather well in geopolitical terms thanks to the polarization and continuing fragmentation of the Arab world. There again, an Israeli–Iranian confrontation could be in the making precisely because the two countries now see the historic opportunity to stamp their hegemony on the considerably weakened Arab domain around them, and could attempt to extend their reach into the other's zone of influence. Indeed, the July–August 2006 Hezbollah–Israel war was seen by many in this very light – a bloody proxy war between Iran and Israel, but one that took place uncomfortably close to Israel itself, even exposing its northern hub (Haifah) to air attack by Hezbollah.

Moreover, there is slowly emerging evidence to suggest that Iran's nuclear activities and its continuing quarrel with the international community are encouraging nuclear-related investments elsewhere in the region too. In both Saudi Arabia and Egypt, for instance, the matter is being discussed at high levels. This proliferation-by-stealth is likely to make this already insecure and unstable region even more so, particularly for Iran itself, even before Iran's programme is satisfactorily put to rest. This is a major concern for the West, with fears of nuclear weapons getting into the wrong hands and being used against Western interests in the region providing an added impetus for the West to ensure that Iran does not produce nuclear weapons.

IRAQ AND AFTER: CLASH OF THE NEOCONSERVATIVES

Evidence of Tehran's strong hand in Iraq, both in its relations with Baghdad's new masters and in close links with the Shia and Kurdish communities of the country, has sent a ripple of fear across the Arab world and also Turkey. As already noted, since early 2005 Iraq's

Arab neighbours have been much more open in their criticism of Iran's growing role in Iraq. King Abdullah II commented in late 2004 about the rise of an Iran-dominated 'Shia crescent' out of the Iraq war. He stated that

> If pro-Iran parties or politicians dominate the new Iraqi government, a new 'crescent' of dominant Shia movements or governments stretching from Iran into Iraq, Syria and Lebanon could emerge, alter the traditional balance of power between the two main Islamic sects and pose new challenges to US interests and allies.[55]

He further added:

> ...if Iraq goes Islamic Republic, then, yes, we've opened ourselves to a whole set of new problems that will not be limited to the borders of Iraq. I'm looking at the glass half-full, and let's hope that's not the case. But strategic planners around the world have got to be aware that is a possibility.[56]

Ghazi Yawar, the Iraqi interim president, also raised concerns of Iranian interference in Iraqi affairs in an interview with the *Washington Post* when he said:

> Unfortunately, time is proving, and the situation is proving, beyond any doubt that Iran has very obvious interference in our business – a lot of money, a lot of intelligence activities and almost interfering daily in business and many [provincial] governates, especially in the south east side of Iraq.[57]

These concerns were followed in September 2005 by the pessimistic assessment of the Saudi foreign minister in New York that the USA's policies since the war were effectively handing Iraq over to Iran, despite the efforts of the Arab states in 1991 to ensure that Iraq would not become a base for Iranian ambitions. President Husni Mubarak of Egypt added further fuel to the fire when he said in an interview with al-Arabiya television station on 10 April 2006 that the significant proportion of Shia in Arab lands were more loyal to Iran than their own countries:

> There are Shia in all these countries [of the region], significant
> percentages, and Shia are mostly always loyal to Iran and not the
> countries where they live ... Naturally Iran has an influence over
> Shia who make up 65 per cent of Iraq's population.[58]

Here, we could potentially have an intra-Islamic 'clash of civilizations' of the first order if Iran and the Sunni Arab states fail to find
common ground and cause in Iraq. This much was recognized by the
Muslim leaders of all sides, who in October 2006 met in the holy
city of Mecca to declare that Iraq's unity and territorial integrity was
paramount and that the fundamentals of Islam 'apply equally to the
Sunni and the Shia without exception. The differences between the
two schools of thought are merely differences of opinion and interpretation and not essential differences of faith.'[59]

Tensions between the two neighbours could also resurface, as they
did in 2004 during the July–August crisis in Najaf, which exemplified the problem for Tehran rather well. For all the declarations of
friendship between the two sides, and Iran's continuing expression
of support for the post-Saddam Iraqi leadership, it was Iraq's former
interior minister himself, Falah Hassan al-Naqib, who in mid-July
2004 accused Iran of involvement in unrest in Iraq. Falah al-Naqib
told the London-based Arabic daily *Asharq al-Awsat* that

> Iran's infiltration in Iraq has increased and Tehran has provided
> paramilitary [insurgents] large-scale capabilities ... Without any
> doubt, Iran has a role in attacks against the Iraqi people ... This
> country's infiltration has increased and this is occurring through
> its large-scale providing of capabilities for certain insurgent
> groups ... Iran's meddling in Iraq's internal affairs is very clear and
> undeniable.[60]

He said that Iraqis were well aware of Iran's activities, adding that
the majority of Iraqis, including those in southern Iraq, were suffering from Tehran's activities. Meanwhile his counterpart, the Iraqi
Defence Minister Hazim Sha'lan al-Khuza'i, accused Iran of 'blatant
interference' in Iraq's internal affairs.[61] Speaking on the al-Arabiya
satellite television channel, he announced that he had fresh information on Iranian and Syrian meddling in Iraq:

I have important information regarding the interference into Iraq by these two countries ... The Iraqi people will soon see footage of the confessions of one of the perpetrators who has information about the meddling of these two countries in Iraq.[62]

The Iraqi interim-Prime Minister, Ayad Allawi, speaking on Iraqi television echoed these comments about Iranian and Syrian meddling in Iraq: 'There are countries which host those who are involved in activities that are harmful to the people of Iraq.'[63]

The Governor of Najaf, Adnan al-Zurufi, said on 8 August 2004 that 'there is Iranian support for al-Sadr's group, and this is no secret. We have information and evidence that they are supplying the [Imam] Al-Mahdi Army with weapons and have found such weapons in their possession.'[64] Tehran was quite taken aback by the forcefulness of these attacks from senior Iraqi officials, and in frustration warned that 'Iraqi officials have just begun working and need to be cautious... [as their remarks will] have serious legal and political consequences' for relations between Iran and Iraq.[65] *Jomhuri-yi Islami*, an influential hard-line newspaper, stated in an editorial, also on 8 August 2004, that the interim government was a 'cast of hand-picked actors'. The next day, it opined that the Najaf crisis was a 'premeditated conspiracy to eliminate the forces of resistance' in Iraq: 'the time [has] come for us to get up and go after the crown of Islam, the very existence of the Shia, and the national interests of the Islamic Republic of Iran.'[66]

In response to growing criticism of Iranian involvement in Iraqi affairs, Iranian Foreign Minister Kamel Kharrazi responded by demanding proof from the accusers, saying 'We are confident that they can produce no proof for their claims.'[67] Kharrazi said Iran only provides spiritual support for the Iraqi nation, stressing that Tehran has never been pursuing interference in Iraq:

Although Iran is naturally enjoying a significant influence in Iraq by considering the common affinities between the Iranian and the Iraqi nations, the Islamic Republic has never been seeking interference in Iraq ... Tehran wants nothing but the good for the Iraqi nation, and I hope that a representative and democratically elected government would be soon established in Iraq.[68]

Kharrazi stressed that Iran is strongly against any effort to sow discord in Iraq. Despite the denials of involvement by Iranian officials, there is a general fear that under the new president the Shia issue in the hands of the hard-liners can spell disaster, further testing its relations with the West (notably the EU and the USA, which are being badly strained by Iran's nuclear activities). What the above demonstrates more emphatically are the residual tensions still at play in Iran–Iraq relations, despite regime change in Iraq.

However it is no longer in dispute that Iran's influence in Iraq today (and as a consequence in neighbouring Arab countries) does indeed stretch far and wide. In the south of Iraq Iran has a dominant socio-economic presence via the funding of social and welfare programmes, where even its unconvertible and poor-value currency is widely used. Iranian pilgrims have flocked to the holy cities of Najaf and Karbala after the removal of Saddam, increasing Iranian presence in Iraq. Iranian pilgrims and officials freely mingle with their Iraqi counterparts and Iran's security apparatus has secured a firm footing due to the relative openness in accessing Iraq. In addition Iran's security apparatus has infiltrated the camp of the Anglo-American-trained police and military units of the new Iraqi security forces. As a consequence, Iran today has a strong security and military presence in Iraq as well. Furthermore, due to its close links with the two main Shia parties in Iraq dominating the Iraqi government today (al-Dawa and SCIRI), Tehran also has easy access to the government machinery of the new Iraq. In addition Iran has strong ties with the Iraqi Ayatollahs who are either of Iranian origin or have spent time studying in Qom and Isfahan. The ability to mobilize Iraqi people via the firebrand Muqtadar al-Sadr has added strength to the Iranian influence in Iraq. Routinely, Iran is at pains to show its solidarity with the Iraqis and since end of 2003 has been doing all it can to assist Iraq's temporary rulers in managing the country, even to the point of being accused of internal interference.[69] At the same time it is feared in the GCC capitals and in the Arab East that Iran is trying to create new facts on the ground by actively changing the demographic map of Iraq's oil-rich Basra province through the settling of Iranians in these areas.

Arab fears of Iranian policies and motives have added more urgency to the USA's search for a solution to its 'Iran problem'. Since 2003, Iran and the USA have been locked in two strategic arenas: Iraq and Iran's nuclear ambitions. Combined, they have come to symbolize the tensions in USA–Iran relations since the rise of Iran's own unique neoconservatives. The clash of the American and Iranian neoconservatives has been taking shape in a security environment filled with suspicion and mistrust, and where the competing neoconservative tendencies have been vying for influence. Like their American counterparts, the Iranian neoconservatives are looking to secure Iran's place in the world as a powerful West Asian and Muslim state with interests in several strategic theatres. They are also trying, like their counterparts in the USA, to marry invigorated traditional (including religiously based) values with a muscular, proselytizing foreign policy. Familiarity in this context could breed contempt and raise the danger of the dialogue of the deaf getting out of hand as the neoconservatives in both countries resort to using external tensions (and possible conflict opportunities) as a tool for domestic rejuvenation and suppression of democratic opposition to their agendas.

To add to the problem, the two also seem to be operating in parallel universes at times, apparently bypassing each other. From Washington's perspective, Iran's influence in Iraq gives it tremendous leverage in an oil-rich state of great strategic significance. Tehran's Shia-run state also provides non-Arab Iran with much greater regional reach in a Shia-dominated Iraq, from where it can influence the domestic politics of many of its Arab neighbours. Add to this Iran's growing links with Hamas, which is also popular amongst the Palestinian diaspora communities in Jordan, Lebanon and Egypt, and Tehran's reach would indeed appear long and strong. For the first time in generations, it is Iran that is realizing the geopolitical opportunities presented to it by the actions of the USA in the region and the Soviet collapse, and can express an independent voice on all the core issues of the region, being able to exercise its options in the Arab world with total disregard for the West and the key Arab states. It is a keen awareness of the growing influence of Iran in the region that has prompted Egypt, Jordan and Saudi Arabia to speak out and also to seek clarification from the USA of its policies. The fear in the Arab world of an Iranian–American 'understanding' in Iraq fails to dissipate, thus adding constant pressure to Tehran's carefully cultivated ties with the Arabs formed during the Khatami era.[70]

To address Iran's growing regional power, which is partly a result of the USA's own policies under the Bush administration, Washington has opted simultaneously to tackle Tehran over Iraq and its nuclear programme. The drawing of a link between the two provides a strategic misfit of the grandest proportions, for if nothing else it enables Iran to use its presence in Iraq as leverage in its confrontation over its nuclear programme with the USA. Shia power in this regard can be used against the West, which would further alienate Iraq's Arab neighbours who are fearful of an Iraqi–Iranian axis emerging.

Ironically the crisis in Iraq also provides the most practical opportunity for leaders in Tehran and Washington to try and meet face-to-face. The meeting of the neoconservatives may not yield much in the first instance, but it will at least provide the first publicly known meeting of the US and Iranian hard-liners since the mid-1980s. In response to the governmental deadlock in Iraq and escalating levels of violence there was tentative agreement of talks between Iran and the USA on the situation in Iraq, indicating acknowledgment by the USA of Iranian influence in Iraq and the desperate situation of the Americans. The hope of talks was shattered when, on Monday 24 April 2006, President Ahmadinejad declared that there was no need for Iran–USA talks due to the fact that the Iraqis had resolved their problem over the candidacy of prime minister,[71] with unanimous acceptance of Nouri al-Maliki. Even when talks did take place in 2007 between the two it was hard to see the USA's willingness to lighten its position on Iran's nuclear activities in return for stabilization of Iraq. However it is not hard to see that the diplomatic exchanges between the two sides could diminish the prospect of another war, diffusing tensions that have been built up between the dominant actors in the Persian Gulf.

The situation has been further inflamed, however, by Ahmadinejad recently suggesting that Tehran might withdraw from the UN's nuclear watchdog agency and the NPT, which has increased suspicion in the West that Iranian scientists will pursue the development of nuclear weapons, with no possibility of outside monitoring.[72] In response to this statement by Ahmadinejad, Sean McCormack, the State Department spokesman, said that Tehran appeared 'hell-bent on defying the international community and pursuing a nuclear programme that is of growing concern'.[73] For the neighbouring Arab states they will have the unenviable task of choosing between bad and worse: avoiding war through acceptance by their US ally of the prominence of Iran in Iraq, or risking war between a new US-led coalition and Iran over its nuclear programme if neither side shows sign of moderation.

The other big danger for the Arab world is for the USA to attempt to check the growing power of Iran in the Arab East by trying to break the link in the geopolitical chain Tehran is building between Iran, Iraq, Syria and Lebanon. In bringing down the Assad regime in Syria and the pro-Assad (and therefore pro-Iran) government in Lebanon, the USA would have severed the strategic advantages that Iran would be exploiting through Iraq. Already Syria has been weakened via US-supported withdrawal from Lebanon in the aftermath of Rafiq al-Hariri's assassination. This has undercut Syrian power and influence in the Levant, which is part of the USA's policy in enforcing retraction on the Syrian regime to cause internal weakness and inevitable decay, leading to regime change. Syria no doubt has been weakened, and has therefore been eager to build ties with Iran and establish influence within Iraq. Syria can be seen to have relations with the Sunnis, Kurds and Shia in Iraq. The USA is aware of the importance of these geopolitical ties for Tehran and can act as an obstacle to Tehran's search for friends and allies as its confrontation with the USA escalates, but question marks remain over the effectiveness of this policy. As in the case of Syria, although the party concerned may be weakened it will still look for alternative means to strengthen its hands, thus strangely at the same empowering the country. Any US action in this regard would be counterproductive as far as the Arab states are concerned, and would further deepen the chasm between the USA and the Arab world, putting even more pressure on the USA's regional allies. The USA is already seen as being an interferer in Arab affairs, therefore any attempt to break geopolitical links and alliances is likely to increase the level of anti-Americanism in the Arab world and thus raise the spectre of instability even further in the region.

US POLICY OPTIONS

The question that has arisen naturally in this stand-off and confrontation between Iran and the USA is: what are the viable policy options that are available to the USA? The breaking of the geopolitical links and alliances that Iran has been trying to forge is an option but it is difficult to see how this would have an impact upon its nuclear programme and it appears to be a long-term strategy rather than one that could have immediate impact. Three options that could be taken up by the USA come to mind, but each option poses dilemmas and difficulties:

1. Air strikes

This has been much touted amongst US policymakers but will pose many difficulties if chosen. First, a number of Iranian nuclear facilities remain unknown to the Security Council, and many are underground. Second, those that are known are located near large population centres. Therefore any air strike would result in the death of many innocent people. This would heighten anti-Western sentiments in Iran (especially anti-American sentiments) and put a dent in Western plans to win the hearts and minds of the Iranian people – a fact stressed by Condoleezza Rice in one of her recent trips to the Middle East.

There are reports to suggest that Israel is preparing potential air strikes. The government recently leaked a contingency plan for attacking on its own if the USA does not do so. Its plan involves air strikes, commando teams, possibly missiles and even explosives-carrying dogs to attack Iranian targets.[74] Israel, which bombed Iraq's Osirak nuclear plant in 1981 to prevent it being used to develop weapons, has built a replica of Natanz for target practice, according to Israeli media, but US strategists do not believe Israel has the capacity to accomplish the mission without the use of nuclear weapons.[75] The possibility of air strikes via the use of Israel by the USA or pre-emptive action by Israel would be catastrophic for both the West and Israel in terms of security and stability in the Middle East.

2. Sanctions

This action seems to be the most likely, but again there are various disagreements in the Security Council. The USA, UK and France seem to agree on the imposition of sanctions but China and Russia do not. This disagreement is dictated by national interest, with China and Russia both having significant economic interests in Iran. This can be seen via Russia's arduous attempts to diffuse the nuclear crisis. Russia has insisted that it is opposed to moves by the USA and its allies to impose sanctions against Iran. At a meeting in Moscow, Russian officials met delegates from the USA, the UK, France, Germany and China to discuss the latest moves regarding Iran's nuclear programme. Afterwards Russian spokesman Mikhail Kamynin insisted that neither the sanctions route nor the use of force would lead to a resolution of the problem.[76]

In addition China is a net importer of oil to fuel its growing economy, and its multi-billion-dollar oil agreements with Iran will surely determine Chinese opposition to any sanctions against Iran. For example, the Chinese state oil giant Sinopec Group in 2004 signed a $70 billion oil field development and liquefied natural gas agreement with Iran: this was China's biggest energy deal.[77] Also the Chinese state oil trader Zhuhai Zhenrong Corp agreed earlier in the same year to buy over 110 million tons of LNG from Iran over 25 years for $20 billion.[78] In January 2006 Iran's North Drilling Company (NDC) and the Hong Kong-registered China Oilfield Services Ltd signed an oil exploration agreement for the management, repair and maintenance of the Alborz semi-floating platform, currently being constructed by the Iranian Offshore Industries Company.[79] A three-year contract with an estimated cost of $33 million will enable Iran, with China's help, to move its exploration activities to the deep waters of the southern Caspian. The consequences of sanctions are daunting for the emerging giants of Asia, with the price of a barrel of oil expected to rise to $100 if oil from Iran is cut off. Such an eventuality would lead to excessive hikes in domestic fuel prices in the West. Politically this would be suicidal for Western governments.[80]

3. War

This might seem the most unlikely option and a far off reality.[81] However, would the USA engage in war without a UN mandate like it did in Iraq? The answer would be difficult to find in Washington's corridors of power. The USA at the moment is over-stretched in Iraq, with the situation continuously deteriorating. In addition the situation in Afghanistan is far from stable and pressure is increasing on the Bush administration to rebuild New Orleans in the aftermath of the destruction caused by Hurricane Katrina on 23 August 2005. War in Iran would be suicidal for the USA in terms of the wider Middle East, further endangering the USA's national interest. In addition, this option is not likely to gain the support of the European allies that showed their opposition to the US-led military campaign against Iraq. Even the UK, which supported the war in Iraq, has dismissed war against Iran as an option. UK Foreign Secretary Jack Straw stated at the Labour Party's annual conference in 2005 that

> there is no question of us going to war against Iran. Why? Because it's not going to resolve the issue. No one is talking about going to war against Iran … This can only be resolved by diplomatic means and by diplomatic pressure.[82]

Indeed his removal from the Foreign and Commonwealth Office in 2006 may well have been linked to his outspoken opposition to the use of force against Iran, but change of personnel does not seem to have changed the UK's position in this regard.

From the three policy options, the prospect of a preventive air attack on Iranian nuclear facilities is gaining momentum but this course of action would pose dilemmas in terms of oil supply to world markets. In addition, Iranian reaction would significantly compound the on-going difficulties of the USA in Iraq and Afghanistan. The encouragement of Iranian proxies such as Hezbollah to attack the interests of the USA in the Levant, causing the USA to enter a new circle of violence, would raise the stakes further for Washington – which it does not need right now given the instability in Iraq and Afghanistan.[83]

CONCLUSION

Ahmadinejad came to power aiming to draw Iran closer to the Muslim world and its Arab neighbours. In practice, he may have done the reverse due to his handling of the nuclear crisis and growing tensions with the West. He said in a major news conference after his election victory that he would 'give priority to the establishment of relations with our immediate neighbours, then with countries that once fell within the zone of Iran's civilization, then with Muslim states'.[84] Yet, Ahmadinejad's policy pronouncements have unsettled nerves at home and abroad, and have again raised suspicions of Iran's motives and strategic objectives in the region. His election victory has not changed the structures of power, however, nor the relationship between the institutions of power, which continue to be dominated by the conservative hierarchy in place since the 1979 Iranian revolution.[85] In the final analysis, despite his neoconservative leanings, President Ahmadinejad has to govern a modern, complex and wayward state, as well as rule over a restless population that no longer responds positively to pressures from above, which is at the same time desperate for its fair share of Iran's bounties. We would submit that the president will find moving the goal posts, in terms of the national agenda, a lot harder than even delivering on his lofty election promises. Geopolitical realities today, as well as 16 years of constructive policymaking at home, have their own policy momenta, which cannot easily be dismissed or bypassed.

Iran's role perception can certainly be modified under different leaders and changing international conditions, and its policies altered to meet its new priorities, which is already happening under President Ahmadinejad. But how far a post-revolutionary state can be run by a neo-revolutionary president is a question that merits further investigation. Our suspicion is that in the medium-term it will probably have to be the neo-revolutionary who has to change, given Iran's shifting demographic balance, its economic difficulties, its role in the international political economy as a major hydrocarbons producer, and the pressures associated with geopolitics. It is with these realities in mind that we can note two new proposals for regional security coming forth in the short time that Dr Ahmadinejad has been president.

The first relates to the proposal put forward by the Iranian Deputy Foreign Minister for Arab-African Affairs, Muhammad-Reza Baqeri, at the regional security conference led by the International Institution for Strategic Studies (IISS) in Manama in early December 2005. At this event, Iran was represented at a high level, indicating the importance that Tehran continues to attach to security dialogue with its Arab neighbours in the Persian Gulf. Mr Baqeri welcomed the IISS initiative and formally proposed the adoption of a regional security regime, but with the usual caveat:

> the security set-up should include a timetable for departure of foreign military forces from the region ... [because] the increased presence of alien military forces in the region has led to more chaos, strengthened radicalism and terrorism and postponed the growth and development of the region.[86]

Of course, such conditions were unlikely to be welcomed by the GCC, who not only host the American military but actually view the presence of American and Western forces in terms of their own security and survival requirements. Nonetheless, the Iranian deputy foreign minister did recommend the adoption of some interesting security measures, notably 'a governmental and non-governmental war against terrorism, a program to rid the region of weapons of mass destruction and rejection of the theory of regional balance'. These generalities provide a basis, albeit a slim one, on which to build confidence into the future.

The second security pronouncement of the new administration was articulated by President Ahmadinejad himself, who on the margins of the OIC summit in Mecca proposed the establishment of an Islamic defence and security pact. Though it is still unclear how the OIC members responded to this proposal, it is interesting to note that the new administration is putting much more emphasis on the need to improve relations with the Muslim world than previous administrations under Rafsanjani and Khatami. His offer of sharing Iran's nuclear technology for scientific advancements in the Muslim world could be seen in the same light as Iran trying to build alliances and relations with fellow Muslim countries. So, while his security pact offer may be broader than a pan-Persian Gulf one, the fact that he has shown sensitivity towards the ongoing security dilemmas of the Muslim world can be seized upon to build confidence across the waterway. Furthermore, placing regional security in a wider, Islamic context could be beneficial in terms of enabling the parties to underplay the role of the Western powers for advancing their agenda and interests in the Muslim world.

Nevertheless, the dawn of post-détente in Iran's regional policies is unlikely to be warmly received by the neighbourhood, despite the continuing exchange of niceties between the new administration and its neighbours and high-level visits by the president and his emissaries to the neighbouring Arab states. The real irony is that Iran's radicalizing tone is taking place just as Iraq may, very slowly, be finally emerging from the dark shadows of the 2003 war. The year 2005 began with elections in Iraq and it also ended thus, with Iraqis voting in large numbers on 15 December to elect their new four-year parliament. According to official sources, as many as 11 million people cast ballots, which would put the voter turnout at more than 70 per cent. Massive participation across Iraq in these elections heralded the pre-eminence of politics over violence in that country, but what this means for Iran as well as Iraq's other neighbours remains to be seen. One thing is certain, however, and that is that the return of the political process to Iraq will further complicate relations of the GCC states with Iran, with the latter being assumed to be making strategic gains in Iraq. The policy initiatives of President Ahmadinejad himself towards Iraq and his southern neighbours could become increasingly more complicated as Tehran and its GCC counterparts embark on the interpretation of the new Iraqi political elite from their own narrowly defined perspectives. How they see the new Iraq will have a direct bearing on how they see each other in the years to come; if current evidence is anything to go by they are likely to see developments in Iraq in zero-sum terms and thus remain suspicious of the other's actions and motives. None of this provides a recipe for happy coexistence, particularly under the leadership of Iran's neoconservatives (who draw their inspiration from such hardline clerics as Ayatollahs Jannati and Mesbah-Yazdi and their policy strategies from populist and messianic ideas prevalent in Iran).

Since 9/11 the securitization of international politics and the grand geopolitical developments in West Asia have had such a dramatic impact on the Iranian polity that today it has an administration dominated by the security spirit of the revolution, if not indeed by many of its personnel. Policy in Iran (as elsewhere) is not shaped in a vacuum and we would venture to suggest that it is still the wider context that determines the national agenda. To follow President Ahmadinejad's policies we must therefore appreciate the domestic backdrop as well as the regional realities in which they take form. Ultimately then it could be argued that, unlike any other time in the life of the Islamic Republic, while the main threats to its national security may have been eliminated (notably the removal of Saddam Hussein and the Taliban), Iran's own activities (in the nuclear realm, amongst others), policies (which have led to termination of negotiations with the EU3) and political priorities are such that it could now be generating such potentially huge security challenges for the future that it may have little alternative but to embark on the building up of its defences in anticipation of external attack.

At no other time in the recent history of the region has the danger of a self-fulfilling prophecy of militarization coming to pass been greater. When the Iranian president spoke of his election victory as a 'Second Islamic Revolution' in the country he would have had the domestic situation in mind, but in reality he may well have forced Iran to relive the tense and lonely period of the 'First Republic' in the 1980s, when friends and allies were in short supply and when defiance of the international community was the Republic's *modus operandi*. The costs of isolation today, however, could be incalculable in terms of opportunities lost, pressures endured and the high price to be paid by the next generation for the country's rehabilitation.

VI

CONCLUSIONS

The rise of the reformists through victory in local and national elections in the 1997–2001 period meant that a new direction was taking shape in Iranian politics. It is not surprising then that as President Khatami's administration became more entrenched so the conservatives sprung into action, not just for ideological reasons but also to maintain their valuable economic and political power bases. Over a short period of time they forced the departure of several leading reformers and President Khatami's advisors from the political scene (including such major figures as Nouri and Mohajerani), the imprisonment of a number of the key figures from his camp, and the suspension of over a dozen pro-Khatami newspapers. A conservative backlash was in full swing and true to form their methods were extremely stringent and draconian. It was feared that the continuing infighting would result in a general breakdown of the Iranian political system, destabilizing the entire government machinery and creating fertile conditions for the direct involvement of the anti-reform factions and of the military in the political process. Looking back, it is clear that the struggle for power weakened the reformist camp and increased the prospects for violent encounters between the various factions, particularly between pro-Khatami students and the security forces, which in the end led to the collapse of the reformist front.

Reformist political parties were not allowed much room to operate within Iran, therefore Khatami – whose intellectualism appealed to those in favour of wholesale political and social reform – was the principal figure behind the entire reform movement. The reformists challenged the traditional norms established within Iranian politics; they even went as far as questioning the role of the clerical leadership, in particular that of the *Velayat-e Faqih*. The conservatives were quick to fend off this apparent attack on the *Faqih*, and by 2004 had managed to realign their forces and once again become a viable and powerful force.

The key difference between the neoconservatives and the traditional conservatives lies with the former's interest in prioritizing the needs of the destitute masses over anything else for winning back power. They rightly calculated that the support of the masses for the regime would also help them preserve the classical, Khomeini-promoted definition of the Iranian Islamic state. According to the neoconservatives the state should be an interventionist one. In addition they focus their slogans and discourse on social justice and the welfare of the poor but do not devalue such matters as Islamic values and the question of *haq* versus *batil* (right and wrong in religious matters). Mahmoud Ahmadinejad has presented himself as a politician who wants to serve the Iranian nation, in particular those who have been forgotten by previous governments. We have tried to show that from his stance it is clear that his social and religious background has influenced his every move and statement. In him we find an interesting combination of religion and new-style politics. It is this combination that has resulted in Ahmadinejad being referred to as a real phenomenon in modern Iranian politics.

The emergence of a new urban-based social class, consisting mostly of migrants starting new lives in Tehran – consequently swelling its population to the 12 million it is today – was part of the changing social structure in post-revolution Iran. These new internal migrants share very similar interests with the Islamic regime; they are religious to the extent that religion is the principal factor in their lives. Ahma-dinejad is an outcome of this social restructuring; however, he and his agenda represent a far more radical shift, even compared to the first revolutionary generation.

Khatami's reforms were an immense threat to these social groups; in their eyes, they felt the regime had been hijacked by unreligious people. Khatami's intellectualism was a source of concern for these traditional conservatives; 'their' Islamic Republic was being un-Islamized right in front of their eyes. The Iranian neoconservatives appealed to the disenchanted lower and middle classes, and they also presented a fresh alternative apart from the traditional conservatives, who were seen as politically impotent when it came to protecting the masses. The neoconservatives also promised to put an end to the widespread corruption within Iranian politics and Ahmadinejad wanted to 'purify' Iran from the many immoralities that had crept into the system.

Ahmadinejad's electoral victory represents a major turning point in Iranian politics. Broadly speaking, the success of Ahamdinejad and the failure of Rafsanjani can be pinned down to two main reasons. First, the former's ability to gain the support of Khomenei, and sec-ond, the latter's inability to convince the people of his sincerity and the plausibility of his policies. Ahmadinejad's victory demonstrates the extent to which Iran remains a deeply polarized society, some 26 years after the revolution. Just as Khatami's success in 1997 and 2001 proved that there was wide support for reform and international in-tegration amongst the Iranian electorate, Ahmadinejad's 2005 vic-tory is evidence that many within Iran support the neoconservatives in their mission to combat poverty, redistribute wealth and preserve the Islamic nature of the state.

Only time will tell whether Ahmadinejad will fulfil his prom-ises and achieve the goals he set out during his electoral campaign. However, what is certain is that the neoconservatives are now part of mainstream politics in Iran – yet with success there also comes mili-tary baggage resulting in the political establishment acquiring a more militaristic face for the first time in over a generation. These changes by Ahmadinejad have not gone unnoticed internally, or indeed externally. Internally the old guard are fearful of the road on which Ahmadinejad may be leading Iran, with fear of their economic and political status being diminished by the new revolution launched by Ahmadinejad. Externally, the military character of the Iranian regime has raised alarm bells and has intensified the stand-off between Iran and the West. The debates about Iran's nuclear programme increasingly have been articulated around these same issues since 2005.

Ahmadinejad's principal internal opposition does not come from reformists, as some may think. A new challenge has begun to rise in the shape of the traditional conservatives, the marginalized 'old guard' within the conservative movement who are wary of the Ahmadinejad phenomenon. This split is likely to be a feature of Iranian politics in the future: how this is dealt with, alongside Ahmadinejad's approach to the Iranian nuclear programme, will determine his popularity and, more importantly, his longevity in power.

The clerics are exerting increased pressure on Ahmadinejad with regards to some of his social policies. They are discontent, for instance, with allowing women into football matches. He has also been accused of deploying a populist agenda in economic policy and in foreign relations, favouring short-term gain instead of long-term stability. How this will affect the remainder of his presidency is unclear, although the elections of the Khobregan Majlis (which as a constitutional body is charged with 'electing' the *Faqih*) was the early indicator of decreasing popularity of President Ahmadinejad. Whether this decrease continues will be seen in the Majlis elections of 2008, which will more than likely bring about an open struggle between the neoconservatives and the reconstituted 'neoreformers'. Where the traditional Right will sit in this struggle is probably going to be the main story of this round of electoral politics, we suspect.

Despite Ahmadinejad's 'revolutionary' nature, his accession to power has not altered the state structure; he remains a staunch supporter of the Leader and does not for a moment entertain the possibility of shifting power away from the Leader's office. Internal challenges within Iran present an obstacle to Ahmadinejad's neoconservative ideology. The president must now govern a modern, complex and evolving state where the population are no longer willing to respond positively to changes from above. We would admit that the president will have a difficult task ahead of him. The realities of geopolitics today, as well as 16 years of reform-oriented policymaking, are factors that cannot be denied or dismissed.

Nonetheless, we still believe that the question should be asked, how far can a post-revolutionary state be run by a neo-revolutionary president? This is a question that merits further investigation. However, bearing in mind facts such as Iran's shifting demographic balance, its economic difficulties, its role in the international political economy as a major hydrocarbons producer and the pressures associated with geopolitics, the neo-revolutionary is indeed being forced to change.

Despite the continuing exchange of niceties between Iran and its Arab neighbours, the current state of Iranian domestic politics is likely to be a source of concern to its neighbouring states. Ironically, the Iranian neoconservatives are pursuing their radical agendas just as Iraq may finally be emerging from the shadows of the 2003 war. As the political process in Iraq is revived, both Iran and the GCC will be looking to make strategic gains in the newly shaped state, thus complicating matters further between Iran and its Arab neighbours.

The events of 9/11 emphasized the need for a more security-centred approach to international relations; this in turn paved the way for an Iranian polity dominated by the security spirit of the revolution. Both internal and external factors shape the Iranian administration's foreign policy, therefore while it is important to consider domestic issues, it will be equally important for Ahmadinejad to be aware of regional realities. Ultimately then, it could be argued that the Islamic Republic is venturing into unprecedented territory; for while the main threats to its national security may have been eliminated, Iran's own policies are such that it could now be generating potentially huge security challenges for the future. Consequently, Iran may have little alternative but to embark on strengthening its defence arsenal in anticipation of any external attack.

The ruling conservative hierarchy have certainly recognized the dangers of an imbalanced foreign policy, and as a result Ayatollah Khamenei commissioned the creation of the non-partisan Foreign Relations Strategic Council in summer 2006 in order to seek the advice of experts in relation to international affairs and the formation of Iran's foreign policy. It will be interesting to see to what extent the advice that is given is actually taken on board by the ruling neoconservative elite gathered around the presidency and in parliament. A key test of the direction of Iranian foreign policy will be the ruling elite's reaction to the ongoing nuclear negotiations converging around the EU package that was tabled in Vienna on 1 June 2006. It is our view that Iran might agree to the suspension of its uranium enrichment programme only to be able to test the credibility of the EU and the USA in terms of what is actually being offered, but beyond that a clear resolution is not yet in sight. It is likely therefore that the nuclear issue will not be solved under the present US administration, making it interesting to see how a new administration will deal with Iran. It is for this reason that the prospects of a military confrontation of sorts cannot yet be ruled out.

If the neoconservatives fail to invest in this historical moment, it is likely that there will be no more real incentives from the West, which would in turn enable the reformist camp in Iran to review its own strategy in order to dislodge the neoconservatives from power. Again, domestic and international have become tied hopelessly together to generate yet more complexities in the case of the Islamic Republic of Iran. We did say at the outset that Iran was an unpredictable country!

APPENDIX

Table 1. Electoral participation: second councils elections, 2003

Province	Electorate	Voters	Participation (%)
Azarbaijan, East	2,350,000	1,096,685	46.67
Azarbaijan, West	1,576,620	977,123	61.98
Ardebil	867,230	335,475	51.37
Esfahan	2,802,257	970,776	34.64
Ilam	350,015	255,822	73.09
Bushehr	525,967	288,327	54.82
Tehran	7,840,698	1,864,311	23.78
Chahar Mahal and Bakhtiari	544,325	341,544	62.75
Khorasan	4,055,943	2,201,208	54.27
Khuzestan	2,232,787	1,293,283	57.92
Zanjan	554,802	353,494	63.72
Semnan	368,600	205,903	55.86
Sistan and Baluchestan	900,575	708,394	78.66
Fars	2,909,965	1,377,065	47.32
Qazvin	725,975	395,758	54.51
Qom	548,136	196,678	54.51
Kurdistan	941,508	497,590	52.85
Kerman	1,175,886	829,731	70.56
Kermanshah	1,316,692	745,074	56.59
Kohgiluyeh and Buyer Ahmad	343,653	271,976	79.14
Golestan	927,771	628,809	72.09
Gilan	1,547,542	1,044,666	67.50
Lorestan	1,095,583	560,761	51.18
Mazandaran	1,599,154	1,065,949	66.66
Markazi	758,343	374,083	49.33
Hormozgan	629,374	417,684	66.36
Hamadan	1,039,163	548,003	52.74
Yazd	598,983	253,605	42.34
Total	*41,127,547*	*20,099,777*	*48.87*

Source: *www.isna.ir*, 3 March 2003.

Table 2. Electoral participation: comparison of the first and second councils elections

First councils election, 1999			Second councils elections, 2003		
Electorate	Voters	%	Electorate	Voters	%
42,000,000	26,000,000	62	41,127,547	20,099,777	49

Source: *http://news.billinge.com*, 10 February 1999; *www.isna.ir*, 3 March 2003.

Table 3. Electoral participation: Seventh Majlis elections, 2004

Province	Electorate	Voters	Participation (%)
Tabriz	1,217,977	378,163	31.79
Aromiyeh	561,902	202,611	36.06
Mahabad	133,849	31,656	23.65
Ardabil	438,811	196,166	44.70
Isfahan	1,288,279	414,559	32.17
Ilam	251,534	170,818	67.91
Tehran	6,047,572	1,965,666	32.50
Karaj	929,047	355,934	38.31
Busher	224,730	91,605	40.76
Najafabad	246,926	89,772	36.36
Shahr-e Kord	231,638	129,121	55.74
Mashhad	1,573,983	744,310	47.28
Ahvaz	837,765	349,011	41.66
Zanjan	339,570	190,518	56.10
Semnan	112,367	56,707	50.47
Zahedan	266,588	179,697	62.41
Shiraz	1,005,404	320,364	31.86
Qazvin	518,736	258,578	49.85
Qum	615,660	311,337	50.57
Sanandaj	367,395	107,708	29.32
Kerman	447,577	208,368	46.55
Kermanshah	676,399	243,157	35.95
Kehkelwih	147,744	147,677	99.95
Gorgan	318,056	200,553	63.06
Rashat	584,853	201,832	34.51
Khorramabbad	355,320	199,013	56.01
Sari	343,540	186,496	54.29
Arak	611,388	200,489	32.79
Saveh	169,818	82,565	48.62
Bander Abbas	412,199	226,187	54.87
Hamadan	447,699	205,906	45.99
Yazd	317,846	135,655	42.68
*All of Iran**	*46,351,032*	*23,709,201*	*51.15*

Source: *www.isna.ir*, 25 February 2004.

* Including provinces not listed here.

Table 4. Electoral participation: comparison of the Sixth Majlis elections, 2000 and Seventh Majlis elections, 2004

Province	Sixth Majlis electorate	Sixth Majlis voters	Participation (%)	Seventh Majlis electorate	Seventh Majlis voters	Participation (%)
Tabriz	1,043,994	566,103	54.22	1,217,977	378,163	31.79
Aromiyeh	474,927	279,320	58.81	561,902	202,611	36.06
Mahabad	111,785	75,713	67.73	133,849	31,656	23.65
Ardabil	363,221	231,080	63.62	438,811	196,166	44.70
Isfahan	1,098,371	571,147	47.45	1,288,279	414,559	32.70
Ilam	203,900	175,432	86.04	251,534	170,818	67.91
Tehran	5,242,993	2,931,113	55.91	6,047,572	1,965,666	32.50
Karaj	785,092	417,706	52.71	929,047	355,934	38.31
Busher	187,275	116,732	62.33	224,730	91,605	40.76
Najafabad	205,518	141,062	68.64	246,926	89,772	36.36
Shahr-e Kord	189,166	142,189	75.17	231,638	129,121	55.74
Mashhad	1,305,677	819,866	62.79	1,573,983	744,310	47.28
Ahvaz	686,419	369,095	53.77	837,765	349,011	41.66
Zanjan	279,724	179,268	64.09	339,570	190,518	56.10
Semnan	96,800	70,460	72.79	112,367	56,707	50.47
Zahedan	213,218	142,974	67.06	266,588	179,697	62.41
Shiraz	842,495	411,314	48.82	1,005,404	320,364	31.86
Qazvin	427,500	285,664	66.82	518,736	258,578	49.85

cont....

Table 4. *cont.*

Province	Sixth Majlis electorate	Sixth Majlis voters	Participation (%)	Seventh Majlis electorate	Seventh Majlis voters	Participation (%)
Qum	510,578	337,078	66.02	615,660	311,337	50.57
Sanandaj	344,975	215,235	62.39	367,395	107,708	29.32
Kerman	375,388	216,523	55.68	447,577	208,368	46.55
Kermanshah	552,705	350,370	63.39	676,399	243,157	35.95
Kehkelwih	116,943	116,024	99.,21	147,744	147,677	99.95
Gorgan	269,440	199,757	74.14	318,056	200,553	63.06
Rashat	504,645	285,536	58.58	584,853	201,832	34.51
Khorramabad	293,011	234,828	80.14	355,320	199,013	56.01
Sari	287,966	204,737	71.10	343,540	186,496	54.29
Arak	389,437	245,528	63.05	611,388	200,489	3.79
Saveh	143,744	94,984	66.54	169,818	82,565	4.62
Bander Abbas	339,719	217,400	63.99	412,199	226,187	54.87
Hamadan	373,929	223,592	59.80	447,699	205,906	45.99
Yazd	267,528	165,559	61.88	317,846	135,655	42.68
*All of Iran**	*38,726,431*	*26,808,423*	*69.23*	*46,351,032*	*23,709,201*	*51.15*

Source: *www.isna.ir*, 10 March 2004.
* Including provinces not listed here.

Table 5. Ninth presidential election, June 2005 – voting by province

Province	Mahmoud Ahmadinejad	Mehdi Karroubi	Ali Larijani	Mohsen Mehralizadeh	Mostafa Moin	Muhammad Bagher Qalibaf	Akbar Hashemi Rafsanjani	Total
Ardabil	34,090 (7.2%)	53,906 (11.3%)	7,766 (1.6%)	111,465 (23.4%)	67,134 (14.1%)	106,272 (22.3%)	95,490 (20.1%)	476,123
Azarbayjan-e Gharbi (West)	75,319 (9.5%)	99,766 (12.6%)	15,435 (1.9%)	163,091 (20.6%)	146,941 (18.5%)	141,289 (17.8%)	151,525 (19.1%)	793,336
Azarbayjan-e Sharqi (East)	198,417 (15.2%)	121,969 (9.3%)	28,075 (2.1%)	378,604 (28.9%)	190,211 (14.5%)	122,160 (9.3%)	268,954 (20.6%)	1,308,390
Bushehr	82,376 (20.3%)	98,148 (24.1%)	8,207 (2.0%)	4,942 (1.2%)	68,547 (16.9%)	46,962 (11.6%)	97,412 (24.0%)	406,594
Chahar Mahall Va Bakhtiari	90,960 (24.8%)	75,044 (20.5%)	23,127 (6.3%)	5,051 (1.4%)	48,356 (13.2%)	64,058 (17.5%)	59,521 (16.3%)	366,127
Esfahan	801,635 (45.6%)	196,512 (11.2%)	73,452 (4.2%)	30,325 (1.7%)	196,261 (11.2%)	198,409 (11.3%)	260,858 (14.8%)	1,757,452
Fars	242,535 (13.7%)	546,633 (30.9%)	61,383 (3.5%)	22,440 (1.3%)	217,122 (12.3%)	273,542 (15.5%)	403,074 (22.8%)	1,766,729

cont....

Table 5. *cont.*

CANDIDATES

Province	Mahmoud Ahmadinejad	Mehdi Karroubi	Ali Larijani	Mohsen Mehralizadeh	Mostafa Moin	Muhammad Bagher Qalibaf	Akbar Hashemi Rafsanjani	Total
Gilan	149,026 (14.8%)	203,941 (20.3%)	50,070 (5.0%)	33,996 (3.4%)	182,321 (18.1%)	171,562 (17.0%)	215,478 (21.4%)	1,006,394
Golestan	56,776 (8.1%)	193,570 (27.6%)	42,334 (6.0%)	8,283 (1.2%)	156,862 (22.4%)	87,522 (12.5%)	155,498 (22.2%)	700,845
Hamadan	195,030 (24.7%)	218,018 (27.6%)	24,002 (3.0%)	20,496 (2.6%)	84,424 (10.7%)	72,986 (9.2%)	175,997 (22.3%)	790,953
Hormozgan	81,054 (13.5%)	177,413 (29.6%)	78,161 (13.0%)	9,679 (1.6%)	153,648 (25.6%)	25,326 (4.2%)	75,601 (12.6%)	599,982
Ilam	32,383 (11.2%)	108,627 (37.6%)	6,783 (2.3%)	3,026 (1.0%)	56,526 (19.6%)	41,082 (14.2%)	40,580 (14.0%)	289,007
Kerman	129,284 (11.2%)	152,764 (13.2%)	221,219 (19.1%)	9,697 (0.8%)	52,896 (4.6%)	112,056 (9.7%)	480,271 (41.5%)	1,158,187
Kermanshah	70,117 (9.8%)	254,780 (35.5%)	22,033 (3.1%)	12,516 (1.7%)	106,804 (14.9%)	115,439 (16.1%)	137,010 (19.1%)	718,699

cont....

cont.....

Khorasan-e Jarubi (South)	101,638 (35.6%)	27,705 (9.7%)	5,716 (2.0%)	4,958 (1.7%)	39,276 (13.8%)	49,043 (17.2%)	57,244 (20.0%)	285,580
Khorasan-e Razavi	377,732 (15.0%)	297,967 (11.8%)	78,976 (3.1%)	33,488 (1.3%)	325,281 (12.9%)	877,665 (34.8%)	527,707 (21.0%)	2,518,816
Khorasan-e Shemali	22,954 (6.6%)	89,551 (25.9%)	16,900 (4.9%)	8,209 (2.4%)	37,330 (10.8%)	100,091 (29.0%)	70,407 (20.4%)	345,442
Khuzestan	232,874 (15.9%)	538,735 (36.7%)	58,564 (4.0%)	20,164 (1.4%)	148,529 (10.1%)	148,234 (10.1%)	319,921 (21.8%)	1,467,021
Kohgiluyeh Va Buyer Ahmad	34,396 (11.0%)	96,459 (30.9%)	20,306 (6.5%)	1,572 (0.5%)	50,954 (16.3%)	52,259 (16.7%)	56,154 (18.0%)	312,100
Kordestan	22,353 (6.4%)	111,249 (32.0%)	10,261 (3.0%)	7,785 (2.2%)	92,884 (27.3%)	48,913 (14.1%)	54,004 (15.5%)	347,449
Lorestan	69,710 (8.8%)	440,247 (55.5%)	31,169 (3.9%)	6,865 (0.9%)	53,747 (6.8%)	70,225 (8.9%)	121,130 (15.3%)	793,093
Markazi	161,669 (28.0%)	104,522 (18.1%)	17,258 (3.0%)	14,058 (2.4%)	65,592 (11.3%)	71,828 (12.4%)	143,118 (24.8%)	578,045
Mazandaran	159,291 (12.0%)	103,229 (7.8%)	464,891 (35.1%)	18,467 (1.4%)	148,408 (11.2%)	116,763 (8.8%)	311,949 (23.6%)	1,322,998

Table 5. *cont.*

CANDIDATES

Province	Mahmoud Ahmadinejad	Mehdi Karroubi	Ali Larijani	Mohsen Mehralizadeh	Mostafa Moin	Muhammad Bagher Qalibaf	Akbar Hashemi Rafsanjani	Total
Qazvin	118,414 (23.8%)	81,569 (16.4%)	24,649 (5.0%)	18,078 (3.6%)	68,366 (13.7%)	77,399 (15.6%)	108,928 (21.9%)	497,403
Qom	256,110 (55.2%)	25,282 (5.4%)	10,894 (2.3%)	14,451 (3.1%)	27,824 (6.05)	25,792 (5.5%)	104,004 (22.4%)	464,357
Semnan	98,024 (34.8%)	25,899 (9.2%)	28,190 (10.0%)	3,873 (1.4%)	26,572 (9.4)	37,059 (13.25)	69,773 (24.8%)	281,390
Sistan Va Baluchestan	47,743 (5.6%)	77,017 (9.0%)	24,954 (2.9%)	7,312 (0.9%)	479,125 (55.7%)	68,605 (8.0%)	155,147 (18.0%)	859,903
Tehran	1,500,829 (30.1%)	415,187 (8.3%)	246,167 (4.9%)	281,748 (5.7%)	648,598 (13.0%)	614,381 (12.3%)	1,274,276 (25.6%)	4,981,186
Yazd	175,206 (38.7%)	58,132 (12.8%)	9,317 (2.1%)	5,186 (1.1%)	60,510 (13.4%)	66,892 (14.8%)	77,924 (17.2%)	453,167
Zanjan	93,309 (20.8%)	62,845 (14.0%)	22,869 (5.1%)	18,568 (4.1%)	68,649 (15.3%)	71,365 (15.9%)	110,698 (24.7%)	448,303

Source: Iranian Interior Ministry, *http://psephos.adam-carr.net/countries/i/iran/iran20052.txt*, 2 July 2005.

Table 6. Voter turnout in the ninth presidential elections, 2005 (sorted after the Ahmadinejad results in the first round)

Province	ROUND 1			ROUND 2		
	Turnout (%)	MA*(%)	HR**(%)	Turnout (%)	MA*(%)	HR**(%)
Azerbaijan(East)	51.25	14.51	19.67	46.8	67.98	29.55
Azerbaijan(West)	44.02	8.93	17.96	37.5	60.18	35.13
Ardabil	54.15	6.93	19.40	49.00	62.93	34.71
Isfahan	58.62	4.64	14.21	59.60	71.83	25.78
Ilam	80.43	10.82	13.55	66.76	51.21	45.81
Tehran	63.68	28.63	24.31	65.20	61.11	28.32
Khorasan (Razawi)	70.99	14.85	20.40	51.25	60.76	35.70
Khorasan (south)	78.59	34.94	19.68	71.88	66.30	32.32
Khorasan(North)	63.55	6.4	19.77	55.67	59.75	38.59
Markazi	62.09	26.79	23.72	60.63	69.70	28.32
Chahar Mahal and Bakhtiari	64.85	22.35	16.17	64.34	71.80	26.49
Bushehr	72.33	19.59	23.16	66.49	55.81	41.82
Khuzestan	55.33	14.85	20.40	51.25	60.76	35.70
Zanjan	65.25	20.06	23.80	61.03	67.62	30.47
Semnan	73.48	33.16	23.60	74.22	71.69	26.18
Sistan and Baluchistan	74.44	5.6	17.74	63.76	44.37	54.35

cont....

165

Table 6. cont.

Province	Round1			Round 2		
	Turnout (%)	MA*(%)	HR**(%)	Turnout (%)	MA*(%)	HR**(%)
Fars	61.36	13.18	21.90	58.52	64.35	32.98
Qazvin	69.23	22.69	20.88	67.04	72.81	25.45
Qum	77.01	53.38	21.68	77.27	73.16	25.05
Gilan	58.40	14.03	20.29	58.52	64.35	32.98
Kerman	77.98	10.85	40.32	77.86	50.71	4.97
Kermanshah	55.38	9.6	17.91	51.20	48.60	4.03
Kehkelwi and Boyer Ahmad	78.48	10.81	17.65	76.11	61.23	32.24
Hormozgan	78.39	12.99	12.25	67.49	59.67	37.70
Mazandaran	65.19	11.58	22.68	65.26	64.57	33.50
Lorestan	67.17	8.4	14.84	60.41	49.70	47.77
Golestan	65.17	8.54	14.84	60.41	49.70	47.77
Kordestan	37.37	5.79	14.00	24.96	49.61	42.37
Hamadan	62.34	22.69	20.88	67.04	72.81	25.45
Yazd	76.02	36.95	16.43	75.49	66.82	30.77

* MA: Mahmoud Ahmadinejad
** HR: Hashemi Rafsanjani

Source: *www.isna.ir*, 28 June 2005.

Table 7. Final result of the ninth presidential race, 2005

Candidate	Votes cast (%)	
	Round 1	Round 2
Mahmoud Ahmadinejad	19.5	64.0
Hashemi Rafsanjani	21.1	36.0
Mehdi Karroubi	17.3	-
Muhammad Baqer Qalibaf	13.9	-
Mostafa Moin	13.8	-
Ali Larijani	5.9	-
Mohsen Mehralizadeh	4.4	-
Cancelled voters	4.2	-

Source: *www.rferl.org/featuresarticle*, 26 June 2005.

Table 8. Results of the eighth presidential election, 8 June 2001

Candidates	Votes	(%)
Muhammad Khatami	21,656,476	78.3
Ahmad Tavakoli	4,387,112	15.9
Ali Shamkhani	737,051	2.7
Abdollah Jasbi	259,759	0.9
Mahmud Kashani	237,660	0.9
Hassan Ghafuri-Fard	129,155	0.5
Mansur Razavi	114,616	0.4
Dr Shahabeddin Sadr	60,546	0.2
Ali Fallahian	55,225	0.2
Mostafa Hashemi-Taba	27,949	0.1

Source: *www.electionguide.org/results.php?ID=542*, 15 June 2001

Table 9. Voter turnout in presidential elections in Iran, 1980–2005

Winner	Eligible voters	Turnout (%)	Date
Mahmoud Ahmadinejad	28,000,000	64.00	June 2005
Muhammad Khatami	42,697,054	63.00	June 2001
Muhammad Khatami	34,909,620	83.49	May 1997
Ali Akbar Hashemi Rafsanjani	33,156,055	50.66	June 1993
Ali Akbar Hashemi Rafsanjani	30,139,589	54.59	July 1989
Ali Khamenei	25,933,802	54.90	August 1985
Ali Khamenei	22,439,930	94.40	October 1981
Muhammad Ali Rajai	22,439,930	64.95	August 1981
Abol Hassan Banisader	20,857,391	67.86	January 1980

Source: *www.rferl.org*, 30 June 2005.

Table 10. Approval figures for Ahmadinejad's first Cabinet

cont....

Candidate Minister	Ministry	Approvals	Denials	Abstentions
Muhammad Reza Eskandari	Agriculture	214	45	24
Masoud Mirkazemi	Commerce	169	85	25
Muhammad Hossein Saffar Harandi	Culture and Islamic Guidance	181	78	20
Mostafa Muhammad-Najjar	Defence and Logistics	205	55	17
Davoud Danesh-Jafari	The Economy and Financial Affairs	216	47	19
Parviz Fattah	Energy	194	56	23
Manouchehr Mottaki	Foreign Affairs	220	47	16
Kamaran Bagheri Lankarani	Health and Medical Education	169	86	27
Mohamma Saeedikia	Housing and Urban Development	222	31	25
Alireza Tahmasbi	Industries and Mines	182	58	30
Gholam-Hossein Mohseni-Ejehei	Intelligence	217	51	13
Mostafa Pour Muhammadi	Interior	153	9C	31
Jamal Karimi-Rad	Justice	191	5⁹	24
Muhammad Jahromi	Labour and Social Affairs	197	5⁹	20

Table 10. *cont.*

Candidate Minister	Ministry	Approvals	Denials	Abstentions
Muhammad Rahmati	Roads and Transportation	214	43	21
Muhammad Mehdi Zahedi	Science Research and Technology	144	101	36
Ali Saeedlou (first choice)	Petroleum	101	133	38
Mohsen Tasalloti (second choice)	Petroleum	77	139	38
Kazem Vaziri-Hamaneh (approved minister)	Petroleum	172	53	34
Alireza Ali-Ahamadi (first choice)	Cooperatives	105	134	34
Muhammad Nazim-Ardakani (approved minister)	Cooperatives	174	51	11
Ali Akbar Ash'ari (first choice)	Education	73	175	31
Mahmoud Farshedi (approved minister)	Education	136	91	21
Mehdi Hashmi	Welfare and Social Security	131	108	36
Parviz Kazemi (approved minister)	Welfare and Social Security	178	61	15

Source: *http://www.freerepublic.com/focus/f-news/1524384/*, 18 November 2005.

NOTES

INTRODUCTION

1   Some of the dates cited in this book provide the date in the Iranian calendar first followed by the Gregorian (Western) calendar in parentheses.

CHAPTER I
REFORM IN IRAN – WHAT WENT WRONG?

1   Gheissari, Ali and Vali Nasr, *Democracy in Iran: History and the Quest for Liberty* (Oxford: Oxford University Press, 2006).

2   Jahanbakhsh, Forough, 'Religious and political discourse in Iran: moving toward post-fundamentalism', *The Brown Journal of World Affairs*, ix/2, (2003), p.243.

3   Berman, Ilan, *Understanding Ahmadinejad* (Washington: American Foreign Policy Council, June 2006).

4   Deputy speaker of Sixth Majlis (Parliament).

5   Former interior minister.

6   Former intelligence officer, Islamic Revolutionary Guard Corps (IRGC).

7   Former commander, IRGC, based in Lebanon.

8   One of the leaders who lead the attacking of the American Embassy in 1979.

9   Former high-ranking IRGC officer.

10   Editor of *Salaam* newspaper, Tehran.

11   Prominent member of the group of students who attacked the American Embassy in 1979.

12   Former senior commander of IRGC ground forces.

13   Buchta, Wilfried, *Who Rules Iran: The Structure of Power in the Islamic Republic*, (Washington: Washington Institute for Near East Policy, 2000), pp.17–19.

14   He was sent to prison for 30 months for 'insulting Islamic values'.

15   The Islamic Revolutionary Guards Corps (IRGC), also known as the 'Pasdaran' (meaning 'guardian'), was established in Iran after the 1979 revolution.

16   See *http://freethoughts.org/archives/0006665.php*.

17   Ibid.

18   At that time, Mahjoob Zweiri was at Tehran University and remembers that most of the reformist elite were attacking President Khatami, accusing him of weakness and asking him to resign. The reasons for accusing him were described in several newspapers, and journalists were arrested, detained and persecuted for their writings. In the same speech he said that it is not wisdom to say everything you know. This message was clear: he had his arrangements to tackle these obstacles, but he could not tell everything.

19   Ayatollah Ali Khamenei has shown his anger for pro-reform newspapers in statements such as: 'Critique and criticism of the government's polices are not bad, but when someone attempts to undermine the foundations of the government, it is treason and not freedom of expression'; 'I am giving a final notice to officials to act and see which newspapers violate the limits of freedom'; 'I am now waiting to see what the officials will do. Stopping these vicious actions is not difficult and I do not care what international organizations will say. We will never care about them.' See *http://freethoughts.org/archives/0006665.php*.

20   This policy was used against newspapers even before Khatami came to power in May 1997. Key events include:

- January 1997: Chief Editor of *Adineh Faraj Sirkuhi* convicted for spreading propaganda against the Islamic Republic of Iran.
- June 1997: Prominent Iranian newspaper editor Morteza Firoozi arrested, held on espionage charges and sentenced to death.
- June 1998: *Jameh* suspended.
- July 1998: Publisher of *Khaneh*, M.R. Zaeri, was arrested, imprisoned, had his licence revoked and was accused him of insulting Islam and publishing photos contrary to public decency.

- August 1998: *Tous* banned.
- August 1998: *Rah-e No* and *Tavana* suspended because they questioned Khomeini's authority.
- September 1998: *Jameh Salem* suspended.
- September 1998: *Asr-e Ma* suspended.

For more details, see *http://freethoughts.org/archives/0006665.php*; *www.rsf.org*; *Daily Telegraph* (London, 9 April 2002); and *www.polpiran.com/reporter2001.htm* (Amnesty International Report, 2001).

21 There are many Iranian intellectuals who were sent to prison because of their involvement in the reform movement :

- Hojjatoleslam Hasan Yousefi Eshkeveri, director of the Ali Shariati Research Centre. He also was a contributor to the magazine *Iran-e Farda*. Arrested 5 August 2000. (Berlin Conference.)
- Akbar Ganji, journalist. (Berlin Conference.)
- Mehrangiz Kar, human rights activist and lawyer. (Berlin Conference.)
- Shahal Lahiji, publisher. (Berlin Conference.)
- Khalil Rostmhkani, translator. (Berlin Conference.)
- Ezzatollah Sahabi, Editor of *Iran-e Farda*. (Berlin Conference.)
- Massoud Behnoud, writer in *Asr-e Azadegan* (Era of the Free) and *Danestani-ha* (Worth Knowing).
- Muhammad Ghoutchani, *Asr-e Azadegan* (Era of the Free).
- Ibrahim Nabavi, journalist and popular satirist.
- Ahmed Zeidabadi, journalist.
- Muhammad Mosavi-Khoeniha, students' activist.
- Emadeddin Bagi, journalist and contemporary historian.
- Akbar Ganji, sent to prison for five years. 'The troublemaker', as he calls himself, argues that Iran's intelligence ministry was behind the killing of those intellectuals because they knew too much about the government's dirty dealings. Lately he signed that ex-president Rafsanjani had valuable information on those murders.

Others were killed:

- Majid Sharif, who was writing in *Iran-e-Farda*, disappeared in October 1998. His body was found later. Killed because of his criticism of the regime and its policies.
- Muhammad Mokhtari disappeared in December 1998 and his body was found later. Killed because of his criticism of the regime and its policies.

- Muhammad-Jafar Pouyandeh, his body was found on 11 December 1998.

- Daryush Forhar and his wife Parvaneh Fourher were stabbed on 22 November 1998. Daryush Forhar was running a modest opposition party. See *www.freemedia.at/bitter.htm* and *www.iranian.com*. The file on this has been closed with the killing of Said Imami (who was accused of giving the orders) in his prison , and later on 'Mostafa Kazemi and Mehrdad Alikhani, former intelligence officials, were sentenced to ten years each in prison' (see *www.news.bbc.co.uk*).

22   *Hambastegi*, No. 145, 9 April 2001. See also Abili, Muhammad, 'Internet and cultural growth in Iran: opportunities and challenges', *Discourse*, iii/3 (2002), pp.101–19; 'History of the Internet in Iran', *Etemad* (Persian morning daily), 18 January 2003; Emrooz, Payman, 'Tehranis also go to Internet cafés', *Social, Economic & Cultural* 35 (1999), pp.50–2.

23   See 'Iran Internet use at risk from conservatives', *www.16beaveergroup. org/mtarchive/archives/*, 18 June 2003. The Iranian government closed more than 400 (out of 1500) cybercafés in Tehran, and asked for new measures to control Internet usage. Theses measures have focused on use of the Internet for political purposes, or visiting sites that affect the Islamic values. 'On November 2001, the Supreme Council of the Cultural Revolution, chaired by president Khatami but dominated by Right wing, ordered all privately-owned Internet Service Providers (ISPs) to shut down or put themselves under government control.' For more see 'Iran', *www.rsf.org* and Hammersley, Ben, 'Iran nets another revolt', *Guardian*, 21 February 2002.

24   *Hambastegi*, No. 145, 9 April 2001.

25   *Agence France Presse*, 2 June 2003.

26   *Farsi*, 14 April 2004.

27   Amuzegar, Jahangir, 'Khatami and the Iranian economy at mid-term', *Middle East Journal*, liii/4 (1999), at *www.sharghnewspaper.com/821010/ polit.htm*.

28   Amuzegar, Jahangir, 'Iran's privatization saga', *Middle East Economic Survey*, xlv/24 (2002), at *http://memri.org/bin/articles.cgi?Page=archives& Area=ia&ID=IA22905*.

29   Farhadian, Mahdy, 'Beyond Khatami's reform era: economic Talibanization or liberalization?', *Iran Analysis Quarterly*, i/2 (2004), pp.7–10.

30   Clawson, Patrick: 'Impact of World Bank Loans to Iran', *www. financialservices.house.org*, 29 October 2003.

31   Ibid.

32   Hooshang, Amirahmadi, 'Current state of civil society in Iran', *Iran Nameh* xiv (winter 1995), pp.79–106 [in Farsi].

33 Sohrab, Behdad, 'From populism to economic liberalism: the Iranian predicament', in Parvin Alizadeh (ed.) *The Economy of Iran: The Dilemmas of an Islamic State* (London: I.B.Tauris, 2000), pp.100–41.

34 The interview was apparently given to *al-Hayat* but it received wide coverage in Iran itself. See *Ettela'at*, 23 June 1997. Rezaie relinquished his position as Commander of the Sepah in September 1997 and soon joined the Expediency Council under the chairmanship of the former President Rafsanjani.

35 With some 20 million votes, Khatami secured 69 per cent of the almost 30 million votes cast in the election, compared with Nateq-Nouri's figure of just 26 per cent. For an analysis of the reformist front's key ideologues see Sadri, Ahmad, 'Still alive: varieties of religious reform in Iran', *The Iranian*, 4 February 2002.

36 It is noteworthy that the commander of the Joint Staff, Brigadier General Firouzabadi, issued a statement in May 1998 criticizing the commander of the Sepah for adopting an overtly political line on domestic issues and for allowing the Sepah to become embroiled in politics. See late April and early May 1998 editions of *Resalat*, *Salam* and *Keyhan*.

37 See *The Echo of Iran*, No. 119, May 1998 at *www.iranalmanac.com*.

38 Reuters, 4 June 1998.

39 See Eisenstadt, Michael, 'The armed forces of the Islamic Republic of Iran: an assessment', in Barry Rubin and Thomas A. Keaney (eds) *Armed Forces in the Middle East: Politics and Strategy* (London: Frank Cass, 2002), pp.231–57.

40 See *The Echo of Iran*, No. 156, January 2002 at *www.iranalmanac.com*. An 80-page pamphlet detailing the clandestine structures and violent activities of the Sepah and intelligence-related personnel was openly circulated in 2000.

41 Some MPs and former MPs have referred to these organs as extra-constitutional and illegal, demanding that they be disbanded. See statement published in reformist paper, *Mardomsalari*, 14 January 2002.

42 Rahman, Hassan Abdul , 'Perspective: comments unworthy of our elite commander', *Iran*, 2 May 1998.

43 Reuters, 26 November 1998 at *www.iranalmanac.com*. Safavi had stated with alarm in 1998 that, 'liberals have taken over our universities and our youth are chanting "Death to Dictatorship" slogans'.

44 The letter is dated 12 July and reached the president's office on 13 July. *Kayhan* and *Jomhuri-ye Islami* newspapers published the text of it in their 19 July 1999 editions.

45 *Iran Report*, Radio Free Europe/Radio Liberty, 19 July 1999.

46 For a detailed discussion of Ayatollah Khomeini's political thought see Brumberg, Daniel, *Reinventing Khomeini: The Struggle for Reform in Iran*

(Chicago: University of Chicago Press, 2001); Martin, Vanessa, *Creating an Islamic State: Khomeini and the Making of a New Iran* (London: I.B.Tauris, 2001); and Moin, Baqir, *Khomeini: Life of the Ayatollah* (London: I.B.Tauris, 1999).

47   See Byman, Daniel, Shahram Cubin, Anoushiravan Ehteshami and Jerrold D. Green, *Iran's Security Policy in the Post-Revolutionary Era* (Santa Monica, CA: RAND, 2001), p.47.

48   See *The Echo of Iran*, No. 130, July 1999, at *www.iranalmanac.com*.

49   Hunter, Shireen, *Iran after Khomeini* (Washington: Praeger, 1992) pp.14–15.

50   It was quite clear that the *Faqih* was originally instated to provide constitutional basis for Khomeini's leadership. Now, with the demise of Khomeini, nobody could claim the religious and political qualifications that Khomeini held himself ... another change about the *Faqih* was that the "single *Faqih*" doctrine was newly introduced by removing the three or five leadership, or the Council of Leadership, clause from the constitution. This doctrine was apparently formulated in order to minimize instability at the highest level in the post-Khomeini era.

(See 'Politics of Theocracy in Iran', at *www.arabia.co.kr/en/docs/Iran-theocracy.htm*.)

51   Article 107 states:

After the demise of the eminent marji' al-taqlid and great leader of the universal Islamic Revolution, and founder of the Islamic Republic of Iran, al-'Uzma Imam Khumayni – quddisa sirruh al-sharif – who was recognized and accepted as marji' and Leader by a decisive majority of the people, the task of appointing the leader shall be vested with the experts elected by the people. The experts will review and consult among themselves concerning all the fuqaha' possessing the qualifications specified in Articles 5 and 109. In the event they find one of them better versed in Islamic regulations, the subjects of the fiqh, or in political and social issues, or possessing general popularity or special prominence for any of the qualifications mentioned in Article 109, they shall elect him as the leader. Otherwise, in the absence of such superiority, they shall elect and declare one of them as the leader. The Leader thus elected by the Assembly of Experts shall assume all the powers of the wilayat al-amr and all the responsibilities arising therefrom. The Leader is equal with the rest of the people of the country in the eyes of law.

(See *www.salamiran.org/IranInfo/State/Constitution/*)

52   Article 109 states that

Following are the essential qualifications and conditions for the leader: Scholarship, as required for performing the functions of mufti in different fields of fiqh, justice and piety, as required for the leadership of the Islamic Ummah. Right political and social perspicacity, prudence, courage, administrative facilities and adequate capability for leadership. In case of multiplicity of persons fulfilling the above qualifications and conditions, the person possessing the better jurisprudential and political perspicacity will be given preference.

(See *www.salamiran.org/IranInfo/State/Constitution/*)

Because of these qualifications, which include the religious aspects, the Leader tends to acquire unlimited authority. He also has to monitor the political process in the country. These responsibilities became clear in Article 110 of the Iranian constitution. Article 110 states that

Following are the duties and powers of the leadership: delineation of the general policies of the Islamic Republic of Iran after consultation with the Nation's Exigency Council, supervision over the proper execution of the general policies of the system, issuing decrees for national referenda, assuming supreme command of the armed forces, declaration of war and peace and the mobilization of the armed forces. Appointment, dismissal and acceptance of the resignation of: (1) the fuqaha' on the Guardian Council; (2) the supreme judicial authority of the country; (3) the head of the radio and television network of the Islamic Republic of Iran; (4) the chief of the joint staff; (5) the chief commander of the Islamic Revolution Guards Corps; and (6) the supreme commanders of the armed forces. In addition to that: resolving differences between the three wings of the armed forces and regulation of their relations, resolving the problems, which cannot be solved by conventional methods, through the Nation's Exigency Council, and signing the decree formalizing the election of the President of the Republic by the people. The suitability of candidates for the Presidency of the Republic, with respect to the qualifications specified in the constitution, must be confirmed before elections take place by the Guardian Council, and, in the case of the first term [of the Presidency], by the Leadership; dismissal of the President of the Republic, with due regard for the interests of the country, after the Supreme Court holds him guilty of the violation of his constitutional duties, or after a vote of the Islamic Consultative Assembly testifying to his incompetence on the basis of Article 89 of the Constitution, and pardoning or reducing the sentences of convicts, within the framework of Islamic criteria, on a recommendation [to that effect] from the Head of judicial power. The

Leader may delegate part of his duties and powers to another person.

(See *www.salamiran.org/IranInfo/State/Constitution/*)

53   Montazari's booklet, 'Hukumat-i mardumi va qanun-i Asasi' [popular government and the constitution] includes his thought about supervision of the jurist. See Bellaigue, Christopher de, 'Iran's last chance for reform', *Washington Quarterly*, autumn 2001, pp.73,75 (at *www.shianews.com*).

54   Arjomand, Said Amir, 'The reform movement and the debate on modernity and tradition in contemporary Iran', *International Journal of the Middle East* 34 (2002), p.728.

55   See n.52.

56   Mojtahed Shabestary has written *A Critique of the Official Reading of Religion* (Tehran: Tarh e No Publications, 2000). His book represents one of the important outputs of reform-era Iran. See also Sadri, Mahmoud, 'Sacral defense of secularism: the political theologies of Soroush, Shabestry, and Kadivar', *International Journal of Politics, Culture and Society* xv/2 (2001), p.261.

57   Jahanbakhsh: 'Religious and political discourse in Iran', p.249.

58   Mahmoud Sadri has summarized the following theories. Theocratic theories include:

1. *Saltantant e Mashroueh*: 'Appointed mandate of jurisconsult in religious matters (*shar'iat*) along with the monarchic mandate of Muslim potentates in secular matters.' This theory has been proposed by well-known Shia *Faqih* such as Muhammad Baqer Majlesi, Ayatollah Abdolkarim and Haeri Yazdi.

2. *Velayat e Entesabi ye Ammeh*: 'General appointed mandate of jurisconsults.' Mulla Ahmed Naragi and Khomeini (before the revolution) supported this theory.

3. *Velayat e Entesabi ye Ammeh ye Sora ye Marje'eh Taqlid*: 'General appointed mandate of the council of the "sources of imitation".' This theory has been proposed by Ayatollah such as Javad Amoli, Beheshti and Thaheri Khorram Abadi.

4. *Velayyet e Entesabi ye Motlaghe ye Faghihan*: 'Absolute appointed mandate of jurisconsult'. Ayatollah Khomeini (after the revolution) had proposed this theory.

Democratic theories include:

1. *Dowlat e Mashrouteh*: 'Constitutional State' (with the permission and supervision of jurisprudents). This theory has been proposed by Shaikh Esma'il Mahllati, Ayatollah Mazabdarni and Tehrani, Tabataba'i.

2. *Khelafat e Mardom ba Nezarat e Marjaiat*: 'Popular stewardship along with clerical oversight'. Ayatollah Muhammad Bagher Sadar has proposed this theory.

3. *Dowalt e Entekhabi e Eslami*: 'Islamic elective state'. Ayatollah Khomeini had proposed this theory after the revolution.

4. *Vekalat e Malekan e Shakhsi ye Mosha*: 'Collective government by proxy. This theory has been proposed by Ayatollah Mehdi Ha'eri Yazdi. See Sadri: 'Sacral defense of secularism', pp.263–4.

59 *Ettela'at International*, 30 January 2006.

CHAPTER II
THE NEOCONSERVATIVES' MARCH TO POWER

1 See 'Iran prepares for first-ever local elections', BBC News, at *http://news. billinge.com*, 10 February 1999; Rabiee, Lara, 'Not in the mood: Iran's local councils elections, four years later', at *www.iranian.com*, 13 February 2003.

2 Article 100 states

'in order to expedite social, economic, development, public health, cultural, and educational programs and facilitate other affairs relating to public welfare with the cooperation of the people according to local needs, the administration of each village, division, city, municipality, and province will be supervised by the council to be named the village, Division, City, Municipality, or Provincial Council. Members of each of these councils will be elected by the people of the locality in question. Qualifications for the eligibility of electors and the candidates for these councils, as well as their functions and powers, the mode of election, the jurisdiction of theses councils, the hierarchy of their authority, will be determined by law, in such a way as to preserve national unity, territorial integrity, the system of the Islamic Republic, and the sovereignty of the central government.'

(See 'The Constitution of Islamic Republic of Iran' at *www.iranchamber. com*)

3 Rabiee: 'Not in the mood'.

4 Ibid.

5 Abdo, Geneive, 'Electoral politics in Iran', *Middle East Policy*, vi/4 (1999), at *www.mepc.org/journal_vol6/9906_abdo.asp*.

6 Ibid.

7 See 'Iran polls are test for reformers', BBC News, at *http://news.bbc.co.uk*, 28 February 2003; Rabiee: 'Not in the mood'.

8   Takeyh, Ray, 'Iran's municipal elections: a turning point for the reform movement?', at *www.washingtoninstitute.org*, 6 March 2003.

9   'Councils elections, challenges and perspectives', at *www.isna.ir*, 3 May 2003; Takeyh: 'Iran's municipal elections'.

10 'Iran reformers suffer poll blow', BBC News, at *http://news.bbc.co.uk* , 2 March 2003.

11 'Iran polls are test for reformers', BBC News, at *http://news.bbc.co.uk*, 28 February 2003. A new debate started after the election of Ahamadinejad in June 2005, about allowing the Guardian Council to monitor the councils elections (local elections). Ahmadinejad's government has proposed a new law that allows the Guardian Council to control the whole issue of councils elections. As it is known elements such qualifying candidates will be the main task that the Guardian Council should deal with before every Iranian election. See 'Monitoring councils elections process has been debated to be transferred to the Guardian Council', at *www. iran-emrooz.net* , 17 May 2006.

12 'Rafsanjani: in analysing councils elections' results look for realities', at *www.payvand.com* , 3 August 2003.

13 Ibid. See also Samii, Abbas William, 'Dissent in Iranian elections: reasons and implications', *Middle East Journal*, lviii/3 (2004), pp.402–23.

14 See 'Rafsanjani: in analysing councils elections results look for realities', at *www.payvand.com*, 3 August 2003.

15 Saghfi, Morad, 'The reform nobody wants anymore', *Islam Review*, 15 (2005), at *www.isim.nl*.

16 Abdo: 'Electoral politics in Iran'.

17 Amuzegar, Jahangir., 'Iran's prospect under the 7th Majlis', *Middle East Economic Survey*, xlvii/17 (April 2004).

18 'Round 12 for Iran's Reformists', Middle East Report Online, at *www. merip.org/mero/mero012904.html*, 29 January 2004.

19 El-Labbad, Mustafa, 'His first 100 days', *Al Ahram* 771, 1–7 December 2005.

20 Ghammari, Behrooz, 'How the reformists lost the presidency – what's the matter with Iran?', at *www.iranian.com*, 5 July 2005.

21 See 'Iran: what does Ahmadinejad's victory mean?', International Crisis Group, at *www.crisisgroup.org/.../iraq_iran_gulf/b18_iran_what_does_ahmadi_nejad_victory_mean.pdf*, 4 August 2005.

22 Most of whom were disqualified by the Guardian Council, which holds the power of veto over all political candidates in Iran.

23 Ghammari: 'How the reformists lost the presidency'.

24 See 'Iran's presidential coup', at *www.opendemocracy.net*, 27 June 2005.

25 'Iran hardliner sweeps to victory', BBC News, at *http://news.bbc.co.uk/2/ hi/middle_east/4621249.stm*, 25 June 2005.

26 Ibid.

27 Ibid.

28 For a comprehensive overview of the election results, including regional turnouts, see Tables 5–9 in the Appendix.

CHAPTER III
THE AHMADINEJAD PHENOMENON

1 Ghammari, Behrooz, 'How the reformists lost the presidency – what's the matter with Iran?', at *www.iranian.com*, 5 July 2005.

2 Interview with Hamid Taqvee, broadcast in English on Iranian television, 26 June 2005.

3 See *www.globalsecurity.org/military/world/iran/ahmadinejad.htm*, 22 March 2006.

4 Tait, Robert, 'A humble beginning helped to form Iran's new hard man', *Guardian*, 2 July 2005.

5 Ibid.

6 Ibid.

7 See 'Iran's new president has a past mired in controversy', at *www.iranfocus.com/modules/news/article.php?storyid=2606*, 25 June 2005.

8 See *www.iranfocus.com/modules/news/article.php?storyid=2606*, 25 June 2005.

9 Branigin, William and Robin Wright, 'Ex-hostages finger Iran's president-elect', *Washington Post*, 10 June 2005.

10 Tait: 'A humble beginning'.

11 Ibid.

12 Ibid.

13 See *www.answers.com/topic/mahmoud-ahmadinejad*, 22 March 2006.

14 See 'Iran's new president has a past mired in controversy' at *www.iranfocus.com/modules/news/article.php?storyid=2606*, 25 June 2005.

15 Ibid.

16 Ibid.

17 See 'Former hostages allege Iran's new President was captor' at *www.cnn.com*, 30 June 2005.

18 See 'Mahmoud Ahmadinejad', at *www.globalsecurity.org*, 6 June 2006.

19 Ibid.

20 See *www.payvand.com/news/03/apr/1142.html*, 29 April 2003.

21 Savyon, Avelet, 'Iran's "Second Islamic Revolution": fulfilled by election of conservative president', Middle East Media Research Institute, at

http://memri.org/bin/articles.cgi?Page=archives&Area=ia&ID=IA22905, 4 July 2005.

22   This organization now has 114 members, all political parties certified by the Interior Ministry.

23   For a discussion of House of Parties election, see article by Nargess Ebrahimi in *Shargh* at *www.sharghnewspaper.com/821010/polit.htm*, 31 December 2003.

24   Savyon: 'Iran's "Second Islamic Revolution"'.

25   See 'The upcoming presidential elections in Iran (Part II)', MEMRI Inquiry and Analysis No. 226, at *http://memri.org/bin/articles.cgi?Page=c ountries&Area=iran&ID=IA22605#_edn28*, 16 June 2005.

26   Savyon: 'Iran's "Second Islamic Revolution"'.

27   *Aftab-e Yazd* , 22 June 2005.

28   *Iran*, 22 December 2005.

29   See *www.sharghnewspaper.com/850620/html/online.htm*, 20 June 2005 and *www.aftabyazd.com/*, 21 June 2005.

30   See 'Iran: what does Ahmadinejad's victory mean?', International Crisis Group, at *www.crisisgroup.org/.../iraq_iran_gulf/b18_iran_what_does_ahmadi_nejad_victory_mean.pdf*, 4 August 2005.

31   See 'The upcoming presidential elections in Iran (Part II)', MEMRI Inquiry and Analysis No. 226, at *http://memri.org/bin/articles.cgi?Page=c ountries&Area=iran&ID=IA22605#_edn28*, 16 June 2005.

32   See *Sharq*, 20 June 2005; *Aftab-e Yazd*, 21 June 2005.

33   *Iran Daily*, at *www.iran-daily.com/1384/*, 1 May 2005.

34   Ibid.

35   See 'Iran leader to set up "Love Fund"', BBC News, at *http://news.bbc. co.uk/2/hi/middle_east/4198906.stm*, 30 August 2005.

36   See 'Iran: what does Ahmadinejad's victory mean?', International Crisis Group, at *www.crisisgroup.org/.../iraq_iran_gulf/b18_iran_what_does_ahmadi_nejad_victory_mean.pdf*, 4 August 2005.

37   Ibid.

38   See *www.president.ir/eng/ahmadinejad/cronicnews/1384/05/12/index-e. htm#b3*. President Mahmoud Ahmadinejad had considered his winning as the second revolution. He thanked after his election 'the blood of the martyrs, a new Islamic Revolution has arisen and the Islamic Revolution of 1384/2005 [the year he won the election] will, if God wills, cut off the roots of injustice in the world'. He believes that 'this wave of the Islamic Revolution will soon reach the entire world'. There is no doubt that this kind of statement from an Iranian politician is new, especially after eight years of reform. There was no mention of the revolution in a global context. See *http://news.gooya.com/President_84*.

39   IRNA, 15 January 2006.

40   See 'Iran president's religious views arouse interest (dangerous ideology)', at *www.freerepublic.com/focus/f-news/1524384/posts*, 18 November 2005.

41   These include prominent figures such as Ali Fallahian (former Minster of Intelligence and National Security); Ahmad Jannati; Ali Younesi (former Minster of Intelligence and National Security); Rouhollah Hosseinian; Gholamhossein Mohseni-Ejehei (Minster of Intelligence and National Security); Mostafa Pour Muhammadi (Interior Minister); Gholamhossein Karbaschi; Ali Razini; Hojjatoleslam Raieesi; Hojjatoleslam Alizadeh; Gholam Reza Naghdi; General Zolghadr; General Allah Karam; Hossein Sharitmadari; Abbas Salimi Namin; Hasan Shaian-Far; Mojtaba Zonnour; Hojjatoleslam Izad-Panah; Hojjatoleslam Meravi; Hojjatoleslam Rahbar; Muhammad Rei-Shahri (former Minister of Intelligence and National Security); Hojjatoleslam Neeiazi; Hojjatoleslam Nezam-Zadeh; Hojjatoleslam Muhammadi-Eraghi; Hojjatoleslam Moalla; Sadeq Ziarati; Mohsen Muhammadi Eraqi; Hojjatoleslam Mir-Sepah; Hojjatoleslam Faker; Ahmad Khatami; Ayatollah Seyyed Hasan taheri Khorramabadi; Ayatollah Javadi Amoli; and Ayatollah Dr Ahmad Ahmadi. See 'Shi'te supremacists emerge from Iran's shadows, from a special correspondent', *Asia Times*, at *www.mesbahyazdi.org*, 9 September 2005.

42   See *www.president.ir/eng/ahmadinejad/cronicnews/1384/05/30/index-e. htm#b4*, 21 August 2005.

43   Aged 46, head of Wheat Self-Sufficiency Programme, founding member of the Jihad Sazandegi, affiliated to the IRGC. See *www.iranfocus.com*, 14 August 2005; *www.khedmat.ir/comments.asp/id=499*.

44   Aged 45, former logistics commander in the IRGC, chairman of IRGC's Centre for Strategic Studies, chancellor of Shahed University (set up exclusively for relatives of 'martyrs' of the Islamic Revolution). See *www. iranfocus.com*, 14 August 2005.

45   Aged 52, former deputy editor-in-chief of ultra-conservative daily *Kayhan*, former brigadier general in the IRGC, former IRGC commander of southern Iran, former director of the Political Bureau of IRGC (for 10 years). See *www.iranfocus.com*, 14 August 2005.

46   Aged 49, brigadier general in the IRGC, joined when it was formed in 1979, took part in the bloody campaign to suppress the Kurds in 1979 and 1980, commander of IRGC operations in Lebanon, Palestinian territories and the Persian Gulf states in the 1980s, head of the Military Industries Organization. See *www.iranfocus.com*, 14 August 2005.

47   Aged 51, chairman of Majlis committee on economy and finance, a leading member of hard-line Islamist faction Abadgaran in the Majlis, former member of the Central Command of the Jihad Sazandegi. See *www. iranfocus.com*, 14 August 2005; *www.khedmat.ir/comments.asp/id=495*.

48   Aged 44, former deputy commander of the Special Division of the IRGC, Imam Hossein University. See *www.iranfocus.com*, 14 August 2005; *www.khedmat.ir/comments.asp/id=508*.

49   Aged 52, chairman of parliamentary Foreign Affairs Committee, former deputy foreign minister and ambassador to Turkey and Japan, former liaison officer between the IRGC and the Foreign Ministry, former vice-president of the Islamic Cultural and Communications Organization, an agency created by the Supreme Leader for export of the Islamic Revolution to other parts of the Muslim world. See *www.iranfocus.com*, 14 August 2005; *www.khedmat.ir/comments.asp/id=515*.

50   Aged 40 (the youngest cabinet member), head of Namazi Hospital in Shiraz, former prosecutor in the investigative committee into medical malpractice in Shiraz, chairman of the Islamic Association of Physicians in the Fars Province. See *www.iranfocus.com*, 14 August 2005; *www.khedmat.ir/comments.asp/id=515*.

51   Aged 59, chairman of the Urban Planning and Development Corporation, former senior officer of the Jihad Sazandegi, former Minister of Transportation. See *www.iranfocus.com*, 14 August 2005.

52   Aged 44, member of the Majlis Research Centre, former senior officer in the Jihad Sazandegi, former head of the Jihad Sazandegi Research Centre, expert in ballistic missile development, former IRGC officer in the Khatam-ol-Anbia garrison of the IRGC. See *www.iranfocus.com*, 14 August 2005.

53   Aged 49, prosecutor and judge of the Special Tribunal for Clergy, formerly special prosecutor in the Ministry of Intelligence and Security, a founding official and member of the staff selection board for the Ministry of Intelligence and Security. See *www.iranfocus.com*, 14 August 2005; *www.khedmat.ir/comments.asp/id=498*.

54   Aged 46, in charge of the Special Department for Security and Intelligence in the office of the Supreme Leader, former deputy minister of Intelligence and Security, former Military Revolutionary Prosecutor. See *www.iranfocus.com*, 14 August 2005; *www.khedmat.ir/comments.asp/id=496*.

55   Aged 49, spokesman of the judiciary, former revolutionary prosecutor in the Zanjan and Qazvin provinces, director of the Taazirat Department (the agency for the implementation of corporal punishment, including flogging in public, and so on) in Qazvin . See *www.iranfocus.com*, 14 August 2005; *www.khedmat.ir/comments.asp/id=503*.

56   Aged 47, deputy chairman for executive affairs of the ultra-conservative Guardian Council, founding member of the IRGC in the Gilan and Mazandaran provinces in 1979, governor of the Zanjan, Lorestan and Semnan provinces, former member of the Secretariat of the State Expediency Council. See *www.iranfocus.com*, 14 August 2005.

57   Aged 47, minister of Roads and Transportation in Khatami's cabinet (the only incumbent in the new cabinet), former head of Universities' *Jihad* (a paramilitary organization affiliated to the IRGC that recruited Islamists in universities), former leadership member of the OSU, key planner of the Islamic Cultural Revolution in 1980. See *www.iranfocus.com*, 14 August 2005; *www.khedmat.ir/comments.asp/id=511*.

58   Aged 51, chairman of Kerman City Council, former professor of mathematics in the University of Shahid Bahonar in Kerman. See *www.iran-focus.com*, 14 August 2005; *www.khedmat.ir/comments.asp/id=512*.

59   'MPs vote for oil minister', See *www.iran-daily.com/1384/2448/html/index.htm*, 12 December 2005.

60   He has BA in communication engineering, used to work with revolutionary courts and also served as a deputy minister of Cooperation. See *www.mellat.majlis.ir*, 22 November 2005. He has since been replaced by Mohamad Abbasi, aged 48.

61   Aged 55, graduated with degree in engineering, used to work with Iranian radio in the Kerman province. See *www.mellat.majlis.ir*, 22 November 2005.

62   Aged 49, graduated in management, participated in the Iran–Iraq war, located at the Kurdistan Front. He worked with Boinyad as an accountant and also worked with Iranian car manufacturer Kodro and Pars. See *www.mellat.majlis.ir*, 22 November 2005.

63   For more information on the cabinet see Table 10 in the Appendix.

64   See *www.president.ir/eng/ahmadinejad/cronicnews/1384/06/03/index-e.htm#b4*, 25 August 2005.

65   See *www.president.ir/eng/ahmadinejad/cronicnews/1385/01/07/index-e.htm#b1*, 27 March 2006.

66   See 'Iranian President: we should build our future on glory of the past', at *www.payvand.com/news/05/sep/1011.html*, 9 February 2005. See also *www.president.ir/eng/ahmadinejad/speeches/index1.htm*.

CHAPTER IV
DOMESTIC POLITICS AND INTERNAL CHALLENGES UNDER AHMADINEJAD

1   See *www.President.ir/eng/ahmadinejad/cronicnews/1384/05/12/index-e.htm#b3*, 3 August 2005.

2   Ibid.

3   Porteous, Tom, 'Reading Iran', *Prospect* 118, 22 January 2006.

4   Khalaji, Mehdi, 'Iranian President Ahmadinezhad's relations with Supreme Leader Khamenei', *Policy Watch* 1147 (Washington Institute for Near East Policy, 2006).

5   Porteous: 'Reading Iran'.

6   Ibid.

7   Ibid.

8   See 'Iran: the struggle for the revolution's soul', International Crisis Group, at *www.crisisgroup.org/home/index.cfm?l=1&id=1673*, 5 August 2002.

9   See 'Iran: what does Ahmadinejad's victory mean?', International Crisis Group, at *www.crisisgroup.org/.../iraq_iran_gulf/b18_iran_what_does_ahmadi_nejad_victory_mean.pdf*, 4 August 2005.

10   Tait, Robert, 'Iranian President appoints hard-line new cabinet', *Guardian*, 14 August 2005.

11   Ibid.

12   See 'Iran President appoints atomic negotiator, advisers' at *www.chinadaily.com.cn/english/doc/2005-08/16/content_469419.htm*, 16 August 2005.

13   Fathi, Nazila, 'Iranian conservatives criticize cabinet nominees', *New York Times*, 22 August 2005.

14   His nomination for oil minister was rejected after heated debate in the Majlis. See *http://www.mehrnews.ir/en/NewsDetail.aspx?NewsID=222211*, 24 August 2005.

15   See 'Iranian MPs approve oil minister', BBC News, at *http://news.bbc.co.uk/2/hi/middle_east/4518300.stm*, 11 December 2005.

16   *Sharq*, 21 June 2005.

17   See 'The upcoming presidential elections in Iran (Part II)', MEMRI Inquiry and Analysis No. 226, at *http://memri.org/bin/articles.cgi?Page=countries&Area=iran&ID=IA22605#_edn28*, 16 June 2005.

18   Savyon, Avelet, 'Iran's "Second Islamic Revolution": fulfilled by election of conservative president', Middle East Media Research Institute, at *http://memri.org/bin/articles.cgi?Page=archives&Area=ia&ID=IA22905*, 4 July 2005.

19   Alamdari, Kazem, 'The power structure of the Islamic Republic of Iran: transition from populism to clientelism and militarization of the government', *Third World Quarterly* 26/8, (2005) pp.1285–301.

20   Ibid., p.1298.

21   It has been suggested that as many as 90 of the 290 deputies in the Seventh Majlis have an IRGC or military background.

22   This notion has been borrowed from Jahangir Amuzegar. See Amuzegar, Jahangir, 'Iran's crumbling revolution', *Foreign Affairs* 82/1 (2003), pp.44–57.

23 Yasin, Kamal Nazer, 'Iran's Revolutionary Guards making a bid for increased power', *Euro Asia Insight*, 19 May 2004.

24 Ibid.

25 Ibid.

26 Ibid.

27 Ibid.

28 Samii, Abbas William, 'The military-mullah complex: the militarization of Iranian politics', *Weekly Standard*, 23 May 2005.

29 Alamdari: 'The power structure'.

30 See 'Rooydad', at *http://rooydad.com/2004/09/blog-post_1094396749016 22214.html*, 5 September 2004.

31 See piece by Emrooz, Mohsen A., at *www.emrouz.info/Showitem.aspx? ID=4900&p=1*, 16 August 2005.

32 For details see Ebrahimi, Zahra, 'It must work much more closely', *Sharq*, 14 July 2005, available at *www.iran.-emrooz.net/index.php?/news2/print/2829/*.

33 Ibid.

34 See 'Observers fear a militarization of Iranian politics', at *www.payvand.com/news/05/apr/1072.html*, 4 November 2005.

35 Alamdari: 'The power structure'.

36 See *www.president.ir/eng/ahmadinejad/cronicnews/1384/10/25/index-e.htm*, 15 January 2006.

37 Ibid.

38 See 'Iran: budget row reflects deputies' domestic, foreign concerns', at *www.rferl.org*, 22 February 2006.

39 IRNA, 24 January 2006.

40 Ibid.

41 *Iran Daily*, 2 February 2006.

42 Ibid.

43 Ibid.

44 Khajehpour, Bijan, 'Protest and regime resilience in Iran', at *www.merip.org* , 11 December 2002.

45 Ahmadinejad and the neoconservatives believe that the Chinese economic model can apply to the Iranian economy. They believe that political reform is not essential to economic reform. Such thought, in fact, is ignoring the realty of Iran's geopolitics; Iran is located strategically on the world's energy map and is an important transit route between the East and the West. This fact is forcing Iran to move towards the West rather than the East; this is not acceptable to the neoconservatives in Iran. The neoconservatives argue that eight years of reform had only increased

the number of Iranians who lived in poverty, and the only way to solve this issue is to follow the Chinese model, which might offer a minimum level of social welfare to ordinary citizens. Those citizens who supported President Ahmadinejad are hoping that his government can offer them this level of life and the basic necessities they require to survive. There is no doubt that any failure to do so will be catastrophic not only to the neoconservatives but also to the Iranian regime in general. See also 'Iran's conservatives mull "Chinese model"', at *www.iranmania.com* , 17 February 2004.

46   Ehteshami , Anoushiravan, 'The political of economic restructuring in post-Khomeini Iran', Institute for Middle Eastern and Islamic Studies, Occasional Paper No.50, University of Durham, (Jul 1995), p.5.

47   'Iran and the Bomb: A government that thrives on defiance', *The Economist*, 6 May 2006, p.25.

48   Khajehpour: 'Protest and regime resilience'.

49   Transparency International Corruption Perceptions Index 2005, at *www.transparency.org*.

50   Transparency International Corruption Perceptions Index 2003, at *www.transparency.org*.

51   Ghazizadeh, Famaz, 'Economic corruption and Iranian officials', at *http://roozonline.com/englis/*, 5 October 2005.

52   See *www.isna.ir*, 29 April 2006.

53   *Ettela't International*, 15 May 2006.

54   Ahadi, Hamid, 'Embassies without envoys', at *http:/roozonline.com*, 26 April 2006.

55   Boghrati, Niusha, 'Islamic dress code to be strictly enforced', at *www.worldpress.org/*, 2 May 2006.

56   See 'Majlis approved a new law of Iranian fashion and dress', at *www.isna.ir*, 15 April 2006.

57   See 'Iran launches Islamic dress drive', BBC News, at *http://news.bbc.co.uk/*, 21 April 2006.

58   See 'President lauds active presence of women in social affairs', at *www.President.ir/eng/*, 24 April 2006; and 'Iran's President vows no dress clampdown', at *www.iranmania.com*, 24 April 2006.

59   See 'Iranian President orders for women's presence in stadiums', *www.isna.ir* , 24 April 2006.

60   Harrison, Frances, 'Iran clergy angry over women fans', BBC News, at *http://news.bbc.co.uk*, 26 April 2006.

61   Dastgir, Mehrangiz, 'Iran women sports ruling vetoed', BBC News, at *http://news.bbc.co.uk* , 8 May 2006; see also 'Supreme Leader opposes Iranian Women in Sports Stadiums', at *http://roosonline.com/english/*, 11 May 2006.

[62] Hafezi, Parisa, 'Iran police crack down on unIslamic women's dress', at *www.iranfocus.com/*, 18 April 2006.

[63] These campaigns started 12 Azer 1362 (3 December 1983) and reappeared on 31 Tir 1363 (22 January 1984), 5 Khordad 1364 (26 May 1985), 4 Tir 1364 (25 May 1984), 30 Ordibehesht 1366 (29 April 1987), 8 Bahman 1366 (28 January 1988), 30 Ordibehesht 1367 (20 May 1988), 22 Farvardin 1368 (11 April 1989), 19 Ordibehesht 1369 (9 May 1990), 24 Ordibehesht 1369 (14 May 1990), 26 Ordibehesht1369 (16 May 1990), 9 Ordibehesht1369 (29 April 1990), 2 Ordibehesht 1370 (23 May 1991), 21 Dey 1372 (11 January 1994), 12 Khordad 1375 (1 June 1996), 27 Mordad1380 (18 August 2001) and 7 Tir 1383 (27 June 2004), and finally a new law about Iranian fashion and dress on 24 Ordibehesht1385 (14 May 2006). See '23 years of tackling shol hijab (loosely draped hijab)', at *www.baztab.ir*, 16 Ordibehesht 1385 (6 May 2006); Balasescu, Alec, 'What the veil says about women', at *http://commentisfree.guardian.co.uk*, 27 April 2006.

[64] Babak, Ganji, 'President Mahmoud Ahmadinejad: a turning point in Iranian politics and strategy?', Middle East Series v/62, Conflict Studies Research Centre, Defence Academy of the United Kingdom (Oct 2005), at *www.defac.ac.uk/colleges/csrc/document-listings/middle-east/05(62).pdf*.

[65] Ibid.

[66] President Ahmadinejad responded to the question about the promises he made to the Iranian people by saying: 'I [Ahmadinejad] am among very rare few politicians that do not usually give promises. I have promised that I will work and we have a good and very coherent program for the advancement of our country', *USA Today*, 12 February 2006.

[67] There is the distinct possibility that a militarized Iran, with a new president backed by a conservative legislature, would engage in confrontation with the West. At first glance it would appear that there is little the international community can do in the short term to affect or to stave off the militarization of the country's politics. But the regime apparently thinks otherwise. In particular, it seems to fear the impact of unfiltered information and it has already started to seize satellite dishes, which are illegal, and fine their owners in an attempt to control news from the outside that could be portraying the regime in a negative manner. Furthermore, Tehran has denounced recent US efforts to support the reformist movement in Iran. The output legitimacy (that is, the performance of the government as set against its electoral promises) of the new conservative consolidation in Iranian politics remains to be tested, and the nuclear issue could be the first high-profile test. (Economic performance is likely to be as important, especially as Ahmadinejad built his electoral manifesto on guaranteeing economic justice.) The conservative consolidation does not end internal disagreements and politicking – Ahmadinejad's difficulties in appointing a cabinet illustrate such bickering – but it does present a unified front of

sorts in that there is little political change in any of Iran's several governing institutions. While this has some benefits for stability, it also sets up a legitimacy crisis for the conservative-dominated regime, because responsibility for decisions and their consequences are now clarified.

68 See 'Iran under pressure', BBC News, at *http://news.bbc.co.uk*, 25 April 2006.

Chapter V
Iran's Regional Role Under the Neoconservatives

1 *Iran Report*, Radio Free Europe/Radio Liberty, 23 October 2006.

2 See 'Asefi hits at PGCC statement on Iranian islands', at *www.irna.ir*, 12 June 2005.

3 Ibid.

4 'Hamas chief vows to support Iran', BBC News, at *http://news.bbc.co.uk/1/hi/world/middle_east/4532570.stm*, 15 December 2005.

5 Ibid.

6 Barnes, Hugh and Alex Bigham, *Understanding Iran: People, Politics and Power* (London: Foreign Policy Centre, 2006).

7 See 'President urges UN to pave way for materialization of world peace', speech at the UN, at *www.president.ir/eng/ahmadinejad/cronicnews/1384/06/24/index-e.htm#b1*, 15 September 2005.

8 Ibid.

9 See Mahmoud Ahmadinejad's speech from the 'World without Zionism' conference, reported in the *New York Times*, also at *http://en.wikipedia.org/wiki/October_30*, 30 October 2005.

10 Ibid.

11 See 'Israel urges UN to exclude Iran', BBC News, at *http://news.bbc.co.uk/2/hi/middle_east/4382594.stm*, 27 October 2005.

12 See 'Annan shocked at Ahmadinajad casting doubt about the Holocaust', Kuwait News Agency, at *www.kuna.net.kw*, 9 December 2005.

13 See *http://en.wikipedia.org/wiki/Mahmoud_Ahmadinejad_and_Israel#endnote_26*, 24 April 2006.

14 See 'Saudis fuming over Iran president's Holocaust, Israel comments', at *www.newsmax.com*, 10 December 2005.

15 See 'Ahmadinejad draws ire of Saudis, Iranians, West over Israel remarks', at *www.dailystar.com*, 10 December 2005.

16 Ibid.

17 Ibid.

18   See 'Iran: Holocaust remarks misunderstood', at *www.cnn.com*, 16 December 2006.

19   See *www.globalsecurity.org/wmd/library/news/iran/2005/iran-051214-irna02.htm*, 24 April 2006.

20   See 'Iranian leader: Holocaust a "myth"', at *www.cnn.com*, 13 December 2005.

21   Saad, Rashu, ' Targeted words: Al-Ahram', at *http://weekly.ahram.org.eg/2005/767/re1.htm*, 9 November 2005.

22   See *www.asianews.ir/en/main1.asp?a_id=733*, 29 October 2005.

23   See *www.isna.ir/Main/NewsView.aspx?ID=News-649691*, 14 January 2006.

24   Ibid.

25   See *www.aftabnews.ir/vdcb8fbrhzbga.html*, 4 February 2006.

26   Ibid.

27   See 'Iran's foreign minister: Ahmadinejad comments misunderstood', at *www.atsnn.com/story/195969.html*, 20 February 2006.

28   See 'Iran President sticks by controversial Israel remark', at *www.khaleejtimes.com/DisplayArticle.asp?xfile=data/middleeast/2005/October/middleeast_October710.xml&section=middleeast*, 28 October 2005.

29   Ibid.

30   Ibid.

31   This text is part of the speech delivered by Ahmadinejad at the opening session of the third   international Quds Conference in Tehran, April 2006. See reporting in the *Daily Star*, 15 April 2006.

32   See *www.irna.ir/en/news/view/line-17/0604145225195631.htm*, 24 April 2006.

33   Ibid.

34   Ibid.

35   Ibid.

36   See 'Iran's nuclear plans are worrisome, say GCC Foreign Ministers', at *www.gulfnews.com*, 3 March 2006.

37   See 'Saudis warn Iran that its nuclear plan risks disaster', at *www.iranvajahan.net*, 16 January 2006.

38   Ibid.

39   Bolton, John, 'Iran's continuing pursuit of weapons of mass destruction', *www.state.gov/t/us/rm/33909.htm*, 24 June 2004.

40   See 'International Developments', at *www.acronym.org.uk*, 1 February 2003.

41   The negotiations for the Trade and Cooperation Agreement (TCA) stalled from June 2003 because of the pending nuclear issues with Iran.

After the signature of the 'Paris Agreement' in November 2004 between the EU3 and Iran on the suspension of nuclear enrichment, the TCA negotiation resumed. Rounds V, VI and VII took place in January, March and July 2005. However, following Iran's breach of the Paris Agreement by resuming uranium conversion at the Isfahan plant in August 2005, negotiations have been halted by the EU3 Commission.

42   Bakhash, Shaul, 'Iran since the Gulf war', in Robert O. Freedman (ed.) *The Middle East and the Peace Process: The Impact of the Oslo Accords* (Gainesville, FL: University Press of Florida, 1998), pp.241–64.

43   See 'Iran mining uranium for fuel', BBC News, at *http://news.bbc.co.uk/2/hi/middle_east/2743279.stm*, 9 February 2003.

44   Ibid.

45   Ibid.

46   Ibid.

47   Salama, Sammy and Karen Ruster, *A Preemptive Attack on Iran's Nuclear Facilities: Possible Consequences* (Monterey, CA: Center for Nonproliferation Studies, Monterey Institute of International Studies, August 2004).

48   See 'IAEA says Iranian "pilot" uranium enrichment plant almost complete', at *www.bellona.no*, 19 March 2003.

49   Hersh, Seymour, 'The coming wars: what the Pentagon can do in secret', *New Yorker*, 24 January 2005.

50   Takeyah, Ray, 'Iran builds the nuclear bomb', *Survival*, xlvi/4 (winter 2004–2005), pp.51–64.

51   Baheli, Muhammad Nima, 'The Iranian case: possible developments on nuclear issue', *Journal of Middle Eastern Geopolitics*, 1 (July–September 2005), pp.77–90.

52   See Mouawad, Jad, 'Looming Iran showdown gives oil trade a new worry', *New York Times*, 19 January 2006.

53   Ibid.

54   Sepehri, Vahid, 'Iran: legislators warn that country has exhausted petrodollars', *www.rferl.org/featuresarticle/2007/02/12a0ffc6-05c1-4265-a73f-a512fb376c12.html*, 2 February 2007.

55   See Wright, Robin and Peter Baker, 'Leaders warn against forming religious state', *Washington Post*, 8 December 2004.

56   Ibid.

57   Ibid.

58   See 'Mubarak's Shia remarks stir anger', Al Jazeera News, at *http://english.aljazeera.net/English/archive/archive?ArchiveId=21914*, 12 April 2006.

59   The declaration was signed by 28 prominent Sunni and Shia scholars and was issued on 21 October 2006, in the name of the OIC. See *Arab News*, 22 October 2006.

60   See 'The memos of Falah al-Naqib', at *www.asharqalawsat.com/details. asp?section=34&article=335671&issue=9863*, 29 November 2005.

61   Al-Khuza'i also said on 9 August that 'Weapons manufactured in Iran were found in Al-Najaf in the hands of those criminals, who received these weapons from the Iranian border.' He accused Iran of being Iraq's 'first enemy', in the same interview with Abu Dhabi-based al-Arabiya television.

62   See 'Iraqi defence minister says has information on Iranian meddling', *www.iranfocus.com/modules/news/article.php?storyid=1123*, 31 December 2004.

63   See 'Iraqi Prime Minister warns Iran, Syria, to stop disrupting peace', at *www.iranfocus.com*, 31 December 2004.

64   See *Iran Report*, Radio Free Europe/Radio Liberty, at *www.rferl.org/reports/iraq-report/2004/08/29-060804.asp*, 17 August 2004.

65   Remarks made by the Iranian Foreign Ministry spokesman, Hamid Reza Assefi. See *Iraq Report*, Radio Free Europe/Radio Liberty, at *www. globalsecurity.org/wmd/library/news/iran/2004/27-170804.htm*, 22 July 2004. Iraqi Foreign Minister Hoshyar Zebari told the *Sunday Telegraph* (4 July 2004) that as many as 10,000 foreign spies had entered Iraq since May 2003.

66   *Iran Report*, Radio Free Europe/Radio Liberty, 17 August 2004; see also *www.globalsecurity.org/wmd/library/news/iraq/2003/11/iraq-031102-irna02.htm* , 3 November 2003.

67   See 'Iran rejects reports over illegal Iranian trips into Iraq', at *www. payvand.com*, 11 February 2003.

68   Ibid.

69   Samii, Abbas William, 'The nearest and the dearest enemy: Iran after the Iraq war', *Middle East Review of International Affairs*, iii/9 (2005), pp.527–46.

70   See Dergham, Raghida., 'The American "dialogue": no one knows what Washington wants', *Dar al Hayat*, 27 March 2006.

71   See Knowlton, Brian, 'Iran closes US door for talks about Iraq', *International Herald Tribune*, 25 April 2006.

72   Ibid.

73   Ibid.

74   See Bake, Peter R., Dafna Linzer and Thomas E. Ricks, 'US is studying military strike options on Iran', *Washington Post*, 9 April 2006.

75   Ibid.

76   See 'Russia says no to sanctions against Iran', EuroNews, at *http:// euronews.net/create_html.php?page=detail_info&article=354743&lng=1*, 19 April 2006.

77 See 'China signs $70 billion oil and LNG agreement with Iran', *Daily Star*, at *www.dailystar.com.lb/article.asp?edition_id=10&categ_id=3&article_id=9713*, 30 October 2004.

78 Ibid.

79 See Ziyadoy, Taleh, 'Iran and China sign agreement to explore oil in the Caspian sea', EuroNews, at *www.jamestown.org/edm/article.php?article_id=2370729*, 1 February 2006.

80 See Brzezinski, Zbigniew, 'Do not attack Iran', *Herald Tribune*, 26 April 2006.

81 See 'Talk to Iran, President Bush', *International Herald Tribune*, at *www.iht.com/articles/2006/04/25/opinion/edmin.php*, 26 April 2006.

82 Bake, Peter R., Dafna Linzer and Thomas E. Ricks, 'Straw: no military action against Iran', *Al Jazeera*, 28 September 2005.

83 Ibid.

84 IRNA, 8 June 2005.

85 Keshavarzian, Arang, 'Clash of neoconservatives? The Bush administration and Iran's new president', *Foreign Policy In Focus*, 10 August 2005.

86 From a speech made by Baqeri Muhammad-Reza, Iranian Deputy Foreign Minister for Arab–African Affairs at the IISS-led regional security conference, Manama, December 2005.

BIBLIOGRAPHY

BOOKS AND ARTICLES

Abdo, Geneive, 'Electoral politics in Iran', *Middle East Policy*, vi/4 (1999) at *www.mepc.org/journal_vol6/9906_abdo.asp*.

Abili, Mohammad, 'Internet and cultural growth in Iran: opportunities and challenges', *Discourse* iii/3 (2002), pp.101-19.

Abotalebi, Ali, 'Iran's June 2005 presidential election and the question of governance', *Iran Analysis Quarterly* ii/4 (2005), at *www.mit.edu*.

Alamdari, Kazem, 'The power structure of the Islamic Republic of Iran: transition from populism to clientelism and militarization of the government', *Third World Quarterly* xxvi/8 (2005), pp.1285-1301.

Amuzegar, Jahangir, 'Iran's prospect under the 7th Majlis', *Middle East Economic Survey*, xlvii/17 (April 2004).

Amuzegar, Jahangir, 'Iran's crumbling revolution', *Foreign Affairs* xxlii/1 (2003), pp.44-57.

Amuzegar, Jahangir, 'Iran's privatization saga', *Middle East Economic Survey*, xlv/24 (2002), at *http://memri.org/bin/articles.cgi?Page=archives&Area=ia& ID=IA22905*.

Amuzegar, Jahangir, 'Khatami and the Iranian economy at mid-term', *Middle East Journal*, liii/4 (1999) at *www.sharghnewspaper.com/821010/polit.htm*.

Arang, Keshavarzian, 'Clash of neoconservatives? The Bush administration and Iran's new president', *Foreign Policy In Focus*, 10 August 2005.

Arjomand, Said Amir, 'The reform movement and the debate on modernity and tradition in contemporary Iran', *International Journal of the Middle East* 34 (2002), p.719–31.

Babak, Ganji, 'President Mahmoud Ahmadinejad: a turning point in Iranian politics and strategy?', Middle East Series v/62, Conflict Studies Research Centre, Defence Academy of the United Kingdom (Oct 2005), at *www. defac.ac.uk/colleges/csrc/document-listings/middle-east/05(62).pdf.*

Baheli, Muhammad Nima, 'The Iranian case: possible developments on nuclear issue', *Journal of Middle Eastern Geopolitics* i/1 (Jul–Sep 2005), pp.77–90.

Bakhash, Shaul, 'Iran since the Gulf War', in Robert O. Freedman (ed.) *The Middle East and the Peace Process: The Impact of the Oslo Accords* (Gainesville, FL: University Press of Florida, 1998), pp.241–64.

Baqir, Moin, *Khomeini: Life of the Ayatollah* (London: I.B.Tauris, 1999).

Barnes, Hugh and Alex Bigham, *Understanding Iran: People, Politics and Power* (London: Foreign Policy Centre, 2006).

Behdad, Sohrab, 'From populism to economic liberalism: the Iranian predicament', in Parvin Alizadeh (ed.) *The Economy of Iran: The Dilemmas of an Islamic State* (London: I.B.Tauris, 2000), pp.100–41.

Bellaigue Christopher de, 'Iran's last chance for reform', *The Washington Quarterly* (Autumn 2001), pp.73,75.

Berman, Ilan, *Understanding Ahmadinejad* (Washington: American Foreign Policy Council, June 2006).

Brumberg, Daniel, *Reinventing Khomeini: The Struggle for Reform in Iran* (Chicago: University of Chicago Press, 2001).

Buchta, Wilfried, *Who Rules Iran: The Structure of Power in the Islamic Republic* (Washington: Washington Institute for Near East Policy, 2000), pp.17–19.

Byman, Daniel, Shahram Cubin, Anoushiravan Ehteshami and Jerrold D. Green, *Iran's Security Policy in the Post-Revolutionary Era* (Santa Monica, CA: RAND, 2001).

Dirasa fi Vilayat Al-Faqih, Vol. 2 (Qum, 1988).

Ehteshami, Anoushiravan, 'The political of economic restructuring in post-Khomeini Iran', Institute for Middle Eastern and Islamic Studies, Occasional Paper No.50, University of Durham (Jul 1995).

Eisenstadt, Michael, 'The armed forces of the Islamic Republic of Iran: an assessment', in Barry Rubin and Thomas A. Keaney (eds) *Armed Forces in the Middle East: Politics and Strategy* (London: Frank Cass, 2002), pp.231–57.

El-Labbad, Mustafa, 'His first 100 days', *Al Ahram*, 771, 1-7 December 2005.

Emrouz, Payman, 'Tehranis also go to Internet cafés', *Social, Economic & Cultural* 35 (1999), pp.50–2.

Farhadian, Mahdy, 'Beyond Khatami's reform era: economic Talibanization or liberalization?', *Iran Analysis Quarterly* i/2 (2004), pp.7–10.

Gheissari, Ali and Vali Nasr, *Democracy in Iran: History and the Quest for Liberty* (Oxford: Oxford University Press, 2006).

Hooshang, Amirahmadi, 'Current state of civil society in Iran', *Iran Nameh* xiv (winter 1995), pp.79–106 [in Farsi].

Hunter, Shireen (ed.), *Iran after Khomeini* (Washington: Praeger, 1992).

Jahanbakhsh, Forough, 'Religious and political discourse in Iran: moving toward post-fundamentalism', *The Brown Journal of World Affairs* ix/2 (2003), p.243–54.

Khalaji, Mehdi, 'Iranian President Ahmadinezhad's relations with Supreme Leader Khamenei', *Policy Watch* 1147 (Washington Institute for Near East Policy, 2006).

Martin, Vanessa, *Creating an Islamic State: Khomeini and the Making of a New Iran* (London: I.B.Tauris, 2001).

Moin, Baqir, *Khomeini: Life of the Ayatollah* (London: I.B.Tauris, 1999).

Porteous, Tom, 'Reading Iran', *Prospect Issue* 118, 22 January 2006.

Rubin, Michael, *Into the Shadows, Radical Vigilantes in Khatami's Iran* (Washington: The Washington Institute for the Near East Policy, 2001), pp.46–77.

Sadri, Mahmoud, 'Sacral defense of secularism: the political theologies of Soroush, Shabestry, and Kadivar', *International Journal of Politics, Culture and Society* xv/2 (2001), p.257–70.

Saghfi, Morad, 'The reform nobody wants anymore', *Islam Review* 15 (2005), at *www.isim.nl*.

Salama, Sammy and Karen Ruster, *A Preemptive Attack on Iran's Nuclear Facilities: Possible Consequences* (Monterey, CA: Centre for Non-proliferation Studies, Monterey and Institute of International Studies, 2004).

Samii, Abbas William, 'Dissent in Iranian elections: reasons and implications', *Middle East Journal*, lviii/3 (2004), pp.402–23.

Samii, Abbas William, 'The nearest and the dearest enemy: Iran after the Iraq War', *Middle East Review of International Affairs*, iii/9, (2005), p.527–46.

Sohrab, Behdad, 'From populism to economic liberalism: the Iranian predicament', in Parvin Alizadeh (ed.) *The Economy of Iran: The Dilemmas of an Islamic State* (London: I.B.Tauris, 2000), pp.100–41.

Takeyah, Ray, 'Iran builds the nuclear bomb', *Survival* xlvi/4 (2004-05), pp.51–64.

NEWSPAPERS AND WEBSITES

Agence France Presse, 'China signs $70 billion oil and LNG agreement with Iran', at *www.dailystar.com.lb/article.asp?edition_id=10&categ_id=3 &article_id=9713*, 30 October 2004.

Ahadi, Hamid, 'Embassies without envoys', at *http:/roozonline.com*, 26 April 2006.

Ahmad, Sadri, 'Still alive: varieties of religious reform in Iran', *The Iranian*, 4 February 2002.

Ahmadinejad, Mahmoud, speech from the 'World Without Zionism' conference, reported in the *New York Times*, also at *http://en.wikipedia.org/wiki/October_30*, 30 October 2005.

Ahmadinejad, Mahmoud, 'President urges UN to pave way for materialization of world peace', speech to the 60th regular session of the UN General Assembly, at *www.president.ir/eng/ahmadinejad/cronicnews/1384/06/24/index-e.htm#b1*, 15 December 2005.

Bake, Peter R., Dafna Linzer and Thomas E. Ricks, 'Straw: no military action against Iran', *Al Jazeera*, 28 September 2005.

Bake, Peter R., Dafna Linzer and Thomas E. Ricks, 'US is studying military strike options on Iran', *Washington Post*, 9 April 2006.

Balasescu, Alec, 'What the veil says about women', at *http://commentisfree.guardian.co.uk*, 27 April 2006.

Boghrati, Niusha, 'Islamic dress code to be strictly enforced', at *www.worldpress.org/*, 2 May 2006.

Bolton, John, 'Iran's continuing pursuit of weapons of mass destruction', *www.state.gov/t/us/rm/33909.htm*, 24 June 2004.

Branigin, William and Robin Wright, 'Ex-hostages finger Iran's president-elect', *Washington Post*, 10 June 2005.

Brzezinski, Zbigniew, 'Do not attack Iran', *Herald Tribune*, 26 April 2006.

Clawson, Patrick, 'Impact of World Bank loans to Iran', at *www.financialservices.house.org*, 29 October 2003.

Dastgir, Mehrangiz, 'Iran women sports ruling vetoed', BBC News, at *http://news.bbc.co.uk*, 8 May 2006.

Dergham, Raghida., 'The American "dialogue": no one knows what Washington wants', *Dar al Hayat*, 27 March 2006.

Fathi Nazila, 'Iranian conservatives criticize cabinet nominees', *New York Times*, 22 August 2005.

Ghammari, Behrooz, 'How the reformists lost the presidency – what's the matter with Iran?', at *www.iranian.com*, 5 July 2005.

Ghazizadeh, Famaz, 'Economic corruption and Iranian officials', at *http:/roozonline.com/englis/*, 5 October 2005.

Hafezi, Parisa, 'Iran police crack down on unIslamic women's dress', at *www.iranfocus.com/*, 18 April 2006.

Hammersley, Ben, 'Iran nets another revolt', *Guardian*, 21 February 2002.

Harrison, Frances, 'Iran clergy angry over women fans', BBC News, at *http://news.bbc.co.uk*, 26 April 2006.

Hersh, Seymour M., 'The coming wars: what the Pentagon can do in secret', *New Yorker*, 24 January 2005.

Khajehpour, Bijan, 'Protest and regime resilience in Iran', at *www.merip.org*, 11 December 2002.

Knowlton, Brian, 'Iran closes US door for talks about Iraq', *Herald Tribune*, 25 April 2006.

Mouawad, Jad, 'Looming Iran showdown gives oil trade a new worry', *New York Times*, 19 January 2006.

Rabiee, Lara, 'Not in the mood: Iran's local councils elections, four years later', at *www.iranian.com*, 13 February 2003.

Radio Free Europe/Radio Liberty, *Iran Report*, at *www.rferl.org/reports/iran-report/* (19 July 1999; 17 August 2004; 22 July 2004; 23 October 2006).

Rahman, Hassan Abdul, 'Perspective: comments unworthy of our Elite Commander', *Iran*, 2 May 1998.

Saad, Rasha, 'Targeted words: Al-Ahram', at *http://weekly.ahram.org.eg/2005/767/re1.htm*, 9 November 2005.

Samii, Abbas William, 'The military-mullah complex: the militarization of Iranian politics', *Weekly Standard*, 23 May 2005.

Savyon, Avelet, 'Iran's "Second Islamic Revolution": fulfilled by election of conservative president', Middle East Media Research Institute, at *http://memri.org/bin/articles.cgi?Page=archives&Area=ia&ID=IA22905*, 4 July 2005.

Sepehri, Vahid, 'Iran: legislators warn that country has exhausted petrodollars', *www.rferl.org/featuresarticle/2007/02/12a0ffc6-05c1-4265-a73f-a51 2fb376c12.html*, 2 February 2007.

Tait, Robert, 'A humble beginning helped to form Iran's new hard man', *Guardian*, 2 July 2005.

Tait, Robert, 'Iranian president appoints hard-line new cabinet', *Guardian*, 14 August 2005.

Takeyh, Ray, 'Iran's municipal elections: a turning point for the reform movement?', at *www.washingtoninstitute.org*, 6 March 2003.

Taqvee, Hamid, interview broadcast in English on international TV, 26 June 2005.

Unattributed, 'A government that thrives on defiance', *The Economist*, 6 May 2006, p.25.

Unattributed, 'Current State of Civil Society in Iran', *Iran Nameh* xiv (winter 1995), pp.79–106 [in Farsi].

Unattributed, 'History of the Internet in Iran', *Etemad*, 18 January 2003.

Unattributed, 'Iran's new president charts hard-line agenda', *New York Times*, 22 August 2005.

Wright, Robin and Peter Baker, 'Leaders warn against forming religious state', *Washington Post*, 8 December 2004.

Yasin, Kamal Nazer, 'Iran's Revolutionary Guards making a bid for increased power', *Euro Asia Insight,* 19 May 2004.

Ziyadoy, Taleh, 'Iran and China sign agreement to explore oil in the Caspian sea', EuroNews, at *www.jamestown.org/edm/article.php?article_id=2370729*, 1 February 2006.

Unattributed online articles

'Ahmadinejad draws ire of Saudis, Iranians, West over Israel remarks', at *www. dailystar.com*, 10 December 2005.

'Annan shocked at Ahmadinejad casting doubt about the Holocaust', Kuwait News Agency at *www.kuna.net.kw*, 9 December 2005.

'Asefi hits at PGCC statement on Iranian islands', IRNA, at *www.irna.ir*, 12 June 2005.

'Councils elections, challenges and perspectives', at *www.isna.ir*, 3 May 2003.

'Former hostages allege Iran's new president was captor', at *www.cnn.com*, 30 June 2005.

'Hamas chief vows to support Iran', BBC News, at *http://news.bbc.co.uk/1/hi/world/middle_east/4532570.stm*, 15 December 2005.

'How the reformists lost the presidency: what's the matter with Iran?', at *www.iranian.com*, 5 July 2005.

'IAEA says Iranian "pilot" uranium enrichment plant almost complete', at *www.bellona.no*, 19 March 2003.

'International Developments', at *www.acronym.org.uk*, 1 February 2003.

'Iran: budget row reflects deputies' domestic, foreign concerns', at *www.rferl. org*, 22 February 2006.

'Iran hardliner sweeps to victory', BBC News, at *http://news.bbc.co.uk/2/hi/middle_east/4621249.stm*, 25 June 2005.

'Iran: Holocaust remarks misunderstood', at *www.cnn.com*, 16 December 2006.

'Iran Internet use at risk from conservatives', *www.16beaveergroup.org/mtarchive/archives/*, 18 June 2003.

'Iran launches Islamic dress drive', BBC news, at *http://news.bbc.co.uk/*, 21 April 2006.

'Iran leader to set up "Love Fund"', BBC News, at *http://news.bbc.co.uk/2/hi/middle_east/4198906.stm*, 30 August 2005.

'Iran mining uranium for fuel', BBC News, at *http://news.bbc.co.uk/2/hi/middle_east/2743279.stm*, 9 February 2003.

'Iran polls are test for reformers', BBC News, at *http://news.bbc.co.uk*, 28 February 2003.

'Iran prepares for first-ever local elections', BBC News, at *http://news.bbc.co.uk*, 10 February 1999.

'Iran president appoints atomic negotiator, advisers' at *www.chinadaily.com.cn/english/doc/2005-08/16/content_469419.htm*, 16 August 2005.

'Iran president sticks by controversial Israel remark', at *www.khaleejtimes.com/DisplayArticle.asp?xfile=data/middleeast/2005/October/middleeast_October710.xml&section=middleeast*, 28 October 2005.

'Iran president's religious views arouse interest (dangerous ideology)', at *www.freerepublic.com/focus/f-news/1524384/posts*, 18 November 2005.

'Iran reformers suffer poll blow', BBC News, at *http://news.bbc.co.uk*, 2 March 2003.

'Iran rejects reports over illegal Iranian trips into Iraq', at *www.payvand.com*, 11 February 2003.

'Iran's conservatives mull "Chinese model"', at *www.iranmania.com*, 17 February 2004.

'Iran's foreign minister: Ahmadinejad comments misunderstood', at *www.atsnn.com/story/195969.html*, 20 February 2006.

'Iran's municipal elections: a turning point for the reform movement?', at *www.washingtoninstitute.org*, 6 March 2003.

'Iran's new president has a past mired in controversy', at *www.iranfocus.com/modules/news/article.php?storyid=2606*, 25 June 2005.

'"Iran's nuclear plans are worrisome", say GCC Foreign Ministers', at *www.gulfnews.com*, 3 March 2006.

'Iran's president vows no dress clampdown', at *www.iranmania.com*, 24 April 2006.

'Iran's presidential coup', at *www.opendemocracy.net*, 27 June 2005.

'Iran: the struggle for the revolution's soul', International Crisis Group, at *www.crisisgroup.org/home/index.cfm?l=1&id=1673*, 5 August 2002.

'Iran under pressure', BBC News, at *http://news.bbc.co.uk*, 25 April 2006.

'Iran: what does Ahmadinejad's victory mean?', International Crisis Group, at *www.crisisgroup.org/.../iraq_iran_gulf/b18_iran_what_does_ahmadi_ne jad_victory_mean.pdf*, 4 August 2005.

'Iranian leader: Holocaust a "myth"', at *www.cnn.com*, 15 December 2005.

'Iranian leader picks hardliners', BBC News, at *http://news.bbc.co.uk*, 14 August 2005.

'Iranian MPs approve oil minister', BBC News, at *http://news.bbc.co.uk/2/hi/middle_east/4518300.stm*, 11 December 2005.

'Iranian president orders for women's presence in stadiums', at *www.isna.ir*, 24 April 2006.

'Iraqi Prime Minister warns Iran, Syria, to stop disrupting peace', at *www.iranfocus.com*, 31 December 2004.

'Islamic dress code to be strictly enforced', at *www.worldpress.org/*, 2 May 2006.

'Israel urges UN to exclude Iran', BBC News, at *http://news.bbc.co.uk/2/hi/middle_east/4382594.stm*, 27 October 2005.

'Mahmoud Ahmadinejad', at *www.globalsecurity.org*, 6 June 2006.

'Majlis approved a new law of Iranian fashion and dress', at *www.isna.ir*, 15 April 2006.

'Monitoring councils elections process has been debated to be transferred to the Guardian Council', at *www.iran-emrooz.net* , 17 May 2006.

'MPs vote for oil minister', at *www.iran-daily.com/1384/2448/html/index.htm*, 12 December 2005.

'Mubarak's Shia remarks stir anger', Al Jazeera News, at *http://english.aljazeera. net/English/archive/archive?ArchiveId=21914*, 10 April 2006.

'New-neoconservatives: regime crisis and political perspectives in Iran', at *www.zmag.org*, 15 August 2005.

'Observers fear a militarization of Iranian politics', at *www.payvand.com/news/05/apr/1072.html*, 4 November 2005.

'Politics of Theocracy in Iran', at *www.arabia.co.kr/en/docs/Iran-theocracy. htm*.

'President lauds active presence of women in social affairs', at *www.president.ir/eng/ahmadinejad/cronicnews/1384/06/24/index-e.htm#b1*, 24 April 2006.

'Rafsanjani: in analyzing councils elections results look for realities', at *www. payvand.com*, 3 August 2003.

'Round 12 for Iran's Reformists', Middle East Report Online, at *www.merip. org/mero/mero012904.html*, 29 January 2004.

'Russia says no to sanctions against Iran', Euro News, at *http://euronews. net/create_html.php?page=detail_info&article=354743&lng=119*, 19 April 2006.

'Saudis fuming over Iran president's Holocaust, Israel comments', at *www. newsmax.com*, 10 December 2005.

'Saudis warn Iran that its nuclear plan risks disaster', at *www.iranvajahan.net*, 16 January 2006.

'Shiite supremacists emerge from Iran's shadows from a special correspondent', Asia Times, at *www.mesbahyazdi.org*, 9 September 2005.

'Supreme Leader opposes Iranian women in sports stadiums', at *http:// roosonline.com/english/*, 11 May 2006.

'Talk to Iran, President Bush', statement signed by various former foreign ministers, *International Herald Tribune*, at *www.iht.com/articles/2006/04/25/ opinion/edmin.php*, 26 April 2006.

'The memos of Falah al-Naqib', at *www.asharqalawsat.com/details.asp?section =34&article=335671&issue=9863*, 29 November 2005.

'The upcoming presidential elections in Iran (Part II)', MEMRI Inquiry and Analysis No. 226, at *http://memri.org/bin/articles.cgi?Page=countries&Area= iran&ID=IA22605#_edn28*, 16 June 2005.

Other news sources

Aftab-e Yazd (21 June 2005; 22 June 2005).

Agence France Presse (2 June 2003).

Asia Times (9 September 2005).

Daily Star (15 April 2006).

Daily Telegraph (9 April 2002).

Etemad (18 January 2003).

Ettela'at International (30 January 2006; 15 May 2006).

Farsi (14 April 2004).

Hambastegi (No. 145, 9 April 2001).

Iran (22 June 2005).

Iran Daily (1 May 2005; 14 April 2004; 2 February 2006).

Mardomsalari (14 January 2002).

Raghida Dergham, Dar al Hayat (27 March 2006).

Sharq (20 June 2005; 21 June 2005; 14 July 2005).

USA Today (12 February 2006).

www.iranalmanac.com

www.iranchamber.com

www.iranfocus.com

www.irna.ir

www.transparency.org

INDEX